The Duke

The Duke

THE AUTOBIOGRAPHY OF
THE CHAMPION TRAINER

David Nicholson

with Jonathan Powell

Foreword by HRH The Princess Royal

Hodder & Stoughton

PHOTOGRAPHIC ACKNOWLEDGEMENTS

The author and publishers would like to thank the following for permission to reproduce their copyright photographs: The Sport & General Press Agency Ltd, Sun, The Associated Press Ltd, The Yorkshire Post, Western Mail & Echo Ltd, Fox Photos Ltd, Gerry Cranham, Bernard Parkin, Findlay Davidson, Frank H. Meads and Dinah Nicholson.

First published in 1995 by Hodder and Stoughton
A division of Hodder Headline PLC

10 9 8 7 6 5 4 3

British Library Cataloguing in Publication Data

Nicholson, David
Duke: Autobiography of a Champion Trainer
I. Title II. Powell, Jonathan
636.12092

ISBN 0 340 66083 X

Typeset by Hewer Text Composition Services, Edinburgh
Printed and bound in Great Britain by
Mackays of Chatham PLC

Hodder and Stoughton
A division of Hodder Headline PLC
338 Euston Road
London NW1 3BH

Contents

Acknowledgements

Researching the life and times of David Nicholson and his family has been rather like turning the pages of racing history over the past seventy years. It is a fascinating journey that has taken me to Devon to meet the splendid old jockey Harry Sprague and to Prestbury for numerous chats with David's mother Di Nicholson, who does not appear to have changed one bit over the last thirty years. David's sister Josie and brother Richard also made notable contributions.

Colin Smith was refreshingly open about his business operation at Jackdaws Castle and Ben Brooks readily helped with background information on the financies of D. Nicholson Racing Ltd.

I have spent many hours in the Cotswolds talking to owners, jockeys, trainers, friends and rivals of David and Dinah Nicholson. None was more lucid and entertaining than the remarkable Roscoe Harvey who is well into his nineties. My thanks to everyone who took the time to assist me, particularly my very good friend Bruce Blair who still appears remarkably sane for someone who has already read every word in this book three times.

Most of all I must thank David and Dinah who made me so welcome on countless visits to Jackdaws Castle during 1994. Theirs is a remarkable story.

Jonathan Powell

Foreword

When I became Master of the Worshipful Company of Farriers in 1984 they generously decided to raise money for the Riding for the Disabled Association of which I am President. One of their ideas to raise funds was a charity race at Epsom and I foolishly volunteered to take part – if they were short of jockeys. So, having had my bluff called, where did I go to get experience and get fit that was not too far from home in Gloucestershire? The 'Duke' of course!

When you are learning something new you need somebody who is knowledgeable and honest, however uncomfortable that may be, to teach you properly. David already had a considerable reputation for both and lived comparatively close by. Thanks to his and Dinah's attention to detail and encouragement, that one race turned into several years of real enjoyment and satisfaction. I cannot thank them enough for the time they gave to an enthusiastic amateur, but there are many other amateurs and budding professionals who have enjoyed the same level of support.

I really did think that the race at Epsom would be my only race, but the friendly atmosphere at Condicote, David's thoroughly professional approach, the general level of horsemanship and the fact that I reckoned my own cross-country riding had improved, encouraged me to continue riding out – the race riding was only an extra!

Moving from Condicote was not easy, and Jackdaws Castle is unique in different ways, but the similarities are more important. The attention to detail, the care of the horses and the close-knit team are the core of their success and are an example to anyone involved in equestrian sport. I suspect the 'Duke' would not be the easiest man to work for, but he has standards and standards are not achieved without hard work and commitment that you are prepared to uphold yourself.

David's record would suggest that those standards are worth pursuing.

This book is as frank and honest as the man, which means it will both annoy and amuse you but it also tells you of the highs and lows that are an integral part of enjoying horses, which David very much does!

Anne

Her Royal Highness
The Princess Royal

Introduction

Jonathan Powell

The journey on horseback from the remote village of Condicote to the most modern training stable in the land lasts barely half an hour. You hack gently along bridle tracks across the roof of the Cotswolds, skirt around the edge of woods, and trot past stone walls built skilfully by hand, before turning downhill towards a block of immaculate new buildings set in the bowl of an ancient stone quarry.

When David Nicholson and his horses set out on this short, picturesque route on a crisp late autumn morning in 1992, it was to propel him irresistibly to the top of his profession after almost a quarter of a century as a racehorse trainer. All morning batches of horses, and their young stable lads, could be seen making their way across the skyline from their previous home in the patchwork of white and black boxes squeezed behind Cotswold House, at Condicote, to new quarters in this extraordinary state-of-the-art jumping yard.

Jackdaws Castle takes its name from the title of the field at Ford Farm that was once the site of the stone quarry. It is a bleak and beautiful setting for the most remarkable development in jump racing in the past twenty years. The distance from Condicote is scarcely four miles. The difference in facilities at Jackdaws Castle for training racehorses is light years apart.

There is room for eighty-eight horses here, with large, spacious boxes, gleaming new accommodation for the trainer and his staff, the most up-to-date advantages imaginable and an infinite variety of gallops, turf and all-weather. You will even find a helicopter landing pad. On a winter's night the twinkling lights of the Plough Inn, far below, at Ford, offer the prospect of welcome shelter from the chill currents of air that can sweep down on man and horse in the stable yard as if from the Arctic.

When David Nicholson accepted Colin Smith's invitation to move to Jackdaws Castle in October, 1992, it was a decision which set in motion his cherished maiden century of winners in his first season in residence. Twelve months later he became champion trainer for the first time. He was champion again in the 1994–95 season, during which his horses earned almost £900,000 in prize money.

It could not have happened at Condicote where he began training a handful of horses in 1968, while still one of the country's leading jump jockeys. Combining the two roles is not for the faint-hearted, but Nicholson was encouraged in the strength of his ambition by the striking success his father had achieved as a jockey and trainer.

Frenchie Nicholson is one of the few men to have won the Gold Cup and Champion Hurdle as a jockey. What's more, he was joint champion jockey in 1944–45. But his finest gift to racing still lay ahead, for in the evening of his career the canny old horsemaster unleashed a conveyor belt of riding talent from his little yard at Prestbury beside Cheltenham racecourse.

David Nicholson was his father's first graduate. Hard though it is to believe now, he rode on the flat at the age of twelve. Thin is one thing. The shape he presented in his teens and early twenties was so cadaverous you could almost see right through him, yet he became one of the finest jump jockeys of his age. He was followed by a veritable host of star names on the flat, from Paul Cook, Tony Murray and Richard Fox through to Pat Eddery and finally Walter Swinburn.

David Nicholson is known universally in the racing world as 'the Duke'. Today he has taken over the mantle of producing young jockeys, with one crucial difference. Nearly all his boys have become jump jockeys. At the last count not far short of one hundred hopefuls had ridden their first winner under his disciplined guidance. It is a figure which he acknowledges with much pride.

To spend a winter's day beside the trainer at Jackdaws Castle is to feel the heartbeat of jump racing. Here at this briskly efficient yard you will find as exciting a team of steeplechasers and hurdlers as has been assembled these past few years.

The jaunty two-mile champion chaser Viking Flagship, neat and lithe, canters eagerly past, as keen a worker as you could wish to see. Nearby is the enigmatic Barton Bank, so gifted, so frustrating; a horse whose habit of trying to demolish the odd fence and whose tendency to break blood vessels in the spring has restricted his accumulation of glory.

The stable is rich in talent in every department: top class hurdlers, promising young store horses, battle-hardened handicappers and any number of four-year-olds fresh from the flat. They, like all the horses here, are given endless schooling practice until they can jump to the manner born. Long tom in hand, Nicholson delegates in a calmer manner than his stern reputation might suggest. Yet, when he speaks, assistants scurry to carry out his orders.

'Jumping is the name of the game,' he insists, stabbing his finger towards a hard-pulling grey clumsily clattering through the tops of hurdles placed across an all-weather gallop.

'He will learn. Broadsword was worse than that when he started. Schooling is vital after a first run, too, despite what some trainers might think,' he declares in a manner that defies argument.

Nicholson is a born leader of men. Stubborn, unyielding even, he is compulsively competitive with an unmistakable hardness at the core. There is a physically commanding presence about the man that tends to defy argument. He is also surprisingly emotional and displays a fierce loyalty to those who work and ride for him.

In another, grimmer age he would have led his men unhesitatingly over the top from the trenches. Yet on a bad day he is like a volcano waiting to erupt with the distant promise of further explosions to come. The large blue eyes set in a bluff, open face are alive with a challenging directness. When he chooses, he can be forthrightly and undiplomatically honest to the point of embarrassment. From time to time his fury has overflowed in belligerent public statements. Jockeys, stewards, race officials and journalists have all felt the full force of his invective. It was always thus.

As captain of the National Hunt Jockeys cricket and soccer teams for many years, Nicholson was widely considered by his own players to be a tyrant. The opposition were less complimentary about his uncompromising will to win. But his players always turned up again the following week, and when the game was over the captain would be the first to shake his opponent's hand and buy him a drink.

Like him or not, David Nicholson is one of the great characters of jump racing. He is a man who likes to dominate. When he tells you what he is going to do or, just as likely, what you are going to do, he can invest it all with a huge sense of importance. He delights many, amuses others and unquestionably infuriates some, but you ignore him at your peril.

His life has changed immeasurably since that momentous move from Condicote to Jackdaws Castle late in 1992. Here, on the gallops in the early mornings before the phone starts its incessant ringing, the Duke is relaxed, like his horses. You sense that his new level of success has brought an inner contentment, for his is now the most powerful jumping yard in the land.

1

Little Frenchie

Stanley Wootton was the man who, more than any other, shaped Frenchie Nicholson's eventful life in racing. Wootton, an Australian, was brought to England in 1907 by his parents, who were eager to promote the burgeoning career of his brother Frank, an outstanding apprentice. Frank Wootton possessed such prodigious talent that he became champion jockey on the flat here in four successive seasons while still a teenager.

Stanley Wootton was a successful jockey, too, but not quite in the class of his brother. He was barely eleven when he rode in his first race but his career was a short one. Increasing weight was already a major problem for him and the First World War put an end to his riding ambitions. He survived the horrors of the Somme and the sinking of the ship taking him to Palestine, where he later won the Military Cross.

When he returned from the war Wootton began training at Treadwell House in Epsom and swiftly developed into the finest tutor of jockeys in the history of racing. In those days if you wanted your son to become a jockey you wrote first to Stanley Wootton at Epsom. He would have upwards of a dozen likely lads at any one time and through discipline, hard work and frequent practice turned many of them into the best young apprentices of their time.

The list of graduates from the Wootton academy bears some of the legendary names of racing in a golden age. Charlie Smirke, Joe Marshall, Arthur Wragg, Ken Gethin, Staff Ingham, Johnny Gilbert, Jackie Sirett, Billy Stott, Vic Smyth, Peter Ashworth, Tommy Hawcroft, Jackie Crouch and Harry Sprague were just some of his boys who became top class jockeys.

Apprentices today who can flit from trainer to trainer without *so much as a goodbye would not have survived five minutes under the regime of Stanley Wootton. A tough, uncompromising man, he ruled by fear and corrected riding errors on the gallops with a painful flick of his long tom, wielded from the saddle of his hack galloping close by. Wootton was known with good reason as a strict disciplinarian.*

He was, in short, a martinet. Wootton was meticulous in everything he undertook and expected his apprentices to be the same. There were no short cuts. His apprentices were taught to be polite and punctual and to turn themselves out immaculately at all times. Disobedience was not tolerated.

Offenders were invariably summoned like naughty school-boys to the billiard room at Treadwell House after evening stables for a stern lecture followed by a few accurate lashes with a horse whip. Every apprentice was expected to box whether he liked it or not. Information about horses and gallops was considered entirely confidential. Anyone caught breaking this rule faced instant dismissal.

Those who survived the harsh early days and could ride soon found the benefits of such a regime. The hours were long, the wages almost non-existent, but to be a Wootton apprentice in the 'twenties and 'thirties was to be in constant demand. Boys were taught the importance of race tactics. They were expected to hug the rails to save ground and always to endeavour to take the shortest route in a race. Wootton liked his apprentices to ride patiently, to conserve the energy of their mounts and gauge the strength of the opposition in front before making a late run for victory. At home they were instructed to ride in a low crouch with a straight back, and elbows and toes tucked in. Any departure from this neat, tidy and effective style brought instant retribution from the trainer's long tom.

If you worked for Wootton, evening stables involved three hours grooming two or three horses. The trainer was a master of detail when he inspected his horses each evening. Grooming tools were expected to be laid out in place, body brush, curry comb, rubber, dandy brush, sponge . . . all neatly in line. The straw in the box had to be twisted back immaculately from the door. Scrapings from the horse's coat were placed in a small heap to show that the work had been done properly.

Sometimes the trainer would run his fingers through a horse's mane, then look bleakly at the lad attending him and growl, 'My

boy, I am filthy after being in the box with you.' Punishment
would swiftly follow.

It was to Wootton's Treadwell House stables that my father
was sent early in 1928. He had spent an unusually nomadic
existence as a young boy. It is said he attended a dozen schools
by the age of twelve.

Father was born on January 13, 1913 at Maltby, near
Rotherham in Yorkshire where his parents farmed. His father
Harry Nicholson was a great character, a tough, no-nonsense,
typically resolute Yorkshireman who made his living from
riding and dealing in horses. He was a good, old-fashioned
horse coper.

Grandfather's schooldays at Rugby ended abruptly the
morning he stuck the sharp end of a quill into a master's heel
during a lesson and cried, 'Revolution!'

He was a happy-go-lucky countryman, full of devilment.
Brown envelopes that he suspected might contain bills were
put at once into a roll-topped desk and remained unopened.
Where finance was concerned he just hoped for the best. He
did not buy a cap in his life. When he needed one he would
just go into the nearest pub, have a drink, pick up the first cap
that fitted and walk out with it on his head.

When Harry Nicholson took a job in America running a stud
in New Hampshire my father, who was aged only five, caused
havoc by splashing a large pot of red paint in all directions the
day that the owner visited his mares and foals. Apparently he
was unmanageable at that stage.

Harry Nicholson used to go rabbit shooting on a marvellous
mare who did not seem to mind when he fired with the rifle
resting between her ears. However much he had to drink on a
night out, he could be sure that she would carry him safely home.
He was a fearless horseman: while in America he is said to have
jumped a fence standing seven feet high on a four-year-old.

Later in his life my grandfather ran a livery yard at Cambridge
for undergraduates. It was during his time there that he rode
from Cambridge to Cheltenham to win a bet of £100. The student who challenged him to attempt this unusual feat set out with
him, but was exhausted after two days in the saddle. Undeterred,
my grandfather carried him on his horse as well on the last leg of
the journey from Andoversford to Cheltenham on the third day.

Undergraduates always relished their time spent hunting with him. You can be sure he gave full value. If he felt they had not had sufficient excitement during the day, he would encourage them to jump in and out of people's gardens as they trotted home on the outskirts of Cambridge.

Later my grandfather moved to France to hunt a pack of hounds for an American near Pau in the Bordeaux region. By the time my father was nine years old he was bold enough to lie up with the leaders in the hunt. It was while he was in the South of France that arrangements were made for him to become apprenticed on the flat in 1925 to Charlie Clout at Lamorlaye.

He was barely twelve when he moved there. He lived in a hostel in the village, ate in cafés and complained for the rest of his life that apart from a paltry wage of a few francs he was also expected to buy his own bootlaces! He stayed in France for three years, and had a handful of race rides but was always going to be too heavy for flat racing.

My father found life impossibly tough at times in the early weeks after his transfer to Epsom in 1928. Within days he had been given the nickname that was to stay with him for the rest of his life: initially the lads at Wootton's called him Little Frenchie because he arrived wearing a French raincoat. Though he was not aware of it at the time, the harsh lessons he learned during seven years apprenticed to Wootton proved the foundation of his own system for producing young jockeys forty years later.

Harry Sprague, a brilliant jump jockey who rode against my father, and later rode for him, was apprenticed to Jack Reardon in Epsom at the age of thirteen, but spent a significant spell with Stanley Wootton. Harry points out one crucial difference between Wootton's system and that employed by my father in the 'sixties and 'seventies: 'Frenchie used similar methods to Wootton but he also advised his apprentices financially. He encouraged them to save, to be sensible with their money. His wife Diana was brilliant with the young boys in their care. She organised and helped them. Together they really looked after their apprentices.

'Frenchie did the same things as my old guv'nor but he was a bit milder in his ways. Times had changed. He was strict, yes, but he could not compete with Stanley Wootton. Nobody could do that. When Frenchie told a boy off, it was soon forgotten.'

Wootton's apprentices were not allowed time off. They were expected to work seven days a week, including Sundays, with just one week's holiday a year. Harry Sprague was paid a shilling a week for the first six months in 1933 – my father earned even less at first. This rose to two shillings a week after six months and to two shillings and sixpence after two years. Wootton's secretary opened a bank account for Father but for a long time he did not earn enough money to make any useful savings. Sometimes there would be apprentices riding in Classic races, like the Derby, still earning less than five shillings a week, although clothes for riding and for going racing were provided by the trainer. In return the boys were given an education and a start in life they were unlikely to find anywhere else in racing.

Some of the boys lived in dormitories at the stables. Those who had lodgings in the town were given a pound a week for their landladies. My father shared digs in Beech Way, Epsom with Sean Magee and Arthur Wragg.

Even in their all too brief spare time apprentices were never free from the control of the trainer. Innocuous visits to the cinema or a local dance had to be vetted by Wootton. Often he would not grant permission. If his boys were riding the next day he liked them to be tucked up in bed by nine p.m. Celebrations were not encouraged. Even when an apprentice had won a Classic he was expected to be back at work the next morning. The pubs in Epsom and elsewhere were out of bounds. Landladies, too, were strict and were likely to report to Wootton if their charges stayed out late.

One of my father's friends at Wootton's was the son of Jimmy Gold, who was a member of the Crazy Gang. It was a connection that gave my parents no end of fun in the following years. Bud Flanagan and Chesney Allen both had horses in training and their attractive crazy quilt colours have been carried with distinction in the 'nineties by Oh So Risky.

Father and his friends used to go to a dance in Epsom on Saturday nights. He never paid to get in, for the good reason that invariably he did not have any money. Refreshment came in the form of a hot cup of tea at the bar. He did not pay for that either but simply rattled the saucer in a manner which suggested he had put some money in. At the end of the evening the boys travelled home on the bus, though they rarely paid a fare. On one occasion fourteen small apprentices squeezed into

a taxi after a night out. They were in such a lively mood that
the driver lost control and they all ended up in a hedge near
the Downs.

One night Father had to conjure up a top hat to wear at a
particularly smart function. Once again penniless at the end of
the evening he tried to sneak on to the last bus home without
paying by climbing through a window. He was spotted by the
conductor, who barred his entry and threw his top hat under
the bus. Father was forced to walk home. Usually when he was
late he was able to attract the attention of the landlady's son by
tossing stones or gooseberries against his window. But this time
he could not raise any response and so slept the night huddled
in the porch.

Sometimes as many as nine or ten Wootton boys would be
riding at the same race meeting. They would cram into the
back of the trainer's massive American car. All the apprentices
were expected to be standing by the car immaculately dressed
when it was time to leave for the races. On one occasion Jackie
Crouch, who later became the King's jockey, climbed behind
the steering wheel and attempted to turn the car round. But his
feet barely touched the pedals and as a result the trainer's pride
and joy was badly scratched along one side. When Wootton
appeared he demanded to know the name of the culprit and
promptly grounded him for a fortnight.

At an early age it was obvious that my father was too solidly
built for a career on the flat. Instead he was given his first ride
over hurdles at sixteen. Once his weight settled, he would have
a steak with an egg on it for breakfast, sometimes with a bottle
of beer, and that would have to last him all day.

Even in his early days as a jockey my father struggled to
control his weight. In the summer, during the break in jump
racing, it would shoot up close to twelve stone. He was pretty
much the ideal shape for a jump jockey – short and square, and
so better able than most to take falls – but he was just a shade
too solidly built for comfort. He had big bones and used to
walk and jog constantly in several sets of clothes, then sweat in
a hot bath. Ten and a half stone was his absolute minimum.

Harry Sprague recalls, 'Frenchie was a brilliant jockey, very
hard to beat, with a dead straight flat back, a typical Wootton
product.'

Father used to ride for Sprague's guv'nor Jack Reardon, but

they had a severe disagreement after he won on a horse called Tough Guy at Hurst Park. Reardon had been lining up Tough Guy for a coup for more than two years. In all that time the horse had not been allowed to run on his merits. When Father was booked to ride him at Hurst Park, his instructions were straight to the point: do not win. When he reached the start he could not find a single trier in the race.

Tough Guy could take quite a hold. He was soon in front, going as slowly as Father could manage, just cantering along. There they stayed for the rest of the race. In the end Father had to win. As he returned to unsaddle he saw Reardon, stony faced and bowler hatted, marching toward his car, a bread roll in his hand.

When racing was over Father called on the trainer at his home in Epsom to apologise and explain what had happened. He found Reardon in a rage, still wearing his bowler hat and clutching the bread roll, marching furiously up and down the lounge.

The moment my father tried to speak Reardon shouted, 'You should have jumped off.' With that Reardon threw the bread roll at him. As he ducked it smashed straight into a glass cabinet behind him.

On another occasion at Fontwell my father found himself going far too well on the run downhill for the last time on a horse that was not supposed to win that day.

'Where are you going?' asked another jockey as he shot past travelling much too fast to take the final bend.

'Straight on,' cried Father before plunging headlong into a spinney at the bottom of the course.

Despite his increasing success, Father had no luck at all in the Grand National. He came down at the first fence on his initial visit there on Jimmy James, owned by Bertram Mills, in 1935. Each subsequent year he would set off for Aintree full of expectation and each time he was disappointed. He fell in all eight attempts in the race and never got further than Becher's second time.

In 1937 he found himself briefly marooned on top of the Chair fence on Didoric and then hung on under the horse's neck as he lumbered towards the water jump. His great pal Tommy Carey, on Ready Cash, called out as he passed, 'Leave go now, Frenchie, or you will find yourself in the drink.'

He used to ride a bit for an American, Bam Blair, who trained in Epsom. Blair's doughty assault on the Grand National on the 40–1 chance Jack Horner in 1925 made a lasting impression on my father. He talked about it for the rest of his life though I suspect the story improved for the telling. What is undeniable is that he backed himself at a long price to complete the course.

According to my father Blair parted company with Jack Horner several times on the way round. At one stage the horse ended up in the canal that runs beside the course after dislodging his rider at the Canal Turn. Luckily Blair was a strong swimmer. He jumped into the water, struck out after his horse, led him back to the bank, remounted him and eventually crossed the line in seventh place. The next year, ridden by a professional, Jack Horner won the National!

It was at Liverpool that my parents first met. My mother Diana Holman had gone there with Fulke Walwyn's first wife Di. Though my father was universally known in racing as Frenchie at that time, his family still called him Denton.

The name of Holman runs like a golden thread through the pages of Cheltenham's history. My mother's great-grandfather William Holman settled in Prestbury in 1834. He trained in the middle of the racecourse, won the Grand Annual Chase five times and trained the winners of three Grand Nationals, Little Charley, Freetrader and Anatis between 1856 and 1860.

The Grand Annual was Gloucestershire's first properly organised steeplechase. The race that William Holman won in 1847 was over a gruelling course through Noverton Lane, over a stone wall into an orchard, across a deep brook with gorse bushes on the take-off side and away through the meadows.

William Holman had six sons. Five of them became jockeys. George, the most successful of all, also won the Grand Annual Chase five times and finished second in the 1870 Grand National on The Doctor. His brother William was secretary and manager of the racecourse and another brother Alfred was much involved with the introduction of the National Hunt Festival.

The youngest of the six brothers, Frederick, managed a stud farm close to the racecourse. Some of its paddocks covered the area which is today used for parking cars. My mother Diana Holman is Frederick's grand-daughter. Her father Bill Holman was a horse dealer. He kept polo ponies in the summer at the family home Lake House and also trained a few jumpers, point-to-pointers and hunters.

My mother was a very stylish rider, tall and elegant in the saddle. She was an original member of the Pony Club, rode to hounds with the Cotswold Hunt, played polo and also rode in a few point-to-points at the age of fifteen. She was always very keen on racing and kept an immaculate scrapbook on the leading jockeys, which she has to this day.

Her view that jockeys are attractive because they are sharp, fit, athletic people, full of life, applies just as much today as it did all those years ago when she was riding out in the mornings for the local trainer Ben Roberts.

Professional jockeys, even the more successful ones, were considered to be little more than servants in those days. Despite their own racing connections at first the Holmans did not entirely approve of their daughter's liaison with my father. It all worked out in the end.

Grandfather would sometimes take a team of horses down to Devon for a fortnight. Sometimes my mother would go with him. They would stay in a hotel for the entire fortnight while the horses ran at five local courses – Totnes, Buckfastleigh, Torquay, Newton Abbot and Devon & Exeter. Only the last two survive now.

My parents became engaged in January, 1938 and were married that June at St Mary's Church in Prestbury. Tommy Carey was the best man, and the ushers included Fergus Adams, Jack Bissill, Teddy Underdown – a fine actor who also rode as an amateur – and my mother's brother, Ron Holman, who later became a highly popular racecourse judge.

The church was packed with friends from the world of racing including Fulke Walwyn, Fred Rimell, Staff Ingham, Gerry Wilson, Tim Hamey, George Archibald, Sean Magee and George Owen. After a short honeymoon touring in the North of England my parents set up home at Woodcote Hurst about a mile from Epsom racecourse.

There was a brief diversion two months later. My father enjoyed watching sport and was a particularly keen cricket fan. For years afterwards he talked of the momentous day he spent at the Oval during the Fifth Test against Australia in 1938 as Len Hutton grittily accumulated most of the runs that took him to the then world record score of 364. Father was outraged that some of the crowd barracked the great man for his slow scoring rate in the early stages of a wonderful innings that broke the Aussies' resistance.

2

Golden Miller and Medoc II

My parents moved from Epsom to Prestbury, on the edge of Cheltenham, soon after war broke out in September, 1939. I was just a few months old at the time and they did not want to bring me up close to the threat of bombing in London. At first they lived at Lake House with my grandparents, less than a furlong from the edge of Cheltenham racecourse. You simply walked out across a paddock, popped over a stile and found yourself on the side of the chase course almost opposite the grandstand.

As a small girl my mother and her friends used to watch the racing from the top of a hay waggon conveniently placed near the stile. Her father Bill Holman, a horse dealer specialising in polo ponies, supplied the starter's hack at Cheltenham for years and also trained a handful of hunter chasers. His owners were local farmers, which probably explains why everything in the yard was for sale. Most of their training was carried out on Cleeve Hill, but in later days he was also able to exercise them in the middle of the racecourse.

Trainers who used the common land up on Cleeve Hill were not allowed to mark out gallops, and it could be very dangerous, particularly on a foggy morning with a quarry on one side and steep drops on the other. But my mother, who usually led the Holman string, seemed to know instinctively where to go. Charlie Piggott, who was Lester's great-uncle, Alf Newey, Ben Roberts and Tim Hamey also trained in or near the village.

During the early months of the war my parents spent a lot of time travelling the country helping my grandfather buy up horses for the Army. These were known as remounts. Bill Holman would find the horses and Father would try them out. Some were quite wild, but he had always been able to sit tight and would have made a useful rodeo rider.

Bill Holman had been a captain in the Gunners in the First World War and was determined to become involved again. Although he was over age and had a gammy shoulder, he joined the RAF but quickly became bored when he was given a desk job. Somehow he wangled a transfer to Transport and was then posted to Palestine where he spent the rest of the war. His duties there included running the local hunt!

He was soon followed out to Palestine by my grandmother. She had acted as a night nurse in the First World War at Cheltenham racecourse and briefly, at the start of the next conflict, found herself working at night again as an inspector in a local aircraft factory. Then she joined the YWCA, who ran canteens for the Services overseas. They sent her out to Palestine, too.

This left my parents to farm the land for them and look after the horses. My father turned out to be a natural farmer. He loved keeping cattle, particularly Herefords, ran chickens and grew lots of vegetables, particularly cabbages, with the help of Italian prisoners-of-war.

The war interrupted his career at his peak. He badly wanted to join up, but failed every medical test going. By then he had broken his collar-bone thirteen times and also his leg, so was considered unfit for military service.

Instead he joined the Home Guard in Cheltenham. Since they could muster only one rifle between the lot of them, they would not have been any more effective than Dad's Army. Training and drill took place regularly at the headquarters of the local Women's Institute, and then the troops headed for the Plough in Prestbury. You can be sure they had a lot of fun.

My father continued riding over jumps until 1955, was in the top four in the jockeys' table fourteen times and was champion once, in 1944–45, when he shared the title with his friend Fred Rimell with fifteen winners apiece. Four of these came one memorable February day at Cheltenham.

During the war racing was reduced and centralised, to cut travelling costs. Sometimes there would be as many as eleven races in a day. Once my father rode in all eleven. To keep him going my mother made up a flask of egg, milk and brandy that he would sip between races through the long afternoon.

Eventually the war prevented any racing at all over jumps for two seasons. Rationing brought one advantage: for the first time in years my father was able to manage ten stone without a struggle. For a year he did not even have a car and so cycled everywhere. Things had barely started again the year that my father was champion.

He was very proud to be one of only a handful of men to have ridden the winners of Cheltenham's two greatest races: the Gold Cup and Champion Hurdle. His Gold Cup victory came on Medoc II in 1942. There were only a few jump meetings that year. I remember him telling me that there was quite a strong public lobby against that National Hunt meeting taking place, but it was allowed to go ahead because the authorities considered that racing offered a useful diversion from the grim realities of war.

There was a further threat to the 1942 Gold Cup from the bitterly cold weather, but the thaw arrived just in time. The meeting was staged, unusually, on two consecutive Saturdays, March 14 and 21, and most of the main Gold Cup contenders ran both times. On the first Saturday the Grand Annual Chase, a handicap, proved to be a full dress rehearsal for the Gold Cup a week later. Medoc II, owned by Lord Sefton, was just beaten by Red Rower with Broken Promise a close third. Savon, another leading candidate, fell and had to be put down.

The following Saturday it was Red Rower who started favourite with Medoc II a 9–2 chance in a field of twelve runners for the Gold Cup, which offered prize money of £495! The outcome was decided by a dramatic incident at the last open ditch where Solarium and Broken Promise held a clear lead. Solarium fell, bringing down Broken Promise.

Next to arrive at the fence was Red Rower. He, too, was brought to a standstill. Somehow my father on Medoc II avoided the carnage. Soon they were out on their own. Red Rower set off in urgent pursuit, but Medoc II was gone beyond recall and won by eight lengths. It was to prove the last Gold Cup until 1945. When all jump racing was cancelled here, Medoc II was sent to Ireland to continue racing.

The Gold Cup is the race that every jump jockey wants to win above all. Even though it was in wartime and so held in front of a very small crowd, there was never any doubt that this triumph gave my father a big thrill. His reward was a cheque for £100 from Lord Sefton.

He always felt he was a bit unlucky not to win a Gold Cup on the peerless Golden Miller. The mighty Miller's accumulation of glory included an unprecedented five victories in the race and a famous triumph in the Grand National. He is the only horse to complete the elusive double in these two races in the same year, 1934. He was a supremely versatile horse and won at every distance from two to four and a half miles.

Father rode a bit for Golden Miller's previous trainer, Basil Briscoe, and used to say he was given his chance on the old horse in the 1938 Gold Cup because by then they had gone through all the other jockeys. He was owned by the redoubtable Dorothy Paget, whose eccentric behaviour was the despair of her trainers. Later she was to play a major part in the lives of my parents.

My father was twenty-four when he rode Golden Miller for the first time in an optional selling chase at Birmingham on February 22, 1937. They won, unextended, by fifteen lengths.

He would surely have taken the Gold Cup on him that year, too, but bad weather early in March caused the National Hunt Festival to be put back for one week. The Champion Hurdle was held seven days later, but snow covered the course on Gold Cup day. The stewards called off the meeting but the decision was taken prematurely at eleven in the morning. It then thawed so rapidly that the course was fit for racing long before the time of the first race. In these more enlightened times all sorts of contingency plans are drawn up in similar circumstances to ensure that major championship races are not lost. Unhappily for the connections of Golden Miller the authorities were not so flexible then.

Father won twice more on Golden Miller in the spring of 1938. At Sandown in January the old horse gave the second, Sporting Piper, no less than thirty-four lbs and outran him on the hill to gain an heroic victory by three quarters of a length. Late in February horse and rider returned to Birmingham for another facile triumph in an optional seller. Though no one realised it at the time, it proved to be the mighty Miller's last victory.

Less than a fortnight later Golden Miller started favourite at 7–4 to win the Cheltenham Gold Cup for an unrivalled sixth time. His presence ensured a record crowd of 19,992, but extremely firm going that spring was not in his favour. Perhaps, too, at eleven, the great old warhorse was past his peak. Certainly he struggled for much of the race but somehow he still led coming down the hill for the final time. It was only on sufferance.

Morse Code pressed him hard round the last bend and held a slender lead approaching the final fence. The Miller fought back so valiantly on the flat that he almost drew level halfway up the steep, pitiless hill. The Miller tried, how he tried, but even his stout heart was not quite enough this time and Morse Code prevailed by two lengths. On the way back the crowd cheered the runner-up as much as the winner.

My father won the Champion Hurdle in 1936 on Victor Norman, trained by his friend Bam Blair, but there was a painful price to pay. Three months earlier he had broken his leg in a race fall. For a long time it seemed unlikely that he would recover in time to ride at the National Hunt Festival.

Jockeys today have to carry a medical record book with details of all their injuries. After every fall they must pass the racecourse doctor's scrutiny before they can ride again. The rules were much more relaxed in my father's time. He was determined to come back for the Champion Hurdle, but the injury had been a severe one and it was touch and go if he would be fit enough on the day of the race. Astonishingly, Victor Norman was his first ride after breaking his leg. Of course the break had not mended properly and his premature return aggravated the damage further. As a result he limped slightly for the rest of his life.

He was exceptionally tough, even by the demanding standards of that time. Once, he rode again within nine days of breaking a collar-bone. On another occasion he came back very swiftly after breaking all the toes in his right foot when he was put through the rails at Kempton. His doctor bandaged each toe tightly and he was able to ride with the help of a special support under his foot.

Although jockeys then wore only flimsy cork helmets for protection, he did not suffer from concussion until his last years of race riding. He did sustain a particularly bad back injury at Fontwell after a fall that catapulted him against a concrete upright. He ended up in a hospital at East Grinstead full of seriously wounded airmen but insisted on being discharged after a fortnight.

His doctor believed that he regained his strength by determinedly throwing up hundreds of bales on to hay stacks the following summer. Years later he aggravated the old injury when he had a nasty fall on the road at home. He also skinned the back of his head horribly as he was dragged along for over a hundred yards. Though he was in great pain, he made light of it all. Nothing put him out of action for very long.

3

Banco with Dorothy Paget

In 1946 my father started training horses as well as riding them. He had already gained some useful practice with two horses sent to him, unofficially, by Charlie Piggott. He began with a small team of jumpers because people in Gloucestershire did not accept that flat horses could be trained successfully at Prestbury.

At first, at the request of an owner, he bought six horses in Ireland with the help of Cyril Harty. All six won but none the less they were abruptly transferred to the owner's previous trainer, Neville Crump, when he returned from the war. It was an early, painful insight into the unpredictable business of training racehorses for a living.

By then my parents were living at Sandford Dene, their home close to Lake House. Their team of racehorses would make its way through the village on the way to the daily assault on the steep slopes of Cleeve Hill. You never quite knew what to expect up there. Once we passed a scantily clad couple entwined under a tree. My mother, who was at the back of the string, was heard to observe, 'Oh dear. It gets more like Piccadilly up here every day!'

Soon after receiving his licence my father bought a useful Irish hurdler called Mr Fitz for £1,000, and could not understand why the horse was so cheap until he was delivered to the yard. Father's bedroom was right over the yard so he could hear everything that was going on.

Mr Fitz proved to be the worst windsucker you have ever seen, but it was a fault that did not stop him winning races. He was successful at the first attempt in England at Cheltenham in October, 1946, and the following year my father won five races in a row on him, including the November Handicap at Liverpool under a big weight.

Father was always on very good terms with the Head family from Chantilly, who have been such a force in French racing for several generations. In 1947 Willie Head brought over a high class horse called Le Paillon, to be ridden by his son Alec in the Champion Hurdle, which was held that year in April.

As my father walked the course with them he did his level best to persuade Willie Head to let him ride Le Paillon the following day. But old Willie insisted he must be faithful to his son, whose lack of knowledge of this unique course showed as he took Le Paillon, the 2–1 favourite, on the scenic route on the wide outside. Le Paillon was beaten by only a length by National Spirit. He must have won with an English jockey. Later that year he gained unexpected compensation in the Prix de l'Arc de Triomphe in Paris!

At the time Father was still riding as first jockey to Fulke Walwyn. He twice won four races in a day at Cheltenham for Fulke, but the two did not always see eye to eye. As I was to discover years later it is not easy to combine the two roles of jockey and trainer.

Once at Cheltenham Father rode a horse that Fulke was very keen to sell for the good reason that he was extremely moderate. He was down to carry 11st. 5 lbs but after Father weighed out Fulke persuaded him to hand him his lightest saddle. The horse finished fifth, running on as if he would improve for the run. No wonder, since he carried almost a stone and a half less than intended. Only the first four were required to weigh in, so Father escaped detection. The horse was subsequently sold.

At Windsor, acting on the trainer's instructions, Father gave one of Fulke's a very quiet ride, finished fifth, although he could have been a lot closer. It led to an appearance before the stewards. At first Fulke did not respond when he was asked by the stewards if he was satisfied with the way his jockey had ridden. He soon spoke up when my father gave him a hefty kick on the ankle.

Father always liked to deal a bit, too. Towards the end of the war he bought a useful novice called Port O'London and sold him on to Fulke Walwyn a fortnight before the Cheltenham Festival with the promise that he would win the novice hurdle on him at the meeting. He duly did so at 5–4.

The next autumn, after a summer's break, the horse reappeared at Fontwell. For some reason Fulke did not expect him to run well that day and suggested he had a quiet run. My father explained that Port O'London was such a good horse he could not fail to win, however he was ridden.

The trainer was adamant and instructed him that if all else failed, he should jump out and make the running because that way the horse was sure to blow up. Down at the start Father discovered there was not a single horse fancied in the race. So he popped out in front, made the running and won with embarrassing ease. Fulke was furious. Father won again on Port O'London next time but their fruitful partnership was coming to the end.

Eventually Fulke told Father, 'Frenchie. You've got the sack.'

'Mine's full. I hope yours is,' he replied quick-wittedly.

In the days before SIS and camera patrols, jockeys were able to pull strokes without anyone spotting any misdemeanours. Once at Wincanton Father set out to ride his own horse Côte d'Azur who was extremely slow. Thick fog enveloped the course like a shroud. Spectators could barely see the last hurdle, let alone the racing out in the country. At Wincanton in those days there were no running rails on the inside on the far side of the track.

So going towards the far turn Father moved to the inside, then suddenly turned right and nipped across the middle of the course and joined the field again going to the second last hurdle. Côte d'Azur appeared to finish full of running as he passed the winning post upsides the sixth horse Jet Meteor, ridden by Bob Turnell.

The trainer of Jet Meteor told Turnell, 'You can't have run very well if Côte d'Azur finished alongside.'

Turnell replied, 'You should have seen where he has been!'

The result of all this subterfuge was that Father was able to sell the horse at a profit. Years later, purely out of devilment, I took the same short cut at Wincanton on one of my own horses, who had no chance that day. I just wanted him to run well and make a show. We finished close behind the placed horse and luckily the stewards remained unaware of the move.

People imagine that everyone involved with racing bets for a pastime. Father was too careful to be a punter and burned his fingers on the two occasions he did put £25 on a horse. He thought Ursulus was a certainty at Taunton one day, but the horse slipped twice on the tight bends there and was beaten.

He was convinced Flaming Steel was an even bigger certainty in a novice chase because he jumped for fun at home. But the horse was startled by a train blowing its whistle as he was just about to take off at a fence and fell. That put Father off betting for life.

Father kept himself in tip-top condition specifically to ride Flaming Steel in the 1949 Grand National. It broke his heart when the horse was taken away by the owner and sent to Tom Yates shortly before Liverpool. Flaming Steel was a difficult, highly strung horse with a kink. He would not come down the ramp of a horsebox and invariably tried to launch himself from the top out into the middle of the yard. He also tended to try to walk backwards or sideways down Cleeve Hill.

All this would have infuriated some trainers but Father liked a challenge, understood him and came to love that horse. He was very excited about his chance at Aintree and believed this was the one to give him an overdue success there. Instead, he was ridden by an amateur, Joe Spencer, who adopted forcing tactics and ignored my father's advice to ride a waiting race. Flaming Steel finished fifth to the 66–1 shot Russian Hero. My father had no doubt he would have gone close to winning on the horse. Even worse, poor Flaming Steel sliced through one of his tendons while schooling a fortnight later and had to be put down.

My father was so upset that he rather lost interest in being a jockey. He simply kept himself fit enough to ride what he wanted. Each summer his weight rose to around twelve stone. He would not go near a sauna or take pills to help him lose weight quickly. He warned me that the more you took off in a sauna or steam bath, the more you would put on afterwards.

Instead, he used to walk off excess pounds. That way he remained exceptionally fit. Just working hard in the yard at home made him sweat. He did not like being idle. If he had a spare afternoon, he would go out for a couple of hours cutting down weeds round the schooling fences or scything nettles. Most mornings he would jump off and lead his mount up the steepest parts of Cleeve Hill on the way to the gallops. At times it was like climbing a mountain. He was very conscious of being fit.

Although he sometimes said he would be just as happy farming rather than training, there is no doubt that my father had a way with horses. He certainly found the key to an apparently useless chaser called Rough Night who had not threatened to win a race in more than thirty attempts over three years for his previous trainers.

He discovered that Rough Night was prone to breaking blood vessels, ate his own bedding and, at times, some of his droppings. Father put him in one of the orchard boxes and left the door open so that he could wander out in the paddock. Soon he developed a taste for apples. The result of all this was that he won five out of his first six races for us and would probably have won the sixth if he had not slipped and fallen at the water jump when he was odds-on at Warwick.

Irish Lizard was probably the best horse my father trained. He was a hardy annual in the Grand National for years, twice finished third and kept going for so long that he became an enormously popular horse in the area. He was the first big love of my sister Josie, who was born on Gold Cup day, 1950. She adored the horse and, as a little girl, often used to hide in his box.

Though he had thin soles on his feet Irish Lizard was a wonderfully sound horse and did not once need a bandage on his legs. That was just as well, because if he had the slightest scratch he thought he was dying. If you shouted or growled at him, he became very upset.

Really he was unusually sensitive for a chaser, not the type you would expect to do well at Aintree, so my mother rode him in all his work because she felt he needed looking after. He gave the impression that he would be far too timid for the mighty fences they had to jump in those days. He even refused at home when Martin Molony came down to school him before his first attempt at the Grand National. It was all so misleading because he had tremendous courage and proved a natural at Aintree after some early hiccups there.

It is doubtful whether Irish Lizard would ever have been sent to race at Liverpool if he had not belonged to Lord Sefton, who owned the course at the time. He possessed tremendous pace for an out-and-out stayer. If my father had any three-year-olds that could go with him over one and a half miles on Cleeve Hill, then he could be sure they would win races.

Irish Lizard was a superb jumper, yet he had a disastrous

introduction to Liverpool when he and my father were forced out through the wing of a hurdle. Nor did he have much luck when he first tackled the Grand National in 1951, for he was one of twelve horses that crashed out at the first fence. Thus, at one dramatic stroke a third of the field was eliminated. No blame can be attached to Irish Lizard. The form book says that he was brought down, but my mother insists to this day that Pat Taaffe, having his first ride in the race, simply fell off him.

Much the same happened the following year when he was ridden by Rex Hamey. This time he was among ten horses put out of the race at the first fence. Once again he did not fall.

Matters improved greatly in 1953. On the opening day of the Aintree meeting on Thursday Irish Lizard gained an overdue victory over the mighty fences in the Topham Trophy ridden by Dick Francis. Two days later, partnered by Bob Turnell, he turned out again in the Grand National and finished a highly creditable third to Early Mist.

By now he was a standing dish at Liverpool. He started favourite for the 1954 Grand National, aged eleven, after winning his last three races including the Christmas Cracker Chase at Aintree in December and the Fred Withington Chase over four miles at Cheltenham.

When Michael Scudamore arrived at Lake House to drive my father up to Liverpool on the Saturday, he asked if he had packed his dinner jacket.

'Why do I need a dinner jacket?' was the reply.

Michael explained that the winner's connections were expected to attend the annual celebration dinner at the Adelphi Hotel in Liverpool.

'Win or lose I will be coming home straight after the race to lock up the chickens,' declared Father.

Irish Lizard finished third to Royal Tan that year to continue the tremendous run of form of horses trained at Prestbury. Four Ten, trained by John Roberts, had already won the Gold Cup at 100–6 and Impney, from Phil Doherty's stable, was second to Sir Ken in the Champion Hurdle. John Roberts had the foresight to have a £1 each way treble on the three at long odds at Christmas.

At home Irish Lizard was such a character that he was aloof from the other horses. It was almost as if he expected to be treated as part of the family. During his summers in the paddocks my sister Josie, who was six or seven at the time, seemed to appoint herself as his personal valet. He could not stand the pigs on a neighbouring farm. If he was downwind of them, it would drive him demented.

In the 1955 Grand National Irish Lizard, by now twelve, was yet again one of the leading fancies at 100–8. Though age was beginning to catch up with him a bit, he duly completed the course in his own time in eleventh place, a few lengths behind my uncle, Brigadier W. Ron Holman, a regular soldier aged forty-one who maintained the family tradition by finishing eighth on Wild Wisdom. The Lizard returned in triumph to the course in November with yet another stirring victory in the Christmas Cracker Chase. You hardly needed to put the old fellow in a horsebox for the long journey to Liverpool; he seemed to know his own way by then. Unfortunately a ricked back caused him to miss the Grand National the following year, but he returned once more at the age of fourteen in 1957.

After much debate among the family it had finally been decided to my enormous delight, and I must admit trepidation, that I would ride him at Liverpool. I was barely eighteen years old and extremely inexperienced over fences, which was why we came down at Becher's Brook on the first circuit. It was the first time the old horse had fallen over the big Aintree fences in sixteen races and it was entirely my fault.

In those days racing at Liverpool was enormously popular. In addition to the Grand National two other meetings were held over the unique fences at the course, the Sefton meeting in November and the Christmas meeting in December. So sometimes the Lizard would run there three times in a season. He twice won the Christmas Cracker Chase towards the end of his career.

Irish Lizard was in training at Prestbury for ten successive years. My father felt his loss for a long time when he was retired to Lord Sefton's estate at Croxteth, Aintree. The grooms there found it impossible to catch him once he was turned out in a field.

I remember going to see him with my parents when he was nineteen. Lord Sefton explained that we would be unable to get near Irish Lizard, but some horses have good memories and his must have been happy ones. Father simply walked into the middle of this big field and called out. At once Irish Lizard came trotting up and stood there rubbing his head up and down on my father's chest. I can tell you it moved us all close to tears.

Michael Scudamore, who rode the horse more than anyone else, was frequently employed by my father in those days. The two became close friends. Once at Chepstow Michael started to make excuses after a race.

'Son, you can't kid one who has kidded millions,' came the reply. It was a phrase he often used.

We did have a Gold Cup winner in the yard at Prestbury for a couple of nights in 1948. His name was Cottage Rake. That was the year the legendary Irish trainer Vincent O'Brien sent horses to the Cheltenham Festival for the first time. Even then, early in his career, Vincent was a master of detail. He was concerned that the horse should be in a quiet, relaxed hotel away from the noisy racecourse stables. There was also a further concern about security. Vincent approached my father, who agreed to take Cottage Rake as a lodger.

Cottage Rake proved to be quite small and light, almost in the mould of a flat horse. Indeed he won the Irish Cesarewitch and the Naas November Handicap over a mile and a half. Father was asked to make sure he was given bran, Guinness and eggs, a diet of sloppy food that horrified our lads.

On the morning of the race his owner Frank Vickerman came to the yard to have his picture taken with his horse. Cottage Rake beat Dorothy Paget's Happy Home by one and a half lengths in the Gold Cup and that evening the O'Briens were very excited when they called to see him. My mother took a photograph of Mrs Vickerman, the owner's wife, sitting on a rickety tricycle belonging to my brother Richard.

Cottage Rake proved to be an outstanding chaser by completing a famous hat-trick in the Gold Cup in the next two years. Ironically my father had seen him as a young horse on a shopping trip to Ireland with Waring Willis. Cottage Rake, Freebooter and Hatton's Grace were all in the same field! None of them had run at the time.

Father used to change in the weighing-room next to Ben Lay, a top class jockey who was also a farmer. 'Farmers to the fore again,' their valet Arthur Lord would say when he found them discussing the price of bullocks between races.

When he had the time my father liked to attend farm sales in the area. He was always on the look-out for a bargain and found one when he paid ninety guineas for a three-year-old grey filly called Staunton at a farm sale near Upton-on Severn. Most people were interested in buying cattle, sheep and farm implements but three thoroughbreds were tacked on to the end of the auction that day.

It was not, in all honesty, the obvious place to find a decent racehorse. But Father struck lucky. He liked Staunton and later passed her on for a decent profit to Hector Smith, who sent her to be covered by a stallion called Wyndham. The product of that union was Windy City, the champion two-year-old of 1951 who, trained by Paddy Prendergast, won the Gimcrack Stakes at York and also top class races abroad.

Each summer my father used to build a large hay-rick in the paddock. He would thatch the top of it to make it waterproof, a skill he picked up from the fence builder on Cheltenham racecourse. It would take him up to a fortnight in the evenings to complete the thatching. He would come in pouring with sweat, have a quick bath, then head for the Plough for his evening pint.

One June I remember him complaining several times that the work was too hot. He had just finished his work of art that particular summer when smoke appeared from the hay-rick. It must have been smouldering for some time. Soon the whole lot went up in flames. No wonder he had been too hot working on top of the rick. The smell of the remains of that charred hay lingered for weeks.

Fire is a constant worry with so much straw and hay stored near horses. One Sunday night in April, 1963 my parents woke to the terrifying sound of flames devouring the wooden barn that formed part of the yard. Sparks from a bonfire next door had set alight the thatched roof of the barn. Three horses were stabled close to the barn but the lads managed to lead them all out in time.

Every horse in the yard was upset by the noise and commotion. As a precaution Father decided to pull out the three runners he had already declared at Hereford on the Monday. It was just as well that my mother managed to persuade him to change his mind. She argued that the three would never be so wound up again in their lives. Tobago and PC Wren both won and Halligan finished second.

My father always struggled to fill the boxes at home. For him twenty-five was a big string of horses. He was a private man and was not entirely comfortable chatting up owners. That was not his style. He had a strict rule against drinking on a racecourse. He maintained that if he had one drink, he would want twenty-one. So he restricted himself to a coffee while he chatted with the owners. The only time I can ever remember him breaking his rule was at Liverpool after the owners of Fighting Kate landed a gamble.

Today the social side of racing is a much more important part of training. In those days thirty-five horses was a big string. Today sixty-five or seventy is the norm. You have to go racing and look after the owners whether you like it or not.

Training horses in Prestbury became quite dangerous in the 'fifties as traffic increased in the area. Part of the road surface in Mill Street leading towards Cleeve Hill was as slippery as glass. After several horses had come down on the road my father took to using the local footpaths instead. One day he was stopped by a fussy PC and booked for breaking the law. He was furious that he should be in trouble for protecting his horses. This led to a rare appearance before Cheltenham magistrates, who fined him a nominal five shillings for deliberately riding along the footpath in Mill Street.

Father's counsel produced a string of witnesses, including John Roberts and my grandfather, who testified that the road had become too dangerous for horses. They also argued that it was the duty of the Council to maintain the road for whatever traffic was likely to use it.

The case developed into farce at one stage with the County Council representative, a surveyor, admitting that he felt like an Aunt Sally standing before the court. Although Father lost the case, he felt he had made his point when the Court ordered the Council to restore Mill Street into a condition fit for horse traffic.

Cannobie Lee was another hardy campaigner trained by my father. He won a total of fifteen races, but like a lot of decent chasers was far from straightforward. He had useful form in Ireland as a young horse but had rather lost the habit of winning. He was a bit of a lad, too: he jumped, kicked out and bucked all the time and had a habit of shedding his riders when he dropped his shoulder. Cannobie Lee was usually ridden at home by my great friend Sam Wilson, whose claim to fame as a jockey is that he won one race over fences at Stratford in 1954.

It took two years for Cannobie Lee to dislodge Sam. When it happened he lay on the ground laughing while Father shouted furiously, 'Get up. Get up.'

By that time Cannobie Lee was always ridden with restraint in his races by Dave Dick and produced with a late challenge because he tended to pull up in front. Sam discovered that he was much happier at home working upsides in front than in behind. That way he would prick his ears and appear to enjoy himself. So Sam kept on at my father to change the tactics.

We had the chance to try it when I rode Cannobie Lee in the Golden Miller Chase at Cheltenham. When I came into the paddock, I asked my father what he wanted me to do.

'I don't know. Ask Sam. He seems to know more about the horse than me,' he replied before walking off.

So I rode the horse alongside the leader, as Sam suggested. The plan was to stay there until popping his head in front at the last moment. That was fine until the one upsides me fell with over a mile still left to run. Cannobie Lee led on his own for a bit before being headed but he fought back on the run-in to snatch the verdict in a photo-finish.

In June, 1955 my father was sent two horses by Dorothy Paget. Soon three more arrived from her previous trainer, Fulke Walwyn. Father, of course, had ridden Golden Miller a few times for her, but it was Dave Dick who suggested she sent the horses to Prestbury. The first two were pretty moderate but gradually over the next five years my parents ended up with nearly all her jump horses.

Dorothy Paget lived at Chalfont St Giles in Buckinghamshire and was a cousin of Jock Whitney, who owned the dual Gold Cup winner Easter Hero. She was an owner of such unlimited means that she made many of our landed gentry seem like smallholders, and for a few eventful years her team of horses dominated my parents' life. At one stage they had thirty of her horses in training or out to grass. This stretched their resources to the limit since there were never more than twenty-five boxes at Lake House. Luckily, they were able to use some of the spare stables in John Roberts' yard near by.

Five Paget horses that came over at an early stage from Ireland were almost too big for the job, all standing 17.2 hands or more.

They were a bit hairy and, at times, unmanageable. After that we arranged for the Irish trainer Dan Moore to take her young store horses first. He would sort them out and send over the better ones.

Miss Paget had a shocking reputation for being selfish, indecisive and bullying her trainers. She liked nothing more than ringing them up in the middle of the night. If you believed half the stories on the racecourse, she had become so antisocial she was impossible for any trainer to handle.

She was a large, obese woman, with a gargantuan appetite, was also a diabetic, did not trust racecourse catering and preferred to take her own hampers of food. When she did appear in public it was invariably in an old shapeless, woollen overcoat and an ancient, unflattering blue hat. She certainly worked her way through a few trainers and had a very public dispute with Basil Briscoe when she moved Golden Miller elsewhere at the height of his fame.

Dorothy Paget was one of those people who operated best at night. She tended to sleep through the day and come alive after dark. This was not welcome news for my father, who liked to be tucked up in bed early every evening when he returned from the pub. He knew of her habit of ringing her trainers late at night and sensibly refused to install a telephone extension in his bedroom. On the few occasions she ventured out to the races at Windsor or the big Festival meetings Father always made the point of leaving before the last race so that he could be home to feed the horses.

For Dorothy Paget backing horses was an obsession. Gambling ruled her life. She bet fortunes, and, though she hated losing, the vast fortune she left behind in the ring became part of racing legend. She also hated the idea of selling horses in case they won for someone else. Most of all she could not bear one of her horses winning if she had not backed it. So you had to be pretty sure that they only ran when they had a good chance or no chance at all.

This caused no end of work for my mother. Every time we had a Paget runner she was expected to go through the form of every horse in the race and comment on their chances in percentage terms.

If one had an outstanding chance, it was assessed as Banco. Then you knew Miss Paget would have a massive punt. My parents sensibly did not want to know about the huge sums involved but those closest to her often hinted that her standard Banco bet was £10,000. That was a quite staggering amount of money in the late 'fifties. If the horse was considered unbeatable, she was in the habit of describing it as double Banco. Then she would punt £20,000 in one go. Dorothy Paget settled at once when her bets lost and expected her bookies to do the same when she won.

Every fancied runner had to be described in percentage terms of Banco. Sometimes it would take my mother two hours to complete her homework on a race. The evening before they ran she would be required to ring Miss Paget's secretary Miss Williams with her views. I suppose the secretary had a Christian name, but we never did learn what it was. Every conversation with her was recorded. In addition my mother had to ring up again when she reached the racecourse to report on the prevailing conditions.

Despite Dorothy Paget's strange behaviour there is no doubt that she was very fond of her horses. She was proud of them all but was not in the habit of visiting her trainers and was often represented at the races by her friend Sir Francis Cassel, a gifted pianist. Everything was black and white in her eyes. There were no grey areas. If you told her once a horse needed soft ground, then she believed it always wanted soft.

My parents found the many stories about Dorothy Paget thoroughly misleading, for she proved to be a surprisingly good and exceptionally generous owner. No one in the family would allow a word against her. She never failed to remember people's birthdays, sent Christmas boxes for all the family and lads and would arrange tickets for Wimbledon or for the International Horse Show at the White City. When I organised a charity horseshow in Prestbury with my friend Sam Wilson, she donated all the prizes in the name of Golden Miller.

Dorothy Paget was overjoyed when my father trained three winners for her, Straight Lad, Prince of Denmark and Primate at Newbury on December 30, 1955. After Primate won the last race she did her best to steer Father towards the bar for an end-of-year celebration but as usual he made his excuses that he had to set off home to look after his other horses. I remember he drove as far as Cricklade and then announced that we would, after all, have a celebration as he pulled up outside a café. That day he treated us all to tea and doughnuts!

Prince of Denmark was a decent horse who could be a handful. After he landed a bit of a touch in a race the newspapers reported that he had smashed the watch belonging to his lad Chris Middleton and also torn the sleeve of his jacket. Miss Paget was on the telephone at once, complained that she had not been told and asked my parents to buy Chris a new watch and suit to be charged to her account.

Yet for all her generosity Dorothy Paget was always checking on her trainers. Sir Francis Cassel and her jockeys were expected to report on the condition of her horses at Prestbury. My parents found themselves in the embarrassing position of being required to file comments on her horses with Sir Gordon Richards, another of her trainers. Each spring they also accompanied Charlie Rogers on a tour of inspection of her horses in Ireland.

One of Dorothy Paget's best animals was Straight Lad, who came to us from Marcus Marsh in Newmarket. He was a tremendous galloper but, though he won eight of his first ten races for my father over hurdles, he never did learn to jump properly. He tended to gallop through the obstacles or kick them out of the way. Straight Lad was so awkward at the business of jumping hurdles that he once came back with a cut on his chest caused by an upright. Another time at Windsor he sent the top bar of the last flight high above the crowd.

I know my father felt Straight Lad was good enough to win a Champion Hurdle. He was one of the favourites for the race in 1957 but was pulled out at the last minute because he was lame. The next season, when he was not quite so effective, he ran very well, ridden by Harry Sprague, to finish a close fifth behind Bandalore.

Straight Lad was also a pretty decent horse on the flat and won the Newbury Autumn Cup for us in 1956. Unusually for a jumper he was not gelded. He eventually became a leading NH stallion.

Desert Fort was a promising chaser that belonged to Dorothy Paget, but his career seemed over when he hurt his hind joint as he slipped into the open ditch in a race at Wolverhampton. Somehow his lad managed to load him up for the journey home that night, but the next morning the full horror of the injury was plain to see. Desert Fort had dislocated the hind joint so badly that the foot was turned upside down.

When the vet tried to ease it back in place it popped out again. He advised putting the horse down, but although the cause seemed hopeless, Father would not hear of it because he was so fond of him. He was determined to give Desert Fort a chance and decided to put the damaged leg in plaster of Paris.

His leg was still healing when Miss Paget died. Since there was no realistic hope of his racing again, and no one would possibly buy him in that state, the executors gave him to my mother. After three months, when the plaster loosened round the limb, Desert Fort was led out to the nearest paddock. To my parents' amazement he then proceeded to gallop round the field. Miraculously the treatment had worked.

An ugly lump above the joint offered vivid testimony of his close brush with death, but when Desert Fort came back into training, the injury did not seem to trouble him at all. Eventually Father felt he was fit enough to race again. He recovered to such purpose that he won the Hurst Park National Trial two years running and several other races. He seemed much happier going right-handed in his races, so he was never asked to tackle the Grand National.

When Desert Fort retired from racing he was turned out in a paddock with some other horses. But he would not stay out. Once he even jumped over the paddock gate and made his way back to his old box. He was like a battle-hardened boxer who could not walk away from the ring, so we used him as a schoolmaster for our apprentices.

Dorothy Paget had been a racehorse owner for fully thirty years when she died of a heart attack, aged fifty-four, in February, 1960. Her passing was a massive blow to my parents. At a stroke they had lost the mainstay of the yard. The executors decided that all the horses should go to the Ascot sales in May. This left only six in training at the end of that season. It was particularly tough on the lads. Most of them had to go, too.

My parents were very concerned about the future. They knew they would have to give up training racehorses or quickly find another source of income. Unbeknown to them salvation was at hand in the tiny shape of a ginger-haired schoolboy who was about to join them to help out in the yard in his spare time at weekends and in his holidays. His name was Paul Cook.

4

They came on bicycles and left in Rolls Royces

Frenchie Nicholson turned dreams into reality for countless small boys who wanted to become jockeys. He was a man of conspicuous integrity, a first class, conscientious, professional tutor who pushed his staff to the limit but always, nearly always, with a twinkle in his eye. He was a no-nonsense sergeant-major, led by example and had no time for those who preferred short cuts or distractions from the job in hand.

Anyone with the slightest interest in horse racing is almost bound to have heard of Frenchie's exploits as tutor and cornerman, quiet motivator, inspired strategist and, when necessary, humane protector of his apprentices. The imprint of his gifts shows in the records of an array of outstanding performers, from his son David Nicholson, Paul Cook and Tony Murray through to Pat Eddery and Walter Swinburn, and of a small army of other substantial talents in between.

Young jockeys who enlisted Frenchie's help gained far more than a vast depth of riding expertise, for he drew on the accumulated lessons and values of a long life, rich in challenges and achievements. What began as an experiment in teaching swiftly developed into a highly efficient business, but profit was not Frenchie Nicholson's motivation. Throughout those heady years you sensed that he fed off the achievements of his apprentices with a pride that you could almost reach out and touch.

Those who endured his training were immediately identified as men who had been battle-hardened in the toughest school. All those lucky enough to pass through his hands tell the same story.

Morning after morning as the Nicholson team scrambled its way up the side of Cleeve Hill like a mountain mule-train the trainer would coax, bully, chivvy, instruct and above all boyishly share with his pupils the basics of the jockey's craft. His rather frighteningly gruff demeanour failed to disguise limitless enthusiasm for the serious task of making horses run like the wind.

Frenchie Nicholson was, above all, a coach. He did not offer flattery. Thus praise had to be earned. He encouraged flair, disliked delegating, worked every bit as hard as his pupils and rarely, if ever, took a holiday. He was a natural teacher, at times severe, with huge authority. All his pupils received the same sound advice to keep their eyes and ears open on the racecourse and their mouths firmly shut.

Yet there was a jaunty, almost cheeky side to his nature which emerged when he shared a joke. His was invariably an earthy sense of humour. Though he disguised it at times, fun was his living, too. When he stayed at Liverpool, and later Southport, during the Grand National meeting he was invariably the life and soul of the party. If there was a column to be climbed in the hotel hall after dinner, he was often the first one to make it to the top with the nimbleness of a mountaineer. Once, on a racing trip to Belgium, he clambered athletically on to a flagpole standing far above a historic square in Brussels.

He set high standards as a matter of course and was contemptuous of others who could not ride properly. Hints and tips garnered from a lifetime at the heart of racing were passed on with the sureness of a drip feed. As a result he produced a conveyor belt of star apprentices in the 'sixties and 'seventies.

A boy who can ride with the skill of a full-blown jockey and still claim a weight allowance is a priceless asset in racing. He is a trainer's main weapon in the enduring battle of wits against the handicapper, as effective as a bantam weight with lead in his gloves.

Frenchie Nicholson was essentially a trainer of hurdlers and steeplechasers. It was only late in his career that he began preparing, sharpening and teaching likely young apprentices on the flat. No one has done it better. It was as if the first forty-seven years of his life had been preparation for that most difficult of roles.

In his more mellow moments he would reflect with a

fair degree of accuracy, 'They came on bicycles and left in Rolls-Royces.'

Paul Cook was the first of many young flat-race jockeys who, under the stern guidance of my father, were to shape the fabric of British race riding. Paul was a fourteen-year-old schoolboy in Cheltenham when, on the advice of his local butcher, he wrote to my father asking for a job at his stables early in 1960.

There was not a vacancy at the time and anyway he was a bit too young; but he was invited to lend a hand in the yard in the school holidays. Though he had never sat on a horse or pony in his life when he came to us, he would cycle to the stables whenever possible, eager to help. At first he was far too small to be put on a horse but he was mad keen and so my parents ended up giving him a few shillings a week pocket money to follow the bigger apprentices around the yard with the grease pot.

After nearly a year of routine work, cleaning tack, sweeping up in the yard and mucking out stables he was allowed to ride Josie's pony or sit on the old steeplechaser Desert Fort on the way back from the Downs. He signed on as an apprentice in April, 1961, five days after his fifteenth birthday. On Sundays at that time I was mad keen to spend the day with Dinah, but sometimes my father would keep me back to give his new apprentice riding lessons. Although he was not a natural and took a long time to learn the basics of riding, Paul displayed so much spirit that he was soon going out each morning on one of the more straightforward horses in the string.

The trainer played his part to the full by buying two horses, Tenor and Balle d'Or, for him to ride in races. It was an early declaration of my parents' commitment to the expensive, time-consuming business of producing apprentices. Tenor later became a brilliant point-to-pointer and my mother was delighted to see him looking so well in retirement in Scotland when he was twenty-seven. Paul Cook duly made his race-riding debut on Balle d'Or at Bath in July, 1962.

My mother recalls, 'For a long time we thought Paul would never make the grade. If he rode with his stirrups too short he usually ended up suffering from cramp. He was just like a frog. His hands would get further and further forward and his legs would slip further and further backwards!'

To encourage him to use his legs more skilfully on Tenor my

mother offered the young apprentice 2sh. 6d. for each horse
that finished behind him in a race at Warwick. It was a lucrative
lesson. That day he earned five shillings. Once, after Paul hit a
horse with undue frequency at Bath, my father ensured that he
did not carry a whip in a race for a month.

Paul Cook's first victory came at Warwick in September,
1963. Paul was beaten a short head by a horse ridden by Joe
Mercer but the stewards upheld his objection for bumping and
gave him the race. Soon he was much in demand. In 1964
Paddy Prendergast, the legendary Irish trainer, snapped him
up for Credo in the Chester Cup after watching him finish
fifth on another horse in a two-mile handicap at Newbury.
At Chester Paul swooped fast and late on Credo to pip Scobie
Breasley and Utrillo in a tight photo-finish.

Prendergast was moved to exclaim, 'That is the best apprentice
I have ever seen. I never thought that a boy could carry out
instructions so exactly.' He later secured first claim on Paul
Cook's services in England and in the Irish Classics in 1965.
Other trainers were impressed, too. Paul progressed so swiftly
that he became champion apprentice in 1964 and 1965.

'Looking after Paul at that time was almost like managing
the Beatles,' my mother said more than once.

Paul recalls, 'Frenchie must have seen something, because he
persevered with me even though I was a hopeless case at first.
The problem was that I could not hold much and was never
really in control. I think it was basically a lack of strength.

'Frenchie always encouraged me. He was so good at giving
his time to you. He worked with us, knew what was expected
of a rider and impressed on all of us the importance of a good
start in a race.'

My parents were adept at keeping their apprentices' feet
firmly on the floor. It is hard to become big-headed when
you are picking up stones from the gallops every afternoon.
Spending-money was restricted, too, so that they could not
waste their hard-earned fees.

Paul Cook confirms, 'When you rode a few winners, Frenchie
would quickly put you back in your place. He would reprimand
you in the nicest way then give you a bollocking for nothing.
Sometimes he would grab hold of you, right or wrong. There
was no point in arguing because he would say, "I am still
learning. You know damn all yet."'

All the boys had constant advice. Father believed that you could not teach what you could not do yourself. He would frequently point out riding faults, insisted that the boys always took the shortest route in a race and drummed into them the importance of using the whip close to your side. He was also a stickler for making a quick start, particularly in the days before stalls.

Until I started training on my own I often rode out alongside the boys at morning exercise, impressing on them the advantage of looking neat and tidy on and off a horse. My mother worked on the manners and politeness of all the apprentices. She always maintained that boys of a certain age, usually in their late teens, become dissatisfied, and the fact that she understood the problem helped them get over it. She tried to find them all digs within half a mile of the yard but it was not an easy task. Some landladies objected to lively boys under their feet all afternoon.

What had begun as an experiment with Paul Cook soon developed into a full-time business for my parents. At first my father did not want to teach apprentices, but it became a matter of making ends meet. Eventually the system became so successful that the apprentices subsidised the training of the horses. One memorable day all six apprentices from the yard were riding at one meeting or another. My father was tickled pink even though he was left to complete evening stables virtually on his own.

Once I remember a journalist asking my father how many runners he had the next day.

'Two,' he replied. After studying the racecards the journalist declared that he could only find one from the yard.

Father explained, 'I have two of the two-legged variety. They are a lot easier to train. They cost less to keep, you don't have to feed them and they earn you a lot more money.'

My mother kept accounts for all the boys, who were paid a weekly wage according to their age and experience. Expenses for travel and other necessary items were deducted from their riding fees and percentages. Whatever remained was divided equally between master and apprentice. Mother ran a building society account for all the boys which was designed to give them a useful nest egg at the end of their indentures.

Father did not like the idea of a hostel and preferred to use Stanley Wootton's system of placing apprentices with landladies

around Prestbury. That way he could be confident they would
be looked after properly and he would have a better chance of
hearing if they misbehaved.

When Paul Cook ended his apprenticeship he was appointed
first jockey to Jack Jarvis at Newmarket in 1966 but found it
hard to cope with life away from home. At the time my godfather
Bruce Hobbs, who also trained at Newmarket, had second claim
on him. Father told Bruce to make sure he kicked Paul's backside
six days a week and twice on Sundays. Bruce replied that he
could handle young jockeys, but it proved to be an unhappy
episode in Paul's life.

He enjoyed some early success, won the 1966 1,000 Guineas
on Glad Rags for Vincent O'Brien and came desperately close
to victory in that year's Derby on Pretendre for Jarvis. But he
found it difficult to adjust to the hectic tempo of Newmarket
after spending his life in the calmer atmosphere of Cheltenham
and lost his job with Jarvis after two seasons. When he turned
freelance in 1968 his career nosedived calamitously but he
showed great strength of character by fighting back in the
'seventies and added another Classic, winning the St Leger
on Touching Wood in 1982.

Despite Paul's setback many many more set out to follow the
same route to fame and fortune. Journalists would frequently
press my father to reveal the methods he used to make his
apprentices so successful. Invariably he would smile, shrug and
attempt to change the subject.

If they persisted he would sometimes admit, 'I am strict. Damn
strict, but always fair. Discipline is the main thing. Without that
the boys are nothing. Manners are crucial. Politeness comes first.
I take particular note of manners when boys come to me for a
job. If any boy is rude or answers back, then he is out in a
flash. I also impress on the landladies not to be soft on them,'
he would insist.

'As a lad I learned the importance of style. Stanley Wootton
always said, "Never be slovenly and you will never be caught
out." More than anything boys must be alert, almost sharp.
Teaching them to ride is not easy. It would be foolish to pretend
that it was. But, if they have the natural talent and are prepared to
listen and work hard, it can be a very rewarding way of making a
living,' he would add.

The cost of running a stable full of likely lads climbed with the years. My parents bought and kept several horses for the boys to start on in races. They also believed it was crucial that one of them should travel with apprentices to even the most distant meetings. Since my father hated driving it was my mother who increasingly shouldered that burden, though in later years, as the boys grew older, they often drove her. At one stage she was travelling around 36,000 miles a year and covered countless more miles on foot walking every course strange to an apprentice to point out its peculiarities.

My sister Josie gave up her work with a local newspaper to help my mother look after the apprentices and share the driving to distant racecourses. During the winter Josie set up her own business called Stable Stars operating as an agent for some major sportsmen including Mick Channon, Emlyn Hughes and John Lowe, the darts player. She was also briefly involved in trying to find sponsorship for an unknown young driver who was desperate to make it to the top in motor racing. The task proved beyond her because, as much as anything, he seemed a bit short on personality. Much later he became world champion. His name? Nigel Mansell. Today my sister lives with her second husband in Tenerife, where they run a business furnishing villas and apartments. Each winter my mother flies out to stay with Josie for two months. They keep in touch with events at home by watching racing on SIS in a pub called the Railway Tavern in Playa de las Americas.

My parents applied the strictest rules for applicants. They did not like to take apprentices who had worked for other stables, although Pat Eddery and Richard Fox were notable exceptions. They preferred all boys to come straight from school and did not normally accept anyone who weighed much over five and a half stone at fifteen. The first thing Father always wanted to know from applicants was the size of their hands and feet. He knew from long experience that this was the best way of telling if a lad was likely to grow too big or heavy.

When Tony Murray joined my parents on a three-month trial he already weighed six stone. His father Paddy had been a jump jockey and my father warned him that Tony, too, would probably become too heavy for the flat. He was small and round, but very intelligent and learned fast. Father always said that if Tony Murray had not been a jockey, he would have been a success in whatever career he chose.

He could ride from the start and he worked so hard at his weight that he never did have to switch to jumping. He developed into one of the best jockeys in the country, rode first for Doug Smith and then was signed up by Ryan Price. When he lived in Newmarket my parents would sometimes stay with him.

Tony Murray won two English Classics – the 1972 Oaks on Ginevra and the 1975 St Leger on Bruni. He was a grave, dedicated young man and was dismayed at the split with Price caused by some of the stable's owners hastening to follow Charles St George's insistence on using other jockeys on their horses. When he was jocked off St George's Classic colt Giacometti Tony declared bitterly, 'We all have a cross to bear. Mine is the cross of St George.'

Later Tony described his apprenticeship as like five years' hard labour. He certainly put it to good use. At the age of twenty-two he finished a close second to Willie Carson in the jockeys' championship in 1972. A photograph of the pair having dinner together at the time offered grim testimony of just how much he suffered in his struggle to contain his weight. Willie was tucking into a massive meal with plenty of chips while poor Tony was toying miserably with a tiny steak and a lone lettuce leaf.

His battle with the scales was a constant nightmare. He spent hours each day in the sauna and when his health began to suffer he approached a specialist in Ireland who discovered that he produced too much sugar and had a thyroid problem. The doctor prescribed a diet sheet that sounded more like a recipe for a hunger strike. For a while his weight settled down but all those years of wasting left their mark and may well have led to the depression that affected him at times. He retired twice, tried to comeback yet again and his premature death in 1992 was a sad end of a fine young man.

My father tended to distrust the telephone. He took the view that if someone rang up he must want something! So he could be rather short on conversation if he answered the phone. My mother was the one who coped with all the trainers who began ringing up looking for likely apprentices to ride their horses. Sunday was the busiest day of the week for my parents. Things became so hectic that my mother had a job to cook Sunday lunch. The first call at around 6.45 would usually come from the veteran trainer Norah Wilmot, who could not sleep. Trainers would then ring non-stop all morning.

The boys were all family to my parents. They knew these youngsters from distant homes needed someone on their side in the world, whether they were right or wrong. By being light they often started on rides that other jockeys could not do the weight on. Many of these were jumpers having a run or two on the flat to prepare them for a hurdling campaign. Frank Cundell, Martin Tate and Michael Pope gave a lot of support in this way.

If the apprentices grew much too heavy, they were allowed to leave after three years. One lad could not ride and behaved badly, so he was sent home quickly. His parents tried to involve a trade union in his case but Father soon put them straight.

So many angel-faced little hopefuls beat a path to my parents' door. It says much for their methods that most of the ones they took on made it as jockeys, including Ian Johnson, Roger Wernham, Fred Messer, Richard Fox, Chris Leonard and Walter Wharton.

John Farrell was a very promising rider and achieved one win before he was forced to give up racing because he suffered so badly from asthma. Some, like Barry Davies, Sooty White, Keith Barnfield and Geoff Shoemark, became jump jockeys.

Richard Fox is a tremendous character who was unlucky not to make it to the top. His first faltering riding lessons at the age of eight were on the backs of giant, gentle hairy-heeled dray horses in Cork. He came into racing on the unlikely recommendation of an Archdeacon but managed only twenty rides rides in four years with Seamus McGrath in Ireland. It was then that his indentures were transferred to my father, who was no doubt influenced by the fact that the previous boy sent over by Seamus had been Pat Eddery.

Richard flew to Birmingham airport where he was met by my mother. As she led him to the waiting car she asked his weight then added quietly that she had three booked rides for him at Chepstow four days later.

He recalls, 'I envisaged Frenchie Nicholson's academy as some great private estate, with endless film shows to explain the finer points of riding and the boys packed off into dormitories at night.'

The reality was somewhat different when the new arrival walked jauntily into the small stable yard at Prestbury.

'This slightly gruff old boy came up looking like the gardener. He was wearing dungarees with holes at the knees and an old cloth cap. When he asked who I was I told him and he introduced himself as Frenchie Nicholson,' he says.

The eager new apprentice was clutching a pitchfork and muck sack in his right hand so held out his left to shake hands with the trainer, who knocked the proferred hand away with a swish of his riding crop and barked, 'Listen, we had better start right by shaking hands properly.'

Thus began a long, friendly and affectionate bond between the old master and the young pupil.

'I was very naive when I moved from Ireland. Frenchie woke me up and I owe him everything. He was a hard taskmaster but always fair,' reflects Fox.

On the days when his apprentices were not riding they would be expected to pick stones off the gallops, help in the garden, collect fruit, mow lawns and cut gorse for schooling hurdles. Some afternoons they would dig a ditch; the next day they would be required to fill it in.

After riding his first treble at Salisbury Richard Fox timed his return to Prestbury just as evening stables ended. He walked, nattily suited, into the yard to be confronted by the waiting trainer, who instructed him to change into his working clothes and took him off to the paddock to cut thistles and nettles for two hours.

When the task was completed the old trainer turned to his unhappy apprentice. 'You think I am a bastard. But I can assure you that if I had not held you back tonight, you would have been in the pub, buying lots of drinks and riding three more winners in the bar. That way you would have had lots of friends tonight and none tomorrow!'

Once Richard Fox was given £20 as a present for riding a winner for Martin Tate. That Christmas he was looking for a small bonus to help pay for his trip home to Ireland but there was none forthcoming in his pay packet.

'Is that all I am getting, Guv'nor?' asked the apprentice.

'Surely you've still got the £20 from Mr Tate,' my father replied.

Later Foxy earned enough money to buy a new car. The next

morning he rang my mother from the garage to say it would not start. It turned out that he had omitted to put in any petrol!

Other hopefuls came to my parents to be jump jockeys and to try to learn the mysterious art of training racehorses. These included Michael Dickinson, Lord Killanin's son Mouse Morris and Brough Scott.

Michael Dickinson arrived at Prestbury with limited experience of point-to-pointing and hunting. His parents Tony and Monica Dickinson had run one of the most successful point-to-point yards in the North and made an enormous impact when they switched fulltime to jump racing. Though he was extremely tall and as thin as a coat-hanger, Michael Dickinson wanted to be a jockey. From the first my father had his doubts.

One day he told Michael, 'You might not make it as a jockey but you will certainly never be short of a job.'

Michael replied, 'What do you mean?'

'You will not need a ladder so you might as well become a window cleaner,' concluded Father!

Later Michael did become a leading professional jockey and it is history now that he changed the face of jump racing when he started training. He broke so many records. Most notable of all he saddled the first five in the 1983 Cheltenham Gold Cup, an extraordinary feat that will never be equalled. More recently he has been training on the flat in America.

Michael offers this generous tribute: 'The Nicholsons were wonderful teachers. The best. They didn't half straighten me out.'

Mouse Morris stayed for the best part of two years. He, too, became a top class jump jockey and is now a leading trainer in Ireland.

Brough Scott, the ageless Peter Pan presenter of Channel 4 Racing, was a sixteen-year-old schoolboy with ambitions to ride in point-to-points when he appeared with his mother at Sandford Dene in 1959. His family lived near by at Buckland Manor, near Broadway. Soon he was riding out with the Nicholson team whenever possible. Even then racing seemed to dominate his life. No one could accuse him of being a playboy.

My father arranged for him to ride out for another trainer, Derek Ancil, near Bicester while he was at Oxford. When it became clear that he was serious about riding, his parents bought him two horses and sent them to Prestbury. One of them was Arcticeelagh, who cost £500 from my uncle Willie Stephenson.

Arcticeelagh was an eight-year-old entire with a mind of his own, but still possessed ability if he chose to employ it. At Epsom in August, 1963, Brough returned from a disappointing ride claiming that a clod of mud had caught Arcticeelagh in the face.

'More likely the clod caught the jockey,' was the unsympathetic comment from the trainer. When the horse ran equally badly next time for Paul Cook, my father decided on drastic measures. He gave the horse a proper, old-fashioned wind-up before his next appearance with Brough in an amateur riders' flat race at Lingfield. Equipped with blinkers Arcticeelagh, a 33–1 shot, bounced into the lead and made all the running.

Two months later Mr B. Scott, claiming a seven lb allowance, rode Arcticeelagh in a handicap hurdle at Chepstow. Crucially the old horse was again fitted with blinkers to make him concentrate. Arcticeelagh and his eager young rider came from well off the pace to snatch victory in a photo-finish. The victorious rider takes up the story.

'You had to grab hold of the old horse and growl at him because he resented the whip. It was my first win over hurdles and, though I say it myself, I felt I had timed our late run to perfection. By the evening I was certain it was the finest bit of riding seen at Chepstow for years. What I did not realise was that the runner-up was subsequently warned off for not trying!'

When Brough came down from university he worked, improbably, in the insurance business in London for a few restless months. But by then race riding had become an obsession and he rejoined my father as assistant trainer.

'Frenchie became my mentor. He wanted you to do everything properly and he enjoyed teaching. He used to ride up alongside quietly on the way home from Cleeve Hill and explain the finer points of riding. Really he was sharing his experience. He mixed being serious with an almost childish sense of humour but he had the knack of making his young jockeys badly want to impress him.

'Quite often the conversation would turn to the days when he was an apprentice with Stanley Wootton, a man he quoted seven days a week. Frenchie always said that Wootton had the eye of a hawk.'

A modest degree of success by Brough Scott encouraged his father to purchase Time, a big, hard-pulling chaser who had started joint favourite for the 1964 Grand National and had run with much promise until falling four fences out. Time was then sent to my father at Prestbury. Brough soon discovered that riding him on Cleeve Hill was a perilous business. Once, on a foggy morning, Time, ridden by Brough, and St Gulliver, partnered by Keith Barnfield, set each other off at the end of the gallop.

'We were pounding along at the beginning of a long funnel, with stone walls rushing by on either side and were horribly aware that we were heading out of control for a quarry straight ahead. A bush marking the front edge of the quarry loomed out of the mist and somehow we managed to steer the two horses round the left edge of the quarry at the last moment,' he recalls.

B. Scott's determined assault on Aintree with Time ended in a fall at the fence before Becher's Brook on the second circuit just when they were starting to make significant progress. Brough eventually became a professional jockey and won exactly a hundred races before turning full-time to journalism.

Years later he was invited to write my father's biography. We all met up in Cheltenham to discuss the details, but as the evening wore on Father became increasingly sombre.

Eventually he declared, 'I cannot possibly go ahead with this book. How can I tell the truth while so many people involved are still alive?' So that was the end of the project.

Tod Ramos was light enough to be a jockey, too, but from the age of nine was set on becoming a painter. Drawn irresistibly to jump racing, he spent two years riding out for my parents in his early twenties while studying at Cheltenham Art College close to the racecourse. He had begun his training at Brighton, but arranged a transfer to Cheltenham after receiving a letter of introduction to my father.

'I don't like amateurs,' he told Tod bluntly when they first met. Even so he agreed to let him ride out at Prestbury. Armed with this invitation Tod presented himself for interview with the head of Cheltenham Art School.

Asked why he had chosen Cheltenham, he replied that it was

the centre of National Hunt racing and, crucially, the greatest trainer of jockeys lived on the edge of the town. It was a novel, not to say unique response for an art student, but it did not prevent Tod Ramos being offered a place. He used to cycle to the yard in time to ride out first lot and then have breakfast with my parents before leaving for college.

Some of his spare time was spent sketching and painting my father and his horses in the yard and on the gallops on Cleeve Hill. In addition, in the early days of his apprenticeship, Walter Swinburn once modelled for one of his art classes wearing the Nicholson racing silks. Tod is now one of the foremost equine artists in Europe and is immensely proud that he rode in a handful of races during his time in Cheltenham. Indeed he even flirted briefly with the idea of becoming a trainer.

He recalls, 'Frenchie had the total authority of a wise, older man. He could be equally adept at building someone up and, if necessary, putting them down through irony. He tolerated me and found me a few rides in hunter chases, but he made it clear he thought I was incompetent and frequently advised me to stick to my paint brushes. He also found some early commissions for me. I treasure the two years I spent with him.'

Ian Johnson started, like all my father's boys, on trial. One morning soon after he arrived, Mouse Davies and Pat Eddery rode up alongside Ian and pulled his feet out of the stirrup irons. Out of control he tried like mad not to overtake those in front of him. After six weeks Ian asked my father if he would be taking him on permanently.

'You're still here, aren't you? Get on with your work,' was the dusty reply.

Ian was a decent mechanic as well as a jockey and used to drive my father and the other boys to the races. One day he felt unable to play the role of chauffeur because he was suffering from hay-fever. Father took over, reluctantly, for the journey to Newbury but lost concentration near Swindon and may well have nodded off. The car nudged an embankment, scraping the front wing and side but luckily no one was hurt. Though the front wheel was also damaged, he carried on as if nothing had happened. When they reached Newbury Father blamed Ian for the accident and left him in the car park to change the wheel.

Both Ian Johnson and Pat Eddery were keen to have a go over jumps, even if it was only schooling the jumpers over hurdles at home. When Pat promptly fell off, Father realised he could not afford to risk the boys being injured during the season. Once flat racing ended early in November he gave Ian his chance. The horse he was riding was travelling too fast, landed on a hurdle and sent Ian flying with such force that he broke his ankle.

Father was so furious he threw his hat on the ground. Not realising that Ian was badly injured he made him hop up the field on his one good leg, then told the head lad to find some Elastoplast, patch him up and send him back in time to ride second lot!

The best of all his apprentices was Pat Eddery, who has been champion jockey ten times. When he arrived in September, 1967 he was terrified by my father and wanted to pack his bags and fly straight back home to Ireland.

He concedes, 'I soon changed my mind when I realised that I had a special guv'nor. He wanted all of us to do well. We were almost part of his family. I know I owe him everything.'

Pat was beaten a short head on one of Eddie Reavey's horses in a selling race at Liverpool. As the two horses passed the line Eddie suggested, 'That kid of yours dropped his hands too soon.'

Quick as a flash Father replied, 'Well, you had better go down and pick them up because he has a better pair of hands than you ever had.'

Pat Eddery proved to be a natural, which was not surprising since his father Jimmy had been champion jockey in Ireland. But he was a lazy rider, too, according to my mother, and needed motivating. In some of his early races he gave up as soon as his horse stopped pulling. One trainer at Warwick complained that Pat did nothing but steer. All he required was experience and guidance.

My parents always maintained that a boy needed at least one hundred rides before he was fit for a horse anyone would bet on. The worst thing that could happen was for an apprentice to win on his first ride. Certainly, Pat Eddery had more than fifty attempts, nearly all of them unplaced, before Alvaro set him on his way in a boys' race over the Derby course and distance at Epsom on April 24, 1969. Naturally Mother walked the course with him before racing. Within a month Pat won four times more on the trusty Alvaro, who was trained by Michael Pope.

He was still claiming a three lbs allowance when my mother

drove him to Haydock one memorable Saturday in August, 1970. He was there principally to ride Vale Royale for my father in a maiden race. Vale Royale had failed to win in ten attempts that season, but the journey was considered worthwhile because he had six more booked rides on the card.

Pat won the first two races, finished third in the next, and then added two more victories in the fourth and fifth races. By the time he strode into the paddock to ride Vale Royale in the sixth race my mother was convinced that he had used up all his luck for the afternoon. But he was on fire that day and brought Vale Royale with a sustained challenge to win by a length. It was an extraordinary achievement by a boy of his limited experience to win five races for five trainers on the same card. He then slept in the back of the car all the way home to Prestbury. My mother has kept the Haydock race card and the complimentary badge to this day.

Father used to say that Pat cared for horses with all his heart. He sensed very early that this boy, above all others, seemed to be in total harmony with a horse. But he was known to take short cuts at evening stables. Once, my father caught him out while showing an owner round the yard. To the casual observer peering over the stable door the horse Pat had groomed appeared to be in immaculate condition. His coat shone with health and vitality. But when Pat was invited to turn the horse round his coat on the other side looked as though it had not been touched by a brush for weeks.

From the start Pat was a quick driver. His first car was a Fiat 850 but he drove like the wind and soon picked up a series of endorsements for speeding. One day after racing he swept into the drive in his new car sending gravel in all directions. Father was not amused.

'Look at that. On a horse that boy is brilliant but off one he has not got the brains to sweep the road,' he told several watching apprentices.

My mother always insists, 'Of all the boys we had, Pat was the one who used to get away with murder. He looked so innocent. You knew, whatever the trouble, it was his fault really, but it was hard to pin things on him.'

She continued to book Pat's rides and look after his business affairs for eight years after he finished his apprenticeship. Really she was the first jockey's agent in this country. She paid Pat's bills, dealt with his VAT and made his life much easier in every possible way so that he could concentrate on riding. She still claims he did not have a cheque book until he married!

My father was overcome with emotion when Pat won the Derby for the first time on Grundy in 1975. Tears of joy poured down his face as he greeted his old apprentice as he came back to unsaddle. Then, embarrased that people might think he was soft by showing his feelings, he hurriedly left the course with my sister Josie. Outwardly he seemed a hard man but underneath it all he was very emotional. I am sure he fed off the success of all his apprentices. They gave him a tremendous boost.

My mother treated Pat like a son and was very proud when he was named as Horseman of the Year in 1976. Pat received his award from the National Sporting Club at a lunch at the Café Royal in London. He spent days worrying about his acceptance speech. Other guest speakers included the Air Chief Marshal Sir Augustus Walker, Judge Michael Argyle, QC, the Duke of Beaufort and Chris Collins. There are no prizes for guessing who made the most succinct address of the day.

My mother still visits Pat and his family at his home near Aylesbury each year in the run-up to Christmas. Usually he and his brother-in-law Terry Ellis, who acts as his agent, take her out to lunch. When she arrives home there is invariably a case of champagne in the boot of her car.

The last boy apprenticed to my father was Walter Swinburn, who won the Derby for the first time in 1981 at the age of nineteen on Shergar. Bright and articulate he looked as though he had just been plucked from the school choir until you noticed the wicked sparkle in his big hazel eyes. He arrived at Prestbury in September, 1977 straight from Rockwell College in Cashel, Co. Tipperary where he had been an outstanding all rounder at sport.

Walter Swinburn and Tony Murray were by far the brightest apprentices at Lake House. Both arrived with a hatful of 'O'-levels. There was one crucial difference with Walter: his parents could afford to buy a decent car for him long before he was ready for one. The son of the Irish champion jockey Wally Swinburn, young Walter was also keen on hunting and showjumping. Years later he became Joint Master of the East Galway Foxhounds and developed a passion for tackling the Cresta Run.

Walter had arranged to meet my father briefly at the Irish Derby at the end of July. Father leaned forward and whispered, 'Come here, son.' It was more an order than a request. When the young schoolboy complied he growled in his ear, 'Get your hair cut before you come over to me.' Age had not softened his views on discipline.

When he arrived at Prestbury Walter Swinburn was only just sixteen. He was small and light and at first found difficulty holding the heavy steeplechasers that my father used to train. Jockeys need to be ambidexterous, to be able to pull the whip through in one smooth movement from one hand to the other. Walter, like his predecessors, was encouraged to carry his whip, saddle, and even his pitchfork in his left hand to help make him as effective on one side as the other.

In his first season, 1978, he won twelve races and the following year was firmly on his way with forty-seven winners. By now my father was not in good health. He suffered from poor circulation caused by a restricted blood supply to his right leg. Then he had a stroke and was unable to exercise the required degree of control on Walter. Increasingly my mother was the one who organised things. She was also doing most of the driving to the races but could not be away as much as before because she needed to look after my father. Luckily my sister Josie was able to help out.

My mother recalls, 'Walter needed a strong boss. When Frenchie was ill I did not have him where I wanted him. Walter ate far too many sweets and let his weight go. Often he would not ride out second lot. I liked him a lot but he needed a man in charge.'

Walter confirms, 'I had heard all about Frenchie being a hard man, but I think I had an easier time compared to other apprentices in earlier years. The guv'nor had mellowed by then but it was still hard enough. My spare time was spent gardening, clearing stones off the path leading to the gallops and picking gooseberries. It was tough at the time but you had to do the jobs and I do not regret it at all.

'I learned the most when the Nicholsons took me racing. All the little things like appearance, tidiness, showing your style on the way to the start. The guv'nor told me to watch Pat Eddery and Joe Mercer. He made a point of checking if I knew the ground, the draw, the horse's form, the obvious dangers. He taught us to be alert,' he adds.

It was during the time my father was ill that my mother slipped while clearing some snow and broke her thigh. Somehow she crawled across the drive to the porch but, though she banged on the door, my father was not well enough to assist. So she just sat there in the snow for two hours until she managed to attract the attention of a passer-by.

With both my parents immobile it was decided to transfer Walter's indentures to Reg Hollinshead. The Swinburns did discuss the possibility of sending him to me but opted for Reg because I did not have any flat horses. I don't mind admitting I was mad keen to sort him out. My parents shared the regret that they could not complete Walter's education and were in no doubt that he would become a star. They felt his potential was limitless, provided he did not become too heavy.

My father's continuing illness in 1979 led to his decision to retire from training at the end of that year. He made the announcement at the October meeting at Cheltenham. During a formal presentation Captain Miles Gosling, chairman of the Cheltenham Steeplechase Company, handed over a clock and honorary life membership to both my parents.

The system of training apprentices has altered dramatically since my father retired. Now, there is no chance of anyone emulating him or other excellent tutors like Stanley Wootton, Sam Armstrong and Reg Hollinshead. That has to be very much to the detriment of racing. In those days boys signed on for up to five years and often worked for little money. In return trainers could afford to have a horse or two of their own in training to give them a start in races.

Now, if you have an exceptional apprentice in your care, there is nothing to stop him walking out at the end of the year. Worse, some seem to be able to leave trainers in the middle of a season. The trouble is that there is no control.

It is so wrong and disappointing, when you have taken the trouble to teach apprentices properly. There is a serious lack of loyalty and racing will suffer because of it. Most flat trainers are far too busy to coach their boys properly. That is one of the reasons so many foreign jockeys are riding here now. The present apprentice system is less than perfect and although the Apprentice School does a good job it probably does not have the scope to go far enough.

Father earned a fair living. In return his boys were taught

everything and ended up with money in the bank and often a good job, too. He kept their feet on the ground and worked them hard, while my mother taught them presentation. It was unique for a jumping trainer to do so well with flat-race apprentices. He liked having the boys around him. They made him feel young. It was business, but it was also fun.

He always enjoyed playing snooker and even partnered Joe Davis in a few matches. When my parents had a house built in the corner of the paddock, my father insisted on installing a snooker room. In the evenings he often took on my brother Richard or the apprentices. Stephen Spendlove was particularly talented at snooker. Pat Eddery played well, too.

Though the master was now on the sidelines his pupils continued to win major races at home and abroad. On the eve of the 1980 season Playboy Bookmakers arranged a reception for my father and invited all his old apprentices to attend. It was a roaring success. Twenty-nine turned up to pay tribute to their mentor. They offered tangible evidence of their respect, too, by subscribing over £1,000 towards an elegant silver salver inscribed with all their names.

We were touched that Playboy Bookmakers also laid on the Frenchie Nicholson Appreciation Nursery. This was due to be run on a televised day at Newbury in August, but when that meeting was washed out by heavy rain, the race was rescheduled at Brighton on October 7, 1980.

Hans Andersen could not have contrived a better result. Only two jockeys who had begun their racing careers with my father were in the field but between them they held the lead throughout the race. Paul Cook led for five furlongs on Wrong Page. Pat Eddery, the most successful of all the graduates from my father's academy, then swept to the front on Aperitivo and stayed there to record a highly popular victory.

'I could not be happier,' Eddery confirmed afterwards. 'Frenchie made me what I am and I shall always be grateful.'

My father made the long journey to Brighton by car and was delighted with the outcome: 'My boys have all had to be triers. That's the secret. They are never going to be any good unless they are prepared to work and work,' he told newsmen.

He suffered a stroke soon afterwards and was in poor health for the rest of his life. It was terribly frustrating for a man who prided himself on his fitness. One of the happiest moments of his retirement came as he watched the 1982 Derby on television. His old boys rode the first three horses to finish that day. Pat Eddery won on Golden Fleece with Paul Cook second on Touching Wood and Tony Murray third on Silver Hawk. My father was a very proud man that night.

He died on April 27, 1984, aged seventy-four and was buried at St Mary's Church, Prestbury, just a short canter from Cheltenham racecourse where he twice rode four winners in a day. We all knew it was more than the end of an era. The death of Frenchie Nicholson signalled the passing of a training system that had made our jockeys the envy of the world.

My father knew Cheltenham better than any other course, so it is entirely fitting that the executive there decided to stage a hurdle race in his memory each autumn. Naturally it is confined to conditional jockeys. I am always keen to have a runner in the race, ground permitting, and was thrilled to win it with Watermead, ridden by David Bridgwater, in 1991.

5

Allergic to horses

One of the oldest clichés in racing is the well-worn story about the star jockey who could ride before he could walk. In the case of David Nicholson it happens to be true. What's more, we have the photographic evidence to prove it. While most children are wheeled around in a pram until they can manage a few tottering steps, David was often led by his nanny, the faithful Mrs Stone, round the village of Prestbury on his favourite pony Snowy.

David Nicholson was born at Epsom on March 19, 1939, but before the year had ended his parents had moved away from the edge of London in the early months of the war to the comparative safety of Cheltenham. At six months he began exhibiting the first worrying symptoms of asthma, a condition that troubles him to this day.

Once, his mother mistakenly bought him some Jersey milk which turned out to be far too rich for his delicate constitution. He also proved allergic to any sort of fat. The result was eczema on his face. Asthma attacks swiftly followed. Wool next to his skin also set off irritating reactions.

His mother cut up the silk petticoat from her wedding dress and made underclothes that protected his skin. Dressing the young Nicholson was a time-consuming business since he became breathless if she stood him up to clothe him. The solution was to dress him lying down.

At one stage his diet was restricted to substitute milk powder, sheep's brains, sweetbreads and some fruit and vegetables. Fish, eggs, jelly and fat were strictly forbidden. His mother, acutely aware that he would panic when he began wheezing in his sleep, seldom enjoyed sufficient rest herself. If necessary she maintained a vigil night after night, using liberal amounts of

Friar's Balsam capsules in a steam kettle placed beside his cot to ease his breathing. Those all too frequent terrifying attacks in childhood frequently left him close to collapse.

At times the attacks were so severe that he could not breathe. His complexion invariably resembled the colour and texture of parchment. In those frantic early years there were dreadful nights when his parents wondered if he would survive until the morning.

His mother worried constantly that the severity of his illness would strain his heart. She paints an uncomfortable picture of a delicate little boy who was never well in his formative years. The situation was so grim that there were days when David Nicholson's parents were relieved to discover he was still breathing. They felt that each of his precious early years was a bonus. Since he was and is hopelessly allergic to horses, the wonder is that David Nicholson has spent his entire life working with them. His story is truly a triumph of resilience.

My first memory is of Snowy, who had once been employed to pull a coal cart in Prestbury. I loved that little old pony as only small children can. Even at twenty he was a hundred per cent, a quiet chap with a beautiful mouth.

From the very start the one thing I ever wanted to do was ride. I was going to be a jockey. Nothing else. I still have pictures of my godfather Bruce Hobbs galloping to victory in the Grand National on the tiny Battleship, an entire horse, in 1938. I can also remember seeing the mighty Prince Regent winning the Cheltenham Gold Cup in 1946 when I was almost seven.

Though I did not quite appreciate its importance when I was young, I was also aware that my father had won the 1942 Gold Cup on Medoc II. Later, as a small schoolboy, by then mad keen on racing, I watched entranced as Martin Molony took the 1951 Gold Cup on Silver Fame by a short head in the tightest possible finish against Glen Kelly on Greenogue. I was standing right on the line and the judge got it wrong. He should have given the verdict to Greenogue!

By the time I was seven Snowy had become a bit too ancient even for me, so my grandfather Harry Nicholson sent down a replacement called Patsy. I used to ride her whenever I could get away from my first school Glengarth, in Cheltenham, which is now one of the houses of residence for the Ladies' College.

I was only seven and a half when I started at prep school at Oakley Hall, Cirencester. By then I was riding out in the mornings on some of my father's jumpers. My parents chose Oakley Hall for me on medical grounds. They were advised that asthma would not be such a problem for me there because Cirencester is so much higher than Cheltenham. It was also considered a bonus that the school was set on gravel. My health certainly improved during term time but deteriorated once I returned to Prestbury in the holidays.

When I was eight, my parents took me to see a specialist in London who announced that I was allergic to thirty-two different things, including dust, horses, jelly, eggs and fish. He prescribed a series of injections once a week but they made me feel even worse, so that course of treatment did not continue for very long. Over the next few years I was sent to several more consultants. They all agreed about the severity of my asthma, but none came up with a cure.

It was soon obvious that I was not going to be a scholar. Sport was my passion; still is. Even in those early days I was extremely competitive. I always wanted to win and could not understand why other boys did not try so hard. Nobody played harder. I was a regular in the cricket and soccer teams at Oakley Hall and captain of the Rugby XV for three years. I was also unbeaten as a boxer at prep school at various weights, even though I took on the heavier boys.

The asthma was still there. I would wheeze and sneeze until my eyes poured. Eczema drove me mad: I could not stop scratching. Luckily it did not affect me so much in term time. My breathing was fine over short distances and I could run 100 yards as fast as anyone. But I could not last 440 yards even if my life depended on it, and when my mother took me away to the seaside in the holidays, I used to sleep all the time.

One well-known old boy from Oakley Hall was Peter Hastings-Bass, who trained at Kingsclere in Berkshire and was a great friend of my father. When I was hard up I would write to tell him how well the school was doing and as sure as a coconut he would write back enclosing a ten-shilling note. It never failed.

All the time I was boarding at Oakley Hall I was only able to ride during the holidays. Nothing was forced on me by my parents, but they simply could not keep me out of the yard.

When I was nine I had the holiday of a lifetime with my uncle, Willie Stephenson, who was married to my father's sister Bobby. Soon I was riding out on two-year-olds for him in the mornings. Although I was tall and far too light, I could always hold horses. I had the knack but not the strength in those days.

Uncle Willie, who trained a big team of around eighty horses at Royston, not far from Newmarket, was always drumming into me the merits of what he called the Royston crouch, a neat, streamlined style which he felt his jockeys should adopt. He was one of the old school, had served a seven-year apprenticeship with Major W. Beatty and later produced quite a stream of useful jockeys including Denis Ryan, Bruce Raymond, Des Cullen, Dennis Letherby and Buster Parnell, who became champion jockey in Ireland.

All five of Willie's daughters could ride well, too, and four of them married into families involved in racing. Marshella married Denis Ryan and is the mother of one of today's leading flat-race riders, Willie Ryan. Gillian, who died tragically in 1993, married Bruce Raymond, another top-flight jockey, and Christine is married to Jamie Douglas-Home, who had a spell as a trainer before turning to writing for a living. Liz and her husband Michael Butcher own and run Gibsons, the famous traditional Newmarket saddlery business which supplies me with a lot of tack.

Uncle Willie rode as a professional on the flat for twenty years and won a number of important races including the Yorkshire Cup and the Manchester November Handicap. He was barely sixteen when he dead-heated on Niantic in the Cambridgeshire, but his weight beat him in the end and in his later years he was extremely round in shape with an extraordinary high-pitched, squeaky voice.

When he started training he was an immediate success and he was immensely proud to join the select band who have trained the winners of both the Derby and Grand National. He took the Derby in 1951 with Arctic Prince and added the Grand National eight years later with Oxo. Uncle Willie also trained the outstanding hurdler Sir Ken, who won the Champion Hurdle three years in succession. In partnership with Ken Oliver my uncle also started the Doncaster Bloodstock Sales in 1962.

He could be a hard taskmaster and gave me a particularly tough time when I was nine on a horse that never stopped bucking one morning. My orders were just to sit in behind on it during a gallop but I was so furious at its non-stop rodeo act that I decided I would get my own back on him for putting me on such an awkward animal.

Two furlongs from the end of the gallop I pulled the horse out from behind the others and kicked it in the belly. You have never seen such acceleration. We sprinted clear and beat the others by at least six lengths but there was hell to pay. Uncle Willie was livid, because I had shown up the horse's true ability in front of the other lads. He gave me a fearful dressing down. The horse was pretty decent and won quite a few races after that. Uncle Willie was a big influence on me and got me revved up to be a jockey at an early age.

Back at home my health swiftly deteriorated again. Often I could not even bend down to lace up my riding boots. My parents converted an attic for me, but I can remember leaning out of the window, time and again, with sweat pouring off me wondering where my next breath was coming from. If you panic, things only become worse. One year my parents built a summer house in the garden which I used as a bedroom during the holidays. The idea was to give me as much fresh air as possible.

Yet, however bad I felt because of my asthma, I seemed to relax as soon as I climbed on to the back of a horse. I started to wheeze the moment I tacked one up, so someone else would saddle a horse for me and my father would then carry me out and put me on its back.

There were a lot of bright scholars at Oakley Hall, but I was not one of them. I still do not know how I managed to squeeze through the Common Entrance exam with a pass rate of fifty-one per cent, which was quite good when you consider I was not really interested in any subject at school. Luckily my headmaster Major Francis Letts was on my side solely because I was very keen on all sport. He understood that my life at school revolved around sport and horses and did not disapprove.

Even so, I would probably have failed my Common Entrance if it had not been for the help of Gerald Lefebve, whose father Len took up training when he finished riding and eventually became a racereader. The Lefebve family lived less than a mile away in Prestbury and Gerald, who was multi-lingual, coached me for two intensive hours' study each morning during the school holidays.

6

The best schoolmaster of all

The best schoolmasters play a discreet, yet often vital part in our lives. We have already heard about the support of Major Francis Letts, David Nicholson's headmaster at Oakley Hall. Later at Haileybury, his housemaster, a stern disciplinarian with the endearing nickname of 'Killer' Cook, left his mark on Nicholson and his class mates with the frequent, forceful application of the cane.

But the schoolmaster to exercise the greatest influence on David Nicholson was a jaunty little bay colt called Fairval, who was to provide him with his first ride on the flat, his first cherished success over hurdles and his first win over fences.

Fairval belonged to Tom Aisthorpe, who had been a friend of Frenchie Nicholson's for many years. In order to ride in public for the first time David Nicholson became apprenticed to his father at the age of twelve while he was still a pupil at Oakley Hall. Another rather more prominent apprentice at the time, Lester Piggott, seemed able to skirt around the problems of school attendance in the same adroit manner in which he later avoided other chores that did not appeal.

David Nicholson was not so lucky. Though he badgered his father constantly to be given the chance to ride on the flat, his opportunities were sensibly limited to the odd race during his school holidays.

The first came on Fairval in the Easter break in the Brandon Apprentice Plate at Newmarket on April 18, 1951. Nicholson, who was barely twelve, was as thin as a gipsy's whippet, weighed scarcely four and a half stone and was the youngest rider in the race, which featured a number of future stars including Jimmy

Lindley, Brian Taylor, Buster Parnell, Frank Storey and Sammy Millbanks.

*   *   *   *

I had been pressing my father for ages to give me a ride and Fairval, who was then five, was the only suitable horse in the yard. He was a beautifully balanced, thoroughly reliable little colt from France with a lovely mouth, did not pull and was a complete gentleman. Whenever possible he was my ride at home.

Since Fairval was set to carry 8st. 9lbs and I touched the scales at barely 4st. 7lbs, he carried a massive amount of dead weight in the form of pieces of lead in the weight cloth. I remember driving up to Newmarket with my parents and walking the course with them, and my mother even came down to the one mile start to see that I was all right. By then I had a few butterflies in my stomach.

Fairval started at 100–6 that day and my orders were to line up half a length behind the others and kick him along the whole way, because he was basically idle. At halfway I picked my whip up and started using it. By the time I reached the finishing line I could not put it down because my hands were in such a muddle and I nearly poked my eye out in my determination to keep hitting the poor little horse.

The race seemed all over and done with in a moment. Everything happened so quickly. Though I was exhausted when we pulled up and too weak to carry back the saddle, I could not wait for the next chance to ride in a race.

When you start to ride in races your knees invariably give way when you jump off because you are not as fit as you think you are. It would have happened to me, too, with Fairval, but luckily Father warned me to hang on to the stirrup iron. It is something I tell everyone who starts race riding for me, including experienced eventers like Princess Anne.

I remember a day when Mark Todd, Ian Stark and Robert Lemieux rode in a charity race at Kempton. All three are world class riders but Ian and Robert fell straight down afterwards because their legs betrayed them. Mark Todd was even worse, probably because he had been wasting too hard to make the weight. He collapsed in the weighing-room and needed oxygen.

I was not much better after riding Fairval. When we reached

Prestbury that night my father took me to see the horse, who had weals all over him. I was horrified, because I loved that horse. I dread to think how many times I must have hit him. Father blamed himself a bit because he had forgotten to tell me not to pick up my stick.

My first ride as an apprentice proved an invaluable lesson, because my father insisted on the spot that I was not to pick up my whip again in a race until I knew how to use it. I waited four long years before he gave his consent and by then I was able to kick and push one along.

That is exactly what half the jockeys cannot do today. They do not seem to know how to nudge and push a horse in the classic manner displayed by Joe Mercer for so many years on the flat. Instead, as soon as a horse comes off the bridle, they cannot wait to pick up their whips.

My father taught me so much about the intricacies of race riding, while my grandfather Bill Holman, who had retired from training by then, did his best to guide me through the complexities of dressage and cross-country. I could not stand dressage. There was a terrible fuss after I won the boys' individual prize at a Pony Club one-day event held at Highgrove long before it became the home of Prince Charles. Though I was only twelve someone objected because I was a professional jockey. It was a petty complaint and quickly overruled.

Towards the end of the summer holidays I was given my second chance on Fairval in another apprentice race at Haydock. The form book tells you that Jimmy Etherington won on Xebec, but I was beaten less than a length into third place and probably should have won.

In those days jockeys did not wear safety helmets or crash hats, just a silk cap tied on as best you could manage. Fairval was slowly into his stride as usual and when he started to race soon after halfway I lost my cap. We were flying at the end and would have won in two more strides. Ten days later Fairval, given a rather more professional ride by my father, won a handicap hurdle at Wincanton. That was the end of my brief but unforgettable glimpse of life as a jockey for 1951, though it became increasingly hard to concentrate on lessons at school when all I wanted to do was ride.

The following year I teamed up with Fairval at Nottingham and Sandown and also began to pick up the odd spare ride for

Phil Doherty, David Hastings and Les Maund. I was always arriving too late at the finish on a horse called Shahjem and should have won at least twice on him, but I realised it was all good practice.

One day in the weighing-room at Bath Father teased me about a horse that had run away with me at home. Michael Beary, a great jockey and a marvellous man, took me to one side and said, 'Don't worry, sonny boy. Pace will hold anything.' I have never forgotten his advice. On another occasion at Bath I was unable to pull up a horse of David Hastings' when we reached the start, so had to complete a full lap of the course before I managed to regain control.

Once I moved on to Haileybury at the age of thirteen, there was still no doubt in my mind that I was going to be a professional jockey. Naturally there was a temptation to leave school early to be a full-time apprentice, but my parents felt it was important that I should have the chance to develop and go as far as possible at Haileybury.

Though I did not appreciate it then in my impatience to ride, time spent at school usually stands you in good stead. Certainly two of the very best, Peter Scudamore and Richard Dunwoody, did not lose out by remaining at school longer than most would-be jockeys.

I enjoyed carpentry at Haileybury and all sports but that was the limit of my interest. Daily lessons did not appeal at all. I remember some of the boys at school thought I was big-headed. I could not disguise my desire to be a jockey and was proud that my father was a top class jockey and trainer.

It was around this time that one of my father's lads, Chris Middleton, came up with the nickname that has been with me ever since. Unimpressed with the haughty way I strolled into the yard at the end of term he observed, 'Here comes the bloody Duke.'

My short career as a boxer came to a bruising end at Haileybury but not before I had knocked out the captain of boxing who, at seventeen, was three years older than me. When he came round he told me I was in the school team. I was then badly beaten by a useful fighter from Wellington College. He hit me hard for three rounds, but though I did not go down, he was a decisive winner on points.

I'm sure the fact that I rode so often helped ease the pain when

I was on the receiving end of the cane wielded so forcefully by 'Killer' Cook. Already my backside was like leather from sitting on so many horses. Once Cook heard me swear when one of my laces broke during preparation for corps parade. He seemed to take great pleasure in announcing that he would thrash the life out of me after parade, but it did not hurt too much and I was rather proud that his best shots did not even mark me.

The enduring problem of asthma did not improve in my early teens. So even in the school holidays I did not work in the yard, just rode out two or three lots each morning for a bit of pocket money. I remember my mother taking me to a chemist in Hereford who prescribed a revolting concoction whose main ingredient appeared to be rhubarb. We discovered that I was also allergic to shellfish in addition to so many other things. Even now if I peel a prawn and just touch my face, it will blow up within minutes.

Things improved a bit when on the advice of Frank Cundell, who trained at Aston Tirrold near Didcot, we visited a specialist in Reading who explained that he could not cure my various allergies but felt he could make life more tolerable for me. He prescribed a course of injections at the same time each week. My mother would sterilise the needle and I would then inject myself. After one course ended there would be a short break before I started on a fresh series of injections. They did seem to help.

Soon it became obvious that my time at school was running out. Early in 1955 we had a family discussion about my chances of passing my exams that summer. The choice was to stay on at school and take my exams or earn a living at home. I did not have a moment's hesitation.

I could not wait to return home to work full-time in racing. It was what I had always wanted and both my parents agreed it was the right decision. Things might have been different if I had shown the slightest promise as a scholar, but the truth is that none of my masters tried to persuade me to stay on because they knew I was not academically inclined.

It helped that I was half-prepared for life as a stable lad because I knew what was coming and wanted to do it. By then I was used to people teasing me, although I still rose to the bait sometimes.

My parents knew that I should not muck out horses, but when

I left Haileybury at the end of the Easter Term in 1955, I was determined I was not going to be any different to the other lads in the yard. So I did my two horses at evening stables. I struggled, wore a mask which I hated, poured sweat and used an inhaler; but I did them.

My mother was a very strict disciplinarian, could not stand bad language under any circumstances and was furious when she overhead me swearing in a horse's box at home. I was upset that the horse had been left in such an untidy state but she was not too interested in explanations. 'If I ever hear you repeat those words you will never ride in a race again,' she insisted in a tone that did not encourage any argument.

She says that if I had not been apprenticed to my father, I would not have made the grade as a jockey. Mother is probably right that no other trainer would have put up with my continuing battle with asthma which sometimes prevented me doing as much as the other lads in the yard. For a while I could not travel in a horsebox because my breathing suffered, but eventually I conquered that problem.

I always enjoyed leading up horses at the races and remember looking after Pelopidas, a very good two-mile chaser belonging to Dorothy Paget, and a nice horse called Tough Guy. I cried my eyes out when he was sold after winning a selling race at Kempton.

Though I had continued to ride infrequently on the flat during my time at Haileybury, my first ride over hurdles came on my trusty ally Fairval in a selling handicap at Chepstow on Easter Monday, April 11, 1955, only a fortnight after I left school. I was just sixteen.

At the same time my father took the decision to retire from riding and concentrate fully on training. His last ride was a far from energetic one, also on Fairval, at Cheltenham in March because he was preparing the little horse for a touch at Chepstow and did not want to show him up. He wanted to set me up on a winner, though I did not know it at the time, and had kept going until he felt I was ready to take his place.

Although I was quite tall by then, I was still extremely light at around seven and a half stone and a bit weak, but Fairval looked after me as usual. We came with a steady run from behind, joined the leaders three hurdles from home and were soon involved in a duel with the favourite, Nordest, ridden by the French jockey René Emery.

Fairval was going well enough at the last flight to give me hope, but on the run to the line I was absolutely exhausted. Luckily my father had instilled in me the need to sit still if this happened and not start flapping about in the saddle.

When René Emery started shouting in French at his horse it seemed to encourage Fairval to keep going and we held on by a head in a photo-finish. In the last hundred yards I could not shout or do anything because I had no wind left. I was just going through the motions. One of the stewards told my father that if I had not won, we would have been called in to explain my riding because I did not appear to do very much in the finish.

Father replied sharply, 'That's why he claims a seven pounds allowance.'

I was so excited to win on Fairval but there was not the slightest chance of celebrating, for the very good reason that my father would go mad if he saw any jockey in the bar, whatever the circumstances. It was a Bank Holiday, my race had been the first of the day and before the next race had been run we were on our way home where I was expected to take off my jacket and knuckle down to work at evening stables.

Each lad looked after two horses apiece but my father worked harder than anyone in the yard. In addition he did all the feeding and spent his spare afternoons cutting grass or energetically scything down docks and thistles in the paddock.

Even though I had won on Fairval I was acutely aware that I was not yet fully fit to be a jockey. Asthma prevented me running and really the only way to improve my wind was to ride in races more frequently. I was quickly brought down to earth the next day at Chepstow when I fell off Mariner's Inch over hurdles.

I was earning five shillings a week once I left school and, since my mother did not take anything for feeding me, I thought I was rich. Time was running out for me on the flat because my height had began to shoot up, but I kept my weight as light as possible because I knew I was gaining valuable experience. My father helped by finding a senior jockey to look after me in flat races, but it was obvious I would soon become too heavy.

That summer I rode the only winner of my career on the flat at an evening meeting at Wolverhampton on Desertcar trained by Les Maund. It was, in all honesty, a pretty humdrum race but at least I can claim to have beaten Lester Piggott into second place that day. I walked the course before racing as usual, but there was a bit of a delay when my horse pulled off a shoe at the start. I can remember hitting the front at the furlong pole and going for home as if my life depended on it. Desertcar won by five lengths but I knew that my attention would soon be turned fulltime to jumping.

When I was seventeen I had to face the problem of National Service, which was then compulsory for all young men. Ironically, my age group was the last to be called up before the system ended. I had started to put on weight quite rapidly by then and I think we all knew that my career as a jockey would be finished by two years in the Services. Emergency action was required. Asthma offered my only chance of escape.

So the morning that I was due to take my medical I groomed three of the dirtiest, dustiest horses you have ever seen. By the time I reached Gloucester I was in such a state, coughing, wheezing and sneezing, I could barely breathe. The third doctor on the panel took one look at me, called for a stretcher and sent me home. I have never been so relieved in my life. My father and I had dreaded the thought of my going off to do National Service. He was not keen on the Army. Quite honestly, I dreaded it.

My first car after I passed my driving test was an ancient Morris 1000, reg. no. WDD 199, which my good friend Dave Dick, known to all as Dicko, christened Well Done David. Having a car gave me much more freedom and I often used to stay with Dicko at his parents' home in Warwickshire. He was the man responsible for introducing me to the demon drink in the guise of an apparently innocuous cocktail known as Cherry B. Feeling thirsty and naïvely believing Cherry B to be little more than orange juice, I drank a dozen glasses of the stuff on a Saturday night out with Dicko and was subsequently ill for several days. I have never touched a drop of Cherry B since but that does not stop Dicko claiming today that my enjoyment of a glass or two of brandy means that I now cost more to run than his wife. In all the years that I lived at Prestbury we always walked to Cheltenham races from home. Once we had popped over the stile on the racecourse boundary it took only four or five minutes to reach the weighing-room.

Both my parents rode out each morning. Nearly all the horses were jumpers but my father always liked to have the odd one for the flat. By then Cleeve Hill had become as familiar as our garden. Though the gallops were not marked out I eventually came to know every thistle, each hump and gully so that I could lead the work even in a pea soup fog. It took about forty minutes to walk up the hill to the gallops and on the way back my father would quietly talk to me about ways of improving my riding. Life, for my father, was fun. He taught me never to bear a grudge. Right up until the day of his stroke he was exceptionally fit for a man of his age. Really, he was happiest when he was working, whether it was digging in the garden or showing the boys how a horse should be mucked out.

He liked to win, perhaps because he was a Yorkshireman, was a very keen cricket fan, played a bit when he had the time and never stopped bowling to my brother Richard and me in the garden. We had a pitch marked out at home and were always hitting the ball through the kitchen window.

I remember going with him to watch Gloucestershire play at the County Ground in Cheltenham. When Lancashire were playing in the area, Cyril Washbrook would call in to see the horses with half the team and I recall being very impressed that Father knew the great Aussie allrounder Keith Miller, who was a racing fanatic.

He was a great fan of the Crazy Gang, too, through his connection with Jimmy Gold and once trained for Chesney Allen. It was around this time that I remember my parents taking us all plus Sam Wilson to see one of the Crazy Gang's last shows in Oxford. As we approached the car park my father was fumbling in his pocket for some loose change when my brother Richard, sitting in the back of the car, volunteered, 'I'll pay.'

There was a brief silence before my father, who believed in thrift, replied, 'All right, son . . . but I thought I had brought you up better than that!'

Richard was far too sensible to follow my path as a jockey. As a little boy he did like riding his pony wearing his cowboy outfit, but he has not sat on a horse since the day his pony was stung by a wasp on Cleeve Hill and began acting up. Richard threw a tantrum, jumped off and walked home alone, leaving one of the lads to lead back his pony. Even so Richard was keen on racing while at school; if a horse was fancied, you did not have to tell him twice. He was with me on the day I gave one of John Benstead's a quiet run at Sandown. On the way home I hinted that this horse might win next time. It did just that, at 33–1, and I discovered that my little schoolboy brother had cleaned up in several betting shops in Cheltenham.

Much later Richard had a share in a horse called Casse Noisette II, who won a couple of races for me. My brother is a gifted engineer, and is now the Service Manager with Messier-Dowty. He still lives in Prestbury, but prefers golf these days, and plays off seven, though he retains a solid knowledge of racing and is one of the many shareholders in the Million in Mind syndicate. Luckily he does not suffer from asthma as badly as I do, but his eyes can still stream if he is near a horse, so he has to be careful when he visits us at Jackdaws Castle.

In March, 1957, at the advanced age of eleven, my old friend Fairval had one more vital part to play in my racing education. I had been begging my father for months to allow me to start riding over fences. Although I had done a fair bit of hunting, he resisted until he felt I had gained enough experience of schooling over the bigger jumps at home.

I was finally given my chance on Blenalink, a reasonably secure conveyance, in a handicap chase at Birmingham on February 25 and was thrilled to finish a clear second. So to the Cheltenham Festival, where my next ride over fences came on Irish Lizard, who had reached the venerable age of fourteen, in the National Hunt Chase. He was pretty slow by then but jumped round safely before finishing in the rear.

My next attempt over fences came the following month on Fairval, who by now belonged to my mother, in the Malmesbury Novices Chase over two miles at Wincanton. I would be the first to admit that it is pretty unusual to ask any horse to jump fences for the first time at the age of eleven; in addition, putting two novices together can be a recipe for disaster. But we had formed quite an understanding over the years and, though he was one of the outsiders at 100–8, I knew he would not let me down because we had given him endless schooling at home.

I owe Fairval so much, but I could not make him go if he did not want to. He liked to drop himself out at the start. Even if you persuaded him to set off in front he would be back in last place by the time you reached the first fence. Like a lot of older people he preferred to take his time and that is how he was that day at Wincanton.

Fairval jumped well, started to pick up ground at halfway and came with a flying late challenge between the two leaders at the last fence. One of them, June Mary, the favourite, ridden by Fred Winter, came down but that did not make any difference.

The way Fairval finished I knew that we would win bar a fall at the last fence and he sprinted clear on the flat. After that I felt nothing was going to hold me back as a steeplechase rider. Events at Liverpool eight days later brought home to me that I had an awful lot to learn about riding over fences.

7

Unfinished business at Liverpool

Every jump jockey worthy of the name will tell you about his ambition to win the Grand National. More than one hundred and fifty years after it was first run the race is still the finest sporting spectacle of our age, a matchless, often tumultuous drama that unfolds before a television audience of tens of millions around the world.

Even casual observers who care little for horses and less for racing find themselves caught up in the unrivalled excitement that only Aintree can provide for a few all too brief minutes each year. It is a race that consumes those who dance closest to its flame.

In an increasingly cautious age obsessed with safety, we assemble at Aintree each spring to witness a profound public examination of man and horse that enriches the spirit. Apart from one ignominious exception in 1993, the year of the void race, we have never been disappointed. Nothing in sport can compare with this unique race.

Until recently age was not a barrier to anyone determined to tackle the mighty Aintree fences. The sporting American grandfather Tim Durant was sixty-eight when he completed the 1968 race in fifteenth place on Highlandie after remounting.

David Nicholson was, by comparison, but a boy when he set out to ride Irish Lizard in the Grand National on Friday, March 29, 1957, ten days after his eighteenth birthday. There have been younger jockeys who have ridden in the National, including Nicholson's godfather Bruce Hobbs, who was only seventeen when he won on the tiny Battleship, an entire, in 1938. It is, however, stretching the imagination beyond belief to suggest that anyone has come to this, the world's most formidable horse race, with less experience of riding over fences. Before then Nicholson, quite extraordinarily, had taken part in only four steeplechases.

*   *   *

I will never forget my first visit to Liverpool for the 1952 Grand National meeting immediately after my thirteenth birthday. I loved it. My father and his friends always stayed with a splendid landlady called Mrs Walters in a guest house backing on to the racecourse. Aunty Bobby Stephenson was there, too, as well as Glen Kelly and Bob Turnell.

The grown-ups played pontoon most of the night and I was given the role of banker by my aunt. At one point I was holding £150 for her, which seemed an absolute fortune to me at the time.

When we walked the course the night before the National, won that year by Teal, I amazed everyone by saying I could not see what there was to worry about, and declared that the fences did not seem that big to jump. Bob Turnell and Glen Kelly nearly hit me. I really did not think the fences were as testing as I had been led to believe from listening to my father and tuning in to the radio commentaries. Yet I suspect there would be an outcry if horses had to tackle them today. Basically there was no ground line to help. The fences were stiff and upright. Some years later yellow boards were introduced at the foot of each jump, to give the horses a ground line, and more recently the take-off sides were sloped invitingly. I think they have it right now.

Irish Lizard ran in the National for the second time that year, ridden by Rex Hamey, and was brought down at the first fence. I was captivated by the atmosphere at Liverpool, at the sight of horses working on the course in the early morning mist and then having a pick of grass in the car park. I could not wait to return. I thought then, and still do, that Aintree is a magic place with its own unique appeal.

Since Irish Lizard had been with my father since the age of three and was more a family pet than a racehorse, you can imagine my reaction when his owner Lord Sefton, who was a hard man but very fair, agreed that I could ride him in the 1957 Grand National, which was held on a Friday that year in a bid to boost the attendance.

First, though, he was keen that I should gain experience on the old horse, who was fourteen, at Cheltenham. That was my second ride over fences. My fifth was also on Irish Lizard – in the Grand National.

I walked the course with my father and have to admit I thought the fences looked a bit bigger, now that I was going to ride over them, and were upright with no apron on the take-off side. I also sought the advice of other jockeys who did their best to ease my anxieties by pointing out that the old horse knew his way around the course almost blindfold. Several warned me to prepare for the Canal Turn, where Irish Lizard would automatically jump sharply left-handed to cut the corner.

The tension grew in the final hours before the race and then Lord Sefton, who was the senior steward and the most immaculately dressed man on the racecourse, came into the weighing-room to give us all his annual brisk lecture about not going too fast in the early stages. The idea was to settle people down, but every year we disregarded what he said.

By then I was becoming a bit apprehensive, because the preliminaries seemed to go on for ever. I remember singing and humming 'I never felt more like singing the blues' through the parade.

Once we set off, all I recall is concentrating to make sure I did not make a fool of myself at the Canal Turn. I tried my best to keep out of trouble some way behind towards the outside and, as we negotiated the first few fences, I was loving it.

But I made the mistake of not riding Irish Lizard hard enough into Becher's Brook, which is the sixth fence in the Grand National. He seemed to go straight up and down, was caught out by the drop on the landing side and rolled over. I knew straight away what I had done wrong. I was furious as I picked myself up but happily the Lizard was unscathed. He cantered round on his own and was retired that day. One of my next appointments was at Pony Club camp!

In these more enlightened times anyone attempting to ride in the Grand National with a similar lack of experience would be ruled out, quite rightly, by the much stricter rules that prevail today. Irish Lizard was, in truth, a schoolmaster. I was just an eager pupil, but if you are serious about this business, you cannot have novice riders running around like loose cannons in such an important race. The same applied to some of the dangerous jumpers that used to appear in the Grand National. When the two combine, they are positively lethal.

I could not wait to have another go in the National but it was to be two long years before I was given the chance on Cannobie Lee in 1959. At least I managed a circuit this time but he was not the most willing of horses. He knew how to get out of it and refused at the Canal Turn on the second circuit when a loose horse ran down in front of him. That was all the encouragement he needed to stop, but as he did so he took four horses out with him. I carried straight on over the fence with four other jockeys. You have never seen such panic. We all ran for our lives.

Cannobie Lee was a cunning so-and-so. He knew every trick in the book, so to make him go I used to do things to him that would not be tolerated today. I even hit him between the ears once going to the last fence and then continued to flick my whip while I roared at him.

When I rode him in the 1960 Grand National we tried blinkers to galvanise him. They worked for one circuit, too, but he decided he had done enough at Becher's second time. Cannobie Lee was just behind the leaders approaching the fence but jammed on the brakes with the spectacular result that I flew straight over his head into the bottom of the ditch on the other side.

Several papers the next day showed me crouching perilously in the ditch as the field flew the fence above my head. I was rather wet and uncomfortable, but felt I was safer there than anywhere else unless Cannobie Lee toppled over on top of me. Somehow he remained on the take-off side and all I could see was his blinkered head peering curiously at me over the fence.

I waited until the last runners had thundered past, scrambled out of the ditch and was just congratulating myself on a lucky escape when I was attacked by Willie Robinson, who complained with good cause that my horse had put his mount Team Spirit out of the race. It took Willie four long years before he gained compensation on Team Spirit in the 1964 National.

Despite this reverse I was all set to ride Cannobie Lee once more in 1961 until I dislocated my shoulder at Stratford nine days before Liverpool. It was put straight back in again at the local hospital without anaesthetic, something I would not recommend for the squeamish.

I was in so much pain I was screaming blue murder and gave the nurses and doctors a terrible time but they could not use a local anaesthetic because of my asthma. Paddy Cowley, who had been brought in on a stretcher after we had both come down at the same hurdle, waited patiently for his turn for treatment, saying nothing except for requesting a cigarette. It turned out that poor Paddy had broken his pelvis in several places, yet through it all he did not utter a single word of complaint.

I was told at the hospital that I could not ride for six weeks, so I made my way to London the following evening to see Bill Tucker, a wonderful man who used to patch up all sorts of sportsmen. He fitted a brace so skilfully to my shoulder that I was able to ride, with some discomfort, at Sandown the next day. After that nothing was going to prevent me declaring myself fit to ride in the Grand National a week later, but then Cannobie Lee was pulled out with corns on the morning of the race.

On the course on the day of the National I ran into Bill Rees, who invited me to join him in a bottle or two of champagne to celebrate the birth of his first child. Most of the races that day were on the flat so, relaxed for once, without a ride all afternoon, I was in a pleasantly mellow mood as I wandered down to the last hurdle, three sheets to the wind, to watch the first race. The next thing I rushed out to attend Rex Hamey who took a nasty fall in front of me.

'I've done my ribs. You had better take my place on Vivant in the National,' he groaned.

I tried to protest that after a lively session in the bar I was in no state to ride in any race, let alone the National, but since Rex was clearly out of action I eventually ran back to the weighing-room, where my uncle Willie Stephenson confirmed that I would be on Vivant.

That was the year that two Russian runners took part and Uncle Willie was at pains to make sure that I stayed well out of their way. You can imagine my feelings when I discovered them either side of me as we lined up at the start. I trapped like a greyhound towards the first fence to shake off their attentions. I doubt if I would have passed a breath test but I do not think I rode any the worse for having a few drinks. Vivant was up there with a chance until we fell at the Chair.

My record in the race was already pretty disastrous and I have to admit that did not improve much with the years. At Liverpool you feel that if it is your year, you will win. All I could do was hope that things would improve. I finally managed to finish the race for the first time on Clover Bud in 1962. In those days jockeys' fees hardly paid the bills, so over the years it became a tradition that you were properly rewarded for riding in the Grand National. That year I received £100 in January when I was booked for Clover Bud and another £100 on the day of the race. I also earned myself a rare £5 from Terry Biddlecombe.

Most years we had a bet between us at Aintree and this time we found ourselves hacking round at the back, popping through the gaps, both of us grimly determined to finish for the first time. The duel continued all the way up the long run-in but I took the money on Clover Bud, who came home tenth just in front of Terry on Blonde Warrior, who might have been named after him.

Terry and I had been friends since the days I used to help out at his parents' farm during haymaking. Luckily my asthma prevented me from too much hard labour, and we usually ended up having a few beers at night. He once sold me a shotgun for a small fortune. I paid way over the top, but I am such an indifferent shot it would not have made the slightest difference if I had bought a pair of Purdeys from him. Recently I discovered that the gun is worth considerably more than either of us realised at the time of the transaction.

I fell in the Grand National, yet again, on Avenue Neuilly in 1963 and Ayala in 1964. Although Ayala had won the race the previous year, ridden by Pat Buckley, he subsequently had leg problems and was not the same horse at all the following season. Ayala did not jump a single fence properly with me and scarcely got above the guard rail the whole way round; it was only a matter of time before I fell off him at the Chair.

The horse that I wanted to ride in the Grand National that year was Border Flight, trained by Edward Courage, but I had been jocked off him after we had finished fourth behind Arkle in the Broadway Chase at Cheltenham the previous year. I was very hurt when I later heard that Mrs Courage felt that I had not given him a proper ride. Border Flight, by Airborne, was talented, but a bit soft and I believe I made a considerable contribution to his early education.

It was Paddy Farrell who rode Border Flight in the 1964 Grand National, with the most terrible consequences. Poor Paddy broke his back when the horse came down at the Chair and has been in a wheelchair ever since. Some pictures the next day showed both of us lying on the ground at the same fence.

Three months earlier Tim Brookshaw had also been paralysed in a hurdle race at Aintree. The dreadful injuries to these two highly popular jockeys produced a great wave of sympathy from the public which resulted in the formation of the Injured Jockeys' Fund.

The closest I came to winning the Grand National was in 1965 on Vultrix, a bonny little horse trained by Frank Cundell. Stan Mellor was originally going to ride him but was claimed to partner Frenchman's Cove. I took his place, but when Frenchman's Cove dropped out Stan tried to climb back on Vultrix without success.

Since Vultrix was extremely lazy, I had my whip up going to Becher's first time. We gradually worked our way into the race and were in front of the winner Jay Trump at the Canal Turn second time, but Vultrix was very tired at the end and did well to finish fifth. Frank Cundell told me later that he lay down in his box for two days when he returned home.

A severe attack of jaundice caused me to miss the ride in 1966 on Jim's Tavern, trained by John Hicks. He was a little horse who wanted a lot of motivating and I felt that Nick Gaselee, a leading amateur at the time, was not strong enough for him. I watched the race on television at home at Condicote and was convinced that Jim's Tavern should have won. Instead he came fifth and, apparently, was bucking and kicking within half an hour as if he had not had a race.

It was a matter of some irony that I fell at the first fence on the second favourite Bassnet in the 1967 Grand National won by the 100–1 shot Foinavon in a manner that quickly became legend. Bassnet, trained by Alex Kilpatrick, winged the fence but overjumped. Later people asked me why I had not remounted, but I was not to know that the entire field, apart from Foinavon, would be brought to a halt in a mêlée at the little fence after Becher's on the second circuit. Seldom in the history of the race have so many horses still been going well at this point. The result was that no end of jockeys came back claiming they would have won but for the pile-up, which made headlines around the world. Honey End made up a prodigious amount of ground to claim second place. Afterwards his jockey Josh Gifford was livid at being taken out of the race in such an unexpected way.

Despite my dismal record I set out each time with fresh hope and really believed it was my year on Bassnet the following year, 1968. We were enjoying a terrific run, too, until Bassnet was blinded at the water as five or six horses on the inside tightened him up. The result was that we had nowhere to go and landed on some other horses. I rode yet another faller, Hove, in 1969 and missed a couple of years before finishing the race for only the third time in ninth place on Rough Silk for Frank Cundell in 1972.

My last assault as a rider in the Grand National in 1973 was also pretty brief on Highland Seal, trained by Richard Dening. We were already tailed off when brought to a halt by a loose horse going to Valentines first time. That was the year that Crisp came so agonisingly close to making all the running under top weight of twelve stone. I remember shouting to his jockey Richard Pitman to go on and win the race as they passed me still a long way clear on the second circuit, but it is history now that Red Rum, running in the race for the first time, caught them in the shadow of the post.

What did I do wrong in thirteen attempts to win the Grand National? Well, at least I achieved more than my father, who never did manage to finish the race. It is also true that some of the horses I rode were pretty ordinary, but however you look at it, I had a moderate record round Liverpool.

I have always believed there is more to it than luck. While some of us missed out year after year Michael Scudamore seemed to finish the race almost every time. More recently Neale Doughty, Chris Grant and John White all had superb records at Aintree.

I developed an obsession about riding in the Grand National. It is the world's most prestigious race and I am still as keen as ever to win it as a trainer, although the shape of the race has changed dramatically in recent years. My visit to the course in November, 1993, confirmed my suspicions that the fences had been strengthened a bit after several years during which they had become too soft. Some modifications had been necessary to safeguard the future of the race after the deaths of two horses at Becher's in 1989.

No one in their right minds wants to see horses and jockeys being hurt. So the decision to make alterations to Becher's Brook before the 1990 National, and to introduce some essential qualifications for horses and riders, met with my full approval. The authorities got it right. I do not believe in asking horses to race over traps, and in truth Becher's was a trap. This was put right by regrading the landing side of the fence in order to eliminate the acute backward slope, which tended to catch horses out if they landed short. Other minor changes were also carried out at Becher's.

But unfortunately, mindful perhaps of safety, those in charge took matters a bit too far by weakening the substance of the National fences, too. The solid bases were reduced, to be replaced with more spruce, which was readily kicked out by the horses as they jumped. This, in turn, can cause more problems when horses encounter a stiffer fence.

By November, 1993, I am pleased to say, the fences were strengthened up a bit once more. I did not say anything at the time, because I did not want the wrong people to misinterpret my thoughts. Now, once more, the Grand National is a proper steeplechase over proper fences. The 1994 National was a superb race, beyond criticism, without any traps or injuries to horse and rider. That is how it should be. The 1995 race, on much faster ground, was a marvellous spectacle, too, and it is important to remember that it is seven years since a horse died in the Grand National.

That is why qualifications are necessary. The National should not be a jolly round for anyone who thinks it might be fun to try it. Imagine me driving in the British Grand Prix! The drivers would not stand for it. What is the difference? In this race, above all, horses and jockeys should be of a certain standard. No argument. By removing the traps, introducing a safety limit of forty runners, cutting out inexperienced riders and ensuring that the horses have a reasonable handicap mark, officials could not have done more to improve safety.

I am not sure what the Animal Rights people are protesting about at Liverpool. A racehorse is one of the most loved, and best looked after, of all animals. That is beyond question. There are many important issues for animal lovers to protest about. The Grand National is not one of them.

The race is an institution. I remember being horrified at the time its future was in doubt and doing my bit by donating the proceeds from our annual open day that year and also by sending two teams from Condicote to compete in a major showjumping day, at Ascot, organised by John Dunlop for the fighting fund. Happily, in 1983, Seagram stepped in to redress the balance. Even in the darkest hours I did not believe that this great race was at an end. Equally, whatever the circumstances, I was totally against the idea of trying to re-create it at another racecourse.

It was soon after I retired from riding that girls began riding in the race. I have to say I am not a great advocate of them riding over fences, despite having the pleasure of helping the Princess Royal to achieve her ambition to win a steeplechase. I would not have enjoyed the thought of the Princess competing in the National, even though she has been round Badminton and I appreciate that she is fully capable of hunting one round Aintree.

Yet for all my reservations I thought that Rosemary Henderson did fantastically well to finish fifth in the 1994 Grand National on her own horse Fiddlers Pike. She did everything right, was always in the race, moved into second place going to Becher's second time and, crucially, kept out of everyone's way.

8

Lester Piggott over jumps

It was quite an experience to find myself riding over hurdles against Lester Piggott in the early days. For me, Lester was already a hero when he was a teenager. He was only sixteen when he rode Gay Time in the 1952 Derby for Mrs J. V. Rank (who was my wife Dinah's godmother), finished second, fell off after the post and wanted to object to Charlie Smirke, who had won the race on Tulyar.

While I was at school, I kept a scrapbook full of Lester's cuttings, which I still have at home. I can remember the disbelief I felt when I heard that he had been disqualified for six months in 1954 for foul riding at Royal Ascot on the Derby winner Never Say Die. The truth is that Lester's abrasive style had offended stewards and senior jockeys alike. I think some riders had been looking for the chance to put him in his place.

My second winner over hurdles was Royal Task, owned and trained by Lester's father Keith Piggott. I was probably one of the first of hundreds to be jocked off by Lester. It happened in February, 1957 at Windsor where I had been been booked to ride the favourite, Ocean King, owned by 'Teasie Weasie' Raymond and trained by Keith Piggott.

I had given the horse a quiet run round at Cheltenham before winning a seller easily on him at Sandown in January and was then asked to ride him again at Windsor because Lester was supposed to be on holiday. But when I walked into the weighing-room, there he was pulling on the colours.

As I began to protest, he replied, 'I am riding the horse and you will be paid your fee and percentage.'

Though I was livid, there was nothing I could do. At least it was a profitable exercise. Ocean King won comfortably and I duly received my 10 per cent of the prize.

I remember that spring we all assumed Lester was finished on the flat when he came back from his winter holiday weighing something over ten stone. I should imagine that for a while even he was not sure if he would be forced to switch full-time to jump racing; he certainly never let his weight go again.

Lester, Jimmy Lindley and Brian Taylor all had a few rides over jumps, then decided it was worth the struggle to lose a few pounds in weight because they realised that flat racing was a a bit easier. It is not widely known that Lester won a selling hurdle at Cheltenham on the opening day of the Festival in 1954. Less than three months later he gained his first Derby success on Never Say Die.

Lester would have become a very good jump jockey. We all know he has a first-class brain and he has never been frightened. His nerve is as good as ever, yet most of us who rode against him have been finished for years. He always rode short and I remember a photo of him fully three feet above Prince Charlemagne after a mistake at the last hurdle on their way to victory in the 1954 Triumph Hurdle at Hurst Park.

No one else rode that short over hurdles in those days. Father was always anxious that his apprentices did not copy Lester who, he said, was a law unto himself. All the boys who came to Prestbury were encouraged to copy Joe Mercer, a supreme stylist, as a role model.

I always looked up to Lester. He was a serious, dedicated young boy who wanted to make it. He did not say a great deal, but left the firm impression that nothing was going to stand in his way. He has not changed much with the years except perhaps that he might see more of the funny side of things now. Reputations never counted much with Lester. He just wanted to get on with the job.

I suppose I was sixteen when I made the first of many visits to Wheeler's restaurant, off Jermyn Street in London. It came after I had slipped up on one of those tight bends at the now defunct Wye, an experience that, sooner or later, happened to everyone who rode there. Arthur Freeman, who won the Grand National on Mr What, had agreed to take me back to Willie Stephenson's that night so that I could ride schooling in the morning. But first we caught the train from Kent back to London where we called in

Father's wedding day. From left, Len Lefebve, Ron Holman, George Owen, Charlie Birch, Fred Rimell, Gerry Wilson, Staff Ingham, Frenchie Nicholson, Fulke Walwyn, John Bissill, George Archibald, Gersham Wood, Eric Bailey, Tommy Carey, Tim Hamey (glancing right), Perry Harding and Sean Magee.

Likely lads at Epsom. From left, Frenchie Nicholson, Tommy Carey, Willie Stephenson, Davy Jones and Taffy Taylor.

Father winning the 1942 Gold Cup on the blinkered Medoc II, second left.

A study in elegance. My mother returning from the gallops.

Golden Miller (Frenchie Nicholson) just fails to take the Cheltenham Gold Cup for the sixth time in 1938. Morse Code, the winner, leads Golden Miller (far side) and Macaulay at the last fence.

A lively gathering at an early Champion Jockeys' Dinner. On far side of table from left, Jack Dowdeswell, Ron Smyth, Frenchie Nicholson, Roger Burford and Bob Turnell. Near side from left, Eric Foley, Ben Lay, Tim Molony and Charlie Stalker (valet).

Another Champion Jockeys' Dinner with Terry Biddlecombe at top of table. On his left, Joe Guest, Gene Kelly, D. N., Richard Nicholson, John Haine, Derek Scott, Ron Vibert, Tim Norman and Brough Scott.

Early riding lessons . . . at home on Snowy

. . . and at a local gymkhana.

A winning debut over hurdles for me on Fairval.

D. Nicholson, flat race apprentice.

Our wedding day. Stan Mellor and Johnny Lehane provide a rustic salute.

Everyone in this wedding picture, bar my brother Richard, has ridden winners over jumps. Back row from left, Eddie Harty, Fulke Walwyn, Bill Rees, Frenchie Nicholson, Peter Pickford, Johnny Gamble, Hugh McCalmont, Ivor Markham, Derek Ancil, Tony Curzon, Michael Scudamore, Guy Harwood and Richard Nicholson. Second row, Jimmy Morrisey, Graham Nicholls, Johnny Gilbert, Mick Dillon, Ben Lay, D. N., Stan Mellor, Rex Hamey, Malcolm Smith, Gene Kelly, John Haine, Jeff King and Adrian Major. Front row, kneeling, Clive Chapman, Tim Ryan, Peter Jones, Taffy Jenkins, Johnny Lehane, Dick Broadway, Peter Scudamore (pageboy), Terry Biddlecombe, Josh Gifford, Buck Jones (head bowed) and Tony Biddlecombe.

How to cross Becher's Brook without your horse (Cannobie Lee).

That's me crouching in the Brook as the field thunders over my head.

Heading for victory on Mill House in the 1967 Whitbread Gold Cup pursued by (from left) Kellsboro' Wood (J. Haine), San Angelo (J. Buckingham), La Ina (J. Speid-Soote), Solbina (E. P. Harty), and Woodland Venture (T. W. Biddlecombe).

Stepping out in front on Limonali at Auteuil.

Clear at the last flight on Elan in the 1965 Schweppes Gold Trophy.

Winning the Knobbly Knees competition on the Isle of Wight, supported by John Buckingham (left), Macer Gifford and Victor Dartnall.

Presentation to father at the Playboy Club, flanked by Pat Eddery and myself. At rear from left, Keith Barnfield, Wally Wharton, Barry Davies (partly hidden), Walter Swinburn, Ken Williams (head lad), Richard Fox, Chris Leonard, Paul Cook, Tony Murray and Kevin Davies.

at Jules' Bar, another favourite haunt for jockeys, before heading for Wheeler's early in the evening. I still go there when I am in London.

In those days the younger jockeys respected their seniors and each other far more than seems to be the case today. If not, they were taught a lesson that could be decidedly painful.

Michael Scudamore, who rode for my father and uncle, was one of the best, loved life and was as brave as a lion. I schooled upsides with him from a young age and learned so much from him. He had a big influence on me. He was a good man in the true sense of the word. Later, when I started riding over jumps, he would often give me a lift to the races, though he was not very happy with me one day when I carved him up on the last bend at Kempton. After the race he told my father that if it happened again, someone was liable to put me through the wing.

I also managed to cross the great Fred Winter by squeezing up his inner in a race at Hurst Park, tactics which were definitely not advisable if I intended to continue as a jump jockey. Fred sat me down in the weighing-room with my father, made sure I knew I was out of order and warned me in no uncertain terms of the consequences if I tried it on again.

On the day Mandarin won the King George VI Chase Uncle Willie asked me to ride two novices, Greektown and Granville, both having their first run over hurdles at Kempton. I was told to finish sixth on Greektown, a big, scopey chestnut. My instructions were only marginally different when I came to ride Granville in the final race of the day. This time Uncle Willie asked me to finish seventh, which I managed more or less, although it took me the best part of a mile to pull him up afterwards.

By the time I came back to unsaddle, my uncle had already gone. He was an astute judge, had seen enough to confirm his hopes for the horse and never did ask me how he ran. Three weeks later he rang up to book me to ride Granville again at Market Rasen. Once more Michael Scudamore picked me up for the long journey to Lincolnshire where he was also riding for the stable.

When I walked into the paddock all my uncle said was, 'Don't win too far.'

Granville was always travelling like a winner and was still doing handsprings as we came into the straight upsides the longtime leader Silver Sand, the favourite, whose jockey Johnny Gilbert shouted over to me, 'Steady, matey, you've won.'

I replied, 'Blow you. I'm off,' won readily and then had a bollocking from Uncle Willie for looking round. After we had changed, Michael and I met up with Uncle Willie in the course's tea room, which is a rather grand name for the little tin hut that used to serve that purpose. There, on a long trestle table, was the biggest pile of cash I have ever seen in my life. Much of it was in white fivers. Uncle Willie, his owners and friends were standing around the table counting the money.

It turned out that they had backed an earlier winner and doubled it with Granville at 33–1. They must have won a fortune, because he was backed on the course down to 4–1. It was the biggest touch I have ever been involved with and I did not know a thing about it until afterwards!

After that whenever Uncle Willie asked me to ride for him I did my best to be available. So I was very keen to take up his offer to partner Greektown at Hurst Park the following year. The horse had already won his previous race but I was supposed to be riding Swerford for one my father's best owners, Major-General Sir Randle Feilden, in the same race.

Although the General was Senior Steward of the Jockey Club on three occasions, he liked nothing more than a good bet. My father rang him up, explained my predicament and advised him to have his maximum on Greektown. Josh Gifford took over on Swerford, who had no chance, I won the race on Greektown, who was backed from 6–1 to 11–4, and the General enjoyed a touch.

I was brought up not to worry if an owner or trainer had a big bet on a horse I was riding, just to do my best. Dorothy Paget was certainly the biggest punter I rode for, but I seldom spoke to her because she rarely came racing. Betting was her life and all her messages were relayed through my mother. Once at Birmingham she had a huge bet on one of hers at 33–1 to finish in the first four, which was quite a task given that there were twenty-five runners. Luckily we just crept into fourth place.

An emergency operation to remove my appendix left me on the sidelines early in 1959, but I was so impatient to ride again that I came back at Warwick much too soon, when I was only half fit. The temptation to partner the Liverpool specialist Wyndburgh was irresistible. He had already finished second and fourth in the

Grand National and a few weeks after I won on him at Warwick he finished second again, to Oxo, with Tim Brookshaw riding like a man inspired after one of his stirrups broke on landing over Becher's second time.

It was Tim Brookshaw who came to my rescue that day at Warwick. Wyndburgh was hard work and I just beat Tim on ESB after kicking and pushing my horse along the whole way. But there was a price to pay for my exertions only twenty-one days after my appendix operation.

I blacked out as we pulled up and would have rolled off Wyndburgh's back if Tim had not grabbed me. What's more, he held on to me all the way back to the unsaddling enclosure. That was my second ride of the day and I was so exhausted I quickly gave up my remaining booked mounts.

Though victory at Aintree always eluded me I won the Welsh Grand National three years in succession between 1959 and 1961 on horses owned and trained in Wales. Limonali, who set the ball rolling, was not much more than a novice when he won the Welsh National for the first time at Chepstow in March, 1959. He was trained with skill and understanding by Mrs Posy Lewis quite close to the course at Barry in Glamorgan.

Limonali was a small, lightly built horse with an alarming habit of falling when he began, so Father put me in for the ride and suggested that I should school him round Cheltenham racecourse. From the start we seemed to have an intuitive understanding between us, for Limonali did not make a semblance of a mistake that day.

You could not organise him at his fences or take hold of his head. I quickly learned to ride him with trust, on a loose rein and to just sit up and go with him at each jump. When he beat the previous year's winner Oscar Wilde in the 1959 Welsh National it was his first triumph over fences.

Limonali missed the best part of the next season but I found an ideal substitute in the Welsh-trained Clover Bud, a good tough genuine mare who was prone to making mistakes but stayed for ever in the most testing conditions. Together we won the 1960 Welsh Grand National by fifteen lengths. Later at stud Clover Bud produced National Clover, a wonderfully reliable mare who won twenty-seven point-to-points. So you can imagine my delight to win a race with National Clover's son Go Ballistic in 1994.

Ifor Lewis had taken over the licence from his mother when I rode Limonali to a second success in the Welsh National in 1961. The following year we took the horse to France in April for a crack at the Prix du Président de la République at Auteuil, but when we tried to school him over the bullfinch fence at Lamorlaye he would not have anything to do with it.

So we decided on an emergency plan shortly after dawn one morning while the schooling ground was still locked up. We lifted the gate from its hinges, then Ifor and his head lad Ron Boss, now a trainer, pulled back the curtain of birch in the bullfinch so that Limonali could see he could jump through it.

Local horses, used to this type of fence, jumped fast and low through it and after our early morning sortie Limonali became quite proficient, too. He stepped round in front at Auteuil, to the manner born, jumping quite beautifully for such a small horse and had the entire field stone cold when I fell off him at the final ditch. There seemed to be a crowd of thirty thousand at Auteuil and they clapped and applauded Limonali all the way as he walked back through the middle of the course. It was one of the most moving receptions I have ever witnessed.

When I started riding, jockeys often wore overcoats and galoshes in the paddock to help them keep dry until the last moment. At Haydock, after wasting and sweating on a wet day, I took this a stage further by riding to the start still wearing a lightweight waterproof jacket on Tickle Me, trained by Ifor Lewis. Once there I handed it to the starter's assistant just before the race began. Afterwards the stewards asked me not to do it again, because it confused the commentator, who could not see my colours. Many years later I instructed Allen Webb to do the same thing on one of mine, Colonel Nelson, on a extremely damp afternoon at Towcester. The horse won but Allen, too, was ticked off by the stewards.

My uncle Willie Stephenson provided one of my first major victories as a jockey, on Farmer's Boy in the Imperial Cup at Sandown, which has always been a fiercely competitive handicap hurdle. I had further cause to celebrate because that year the race was held on my twenty-first birthday, March 19, 1960.

I had a bit of luck on the final bend, though I did not appreciate it at the time. Doug Page, riding the Irish-trained favourite Albergo, tightened me up on the rails as we turned out of the back straight. There was nothing I could do except sit and suffer until we reached the home straight. By forcing me to take a pull Doug won me the race, because Farmer's Boy had a wind infirmity.

I had previously had a run-in with Doug in the Champion Hurdle and when he spotted me at Sandown he came past on the outside and, bang, did me properly. I had to drop back or I would have been on the floor.

After his enforced breather Farmer's Boy found a second wind, took up the running between the last two hurdles and though tired on the hill held on well from Albergo, who finished strongly. Farmer's Boy was a bit better than a handicapper and gave me a great ride when he finished third in the Champion Hurdle the following year.

I always enjoyed putting one over the Irish jockeys who liked to give English jockeys a warm reception when we visited Ireland. I will never forget the wind-up two of them gave me in the weighing-room before I rode Herring Gull in the Galway Plate one year. They both tried to knock me down at the first fence but collided with each other instead with the result that one of them fell and the other one was virtually put out of the race. At times in those days in racing it was war.

The day that I won the Imperial Cup also marked the beginning of the end of my life as a bachelor. That night I had a small dinner dance at the Savoy Restaurant in Cheltenham to celebrate my twenty-first birthday. Among the guests invited by my mother were two sisters, Libby and Dinah Pugh, who shared a common interest in racing.

We had met for the first time when they came to the yard to look at a horse called Tinker's Thrift that Libby, having sold some cattle, had just bought from my father. When the girls came into the house, there was D. Nicholson, in slippers and jodhpurs, with his feet up watching Wimbledon on television.

Dinah had just returned from six weeks in the South of France. All I can remember of our first meeting is that she had very short shorts and long brown legs as far as you could see. I coughed and spluttered a bit at the time, but the truth is that I fancied both sisters and so was delighted to hear that they lived near Cheltenham at Temple Guiting. At first I took Libby out, but that ended after a short while and I found another girlfriend Jean

Harper, who later married John Sillett, well known as a player and subsequently manager of Coventry City F.C. However, on the night of my party I started to pay more attention to Dinah and we have been together ever since.

Life was exciting on and off the track but for all the good days a jump jockey enjoys there are plenty of bad ones. One of the worst for me came at Southwell in a three-mile chase on my father's horse Blenalink, owned by Stan Ireland. Blenalink started joint favourite that day and I thought we had won very snugly indeed after I kicked on after the second last and came clear. But when the the field all came past us as I was pulling up I realised, to my horror, that I had ridden a finish a circuit too soon. I could have died.

I set off urgently again on Blenalink but our cause was not helped when he landed in the water jump. I rode like a madman for that final circuit and made up a fair bit of ground but we were still beaten a length and came back to the worst reception I have ever faced. Some irate punters started booing while others threw gravel and stones at me.

Since my father was with me I had a nasty feeling it would be a long journey home. After twenty minutes he looked across at me and said pointedly, 'You won't do that again.'

That was the end of the matter. Even better, because it happened on the Thursday before Good Friday, there was hardly any publicity about my blunder by the time Saturday's papers were published.

Years later my son Philip did the same thing on one of mine, Optimum, in a hunter chase at Stratford. He subsequently told me he could not believe he was winning so easily. I was given the news on the car phone as I drove back from Kempton and so had plenty of time to simmer down before I reached home. At least we are in good company because a lot of jockeys have made the same mistake, including Eddie Harty and, much more recently, Adrian Maguire when he was riding for Jeff King in 1993.

By the time I was twenty-one I was having to work hard to restrict my weight to just over ten stone. My father's long battle with the scales down the years had prepared me for what was to come. At six foot one I was much taller than him and had to be pretty disciplined about wasting because my asthma prevented me spending much time in sauna baths.

A lot of the older jockeys including Arthur Freeman, Dave

Dick and Michael Scudamore were regular visitors to the Turkish baths in Jermyn Street in London before and after racing but my parents did not encourage me to join them.

For ten years I took a pill first thing every morning. I had a friendly doctor who prescribed some pills that used to take away or at least dull your appetite, and had the added advantage of making you feel on top of the world. You had to time this right, because if you took one in the middle of the afternoon you would be far too lively to sleep that night.

My motto was that you could not waste on an empty stomach, so I always had something to eat in the evenings even if I was riding at my lightest the next day. For a while in the 'sixties I also used a plastic sweat chair at home with a steam kettle underneath it to keep up the temperature, and boiled off the odd pound or two by wearing a sweatshirt as well.

When all else failed and I could not shift the weight I relied on a pee pill even though the side effects on me often included cramp and temporary deafness. If I took a pill after riding out one lot it would start to work within an hour. One tablet could make you lose anything between two and four pounds in liquid but you might have to stop two or three times on the way to the races to satisfy the call of nature.

To compensate for this abrupt loss of liquid Terry Biddlecombe and I used to sip a bottle or two of Guinness that we kept under our bench in the weighing-room. It was not, in all honesty, the best way to prepare for a race but we all treated life with a more cavalier spirit. I sometimes wonder if we would have passed the drug tests jockeys are required to take today. Probably not.

Modern jockeys are so well organised that they have a hotline to their own nutritionist, who occasionally appears on race days as well. They work hard at dietary plans, have a physiotherapist on hand beside the weighing-room and call on the best medical advice to help them stay healthy and light. One or two, including Richard Dunwoody, even consult a sports psychologist. But I doubt if they have as much fun as in our day.

9

Playing to win

Sport has provided David Nicholson's living and his main diversion from it. For years he captained the National Hunt Jockeys cricket team with an iron fist, playing with a degree of purpose that is not always expected in friendly matches.

Cricket matches against the friendliest village sides on Sundays were invariably conducted by the skipper, at least, with a severity normally displayed in time of war. He belongs to the battle-hardened school who believe that winning is not the only thing in life, but trying to win is.

There was, however, a useful by-product from these games. Over the years the jockeys' willingness to turn out for any cause ensured that considerable amounts of money were raised for a variety of charities. The Injured Jockeys' Fund was a regular benefactor but many other worthwhile causes had good reason to be grateful for the activities of the NH Jockeys cricket team.

Nicholson, of course, always compulsively competitive, played every match as if his life depended on winning, although some of his team mates approached the summer games with a considerably more relaxed attitude. Fanatical about discipline and personal fitness the captain even demanded squad training at the indoor nets at Northampton during the winter.

'Well, what else do you expect?' he declares in typically forthright tones. 'What was the point of forming a team if we did not intend to win? We tried to play like cricketers, not jockeys.'

So once a fortnight Nicholson and his fellow riders drove to Northants County Cricket Club's indoor school for tuition under the eagle eye of Jock Livingston, an Australian who *was a former Northants batsman, slow left arm bowler and occasional wicket-keeper. Livingston clearly knew his man when he declared memorably, 'If David Nicholson was in charge of England, they would never be beaten.'*

Josh Gifford, whirlwind rider, four times champion and opening bat, would drive up from Sussex; Terry Biddlecombe, blond bombshell, champion jockey and wicket-keeper, from Gloucester. Other regulars at the nets included another champion Stan Mellor, Macer Gifford, Victor Dartnell, Jeff King and Michael Scudamore. A keen team member was John Buckingham, who, although a useful bowler, is best known for his startling victory on Foinavon at 100–1 in the 1967 Grand National.

When most players reached the veteran stage the team was bolstered by the addition of younger players including Peter Scudamore, Graham Bradley, Oliver Sherwood and Steve Smith Eccles. But D. Nicholson, predictably, was captain on a lively tour of Barbados in 1983. Five games were played including one at the Kensington Oval, Bridgetown, two won and three lost but the tour earned a £5,000 sponsorship cheque, part of it for the Injured Jockeys' Fund.

Cricket was not the Duke's only pastime. For a while he was also the forceful captain of the Jockeys soccer team, too. Naturally he required his men to play in the spirit displayed so memorably by Field-Marshal Montgomery when Monty was asked, shortly before the outbreak of war, to form a football side for a friendly game against the crew of the German battleship Gneisenau. Monty picked the very best players available in the Army. They won 40–0.

Do not be misled by the Duke's coathanger frame and slender legs. He was a stout-hearted, hard-tackling defender in the mould of Norman 'Bite Your Legs' Hunter. If he could not reach the ball, he seldom missed the man in possession of it. Finesse was not immediately apparent in the timing of his challenges. Shuddering, bone-crunching commitment, as always with Nicholson, was everything.

When we founded the Jockeys cricket team we wrote to Sir Martin Gilliat, the Queen Mother's private secretary, to ask if we could use her colours, light blue and buff. The Queen Mother agreed and also generously presented a superb silver cup in 1967 for the player who produced the most outstanding perfomance of the year. Today it is the trophy for the Special Cargo and Burnt Oak Chase at Sandown in March. We also signed up two keen racing fans, Ted Dexter and Gary Sobers, as honorary members.

Nets with Jock Livingston were always fun. During the winter we would sometimes drive well over a hundred miles from distant race meetings to Northampton's indoor cricket school at the County Ground. Jock, who became our club chairman, used to say we were the keenest bunch of players he had ever encountered. In our first season alone we arranged eighteen fixtures.

Our annual cricket tours of the Isle of Wight swiftly moved into legend. Jump jockeys in those days really let their hair down during the summer holidays, but many of their antics were unprintable. We used to travel everywhere on the island by coach, though I found it impossible to whip them all in on time. After a lively game at Shanklin our young driver seemed a bit uncertain about driving through the narrow gates of the ground out on to the main road. Eventually he climbed out to check how much room he had to spare.

This was too much for Terry Biddlecombe, who jumped behind the wheel and drove straight through the gates leaving the hapless driver to set off in vain pursuit of his bus. Everyone was beside themselves with laughter. At least Terry pulled up half a mile down the road to allow the poor driver to catch us up.

Terry was a pretty effective wicket-keeper, for the good reason that he always seemed to have some part of his body behind the ball. He did not frighten easily, and scarcely flinched when a bouncer caught him smack between the eyes. On one of our trips to the island I was responsible for cutting his face as we sparred playfully one night after dinner. Blood poured from the wound, but typically he acted as though nothing had happened.

After a riotous night it was Terry, I seem to recall, who was spotted up a lamp-post outside our hotel as dawn broke wearing only a négligé which he had borrowed from a girlfriend. Moments later a road sweeper passed below him, working busily on the pavement. Terry, feeling rather lonely, bid him a cheery good morning. The sweeper looked up, nodded in a friendly fashion, and continued on his way without as much as a second glance.

One year we were based at a holiday camp on the island but the boys caused so much trouble we were not invited back. The first evening all the parasols ended up in the swimming pool. The next night someone drove across the pitch-and-putt course. Whatever the crime, you could be sure the camp's loudspeaker would summon the captain of the Jockeys cricket team to the manager's office at breakfast time the following morning.

Sometimes we would appear on stage at the summer shows on the island, riding hobby horses in a mock race. That's how we first met Felix Bowness, the comedian, who acted as compère. We also enjoyed a diversion on a go-kart circuit until we were thrown off because we were considered a danger to the public. Andy Turnell was unbeatable. Perhaps he should have been a racing driver.

I remember one year a girl on the island seemed to take a shine to just about every member of our side in turn. While she was tucked up in bed with a well-known jockey we decided to pay them a visit, but we had to change tactics when we discovered that the bedroom door was locked. Undeterred we made our way up the emergency staircase outside to the balcony door of the room. That was also locked, so Richard Tate put his shoulder to the door and barged straight through it into the room followed by a posse of giggling jockeys.

You had to admire the way the jockey and his girlfriend did not even pause for one moment in their activities. Really we all felt a bit superfluous to requirements so we pulled out a chest of drawers and lifted the bottom of the bed on to it. Even this did not stop the couple's frenzied display of affection as we made a less than discreet exit.

One of our best cricket trips was to the historic Mount Juliet stud, which used to be the family seat of the McCalmont family. For several days we were treated like royalty by Major McCalmont and his wife. We were so short of players we even called up Richard Pitman to join us.

The parties laid on for us were truly exceptional. One night after racing I had to take to my bath to sober up before dinner. I came down with the best of intentions, was offered a cocktail and was soon away again. Frankly, I was not in a situation to say much during dinner. Later, apparently, I was keen to keep the party going with a few more jars but David Minton put a stop to that by assuring me that everyone was going to bed.

When I got there he locked me in my room and returned to the party.

One night at Mount Juliet I remember dancing round a large, ornamental lily pond with a lively red-haired girl. Despite some serious drinking I could sense something was brewing and I had a nasty feeling I was supposed to end up in the fish pond. The first marauder tried to go for me, then stopped. The next one to appear was Richard Pitman who came on head first. I pushed the girl aside and chopped down on the back of his neck. An uppercut from Mike Tyson could not have been more effective. Richard dropped like a stone and did not move, so my partner and I resumed dancing.

The game on Sunday at Mount Juliet revolved round the apparent early dismissal of one of our best batsmen, Victor Dartnall, to a dubious umpiring decision. It was obvious that he was not out, so when he set off towards the pavilion, I jumped up and told him to go back. A brisk debate ensued before the umpire changed his mind. Victor went on to score a match-winning innings of 90.

Often on a Sunday we would find ourselves playing against famous cricketers of the past, or sometimes against future internationals. That is how we first met Alan Ward, a blindingly fast bowler who turned out for a Brewery XI against us at Derby. Josh Gifford batted for ten minutes against him and came back claiming he never saw a ball. Most of the others had the same problem. No wonder. Within eighteen months Ward was playing for England at the age of twenty-two! Normally I batted at ten with John Buckingham last man in but on this occasion I felt that John deserved to go in ahead of me. He did not agree at first but I insisted. You have never seen a man advance more slowly to the crease. It was as if he was walking to his own execution. After taking guard John looked up to see Alan Ward disappearing into the distance towards his mark.

'Where's he off to?' he asked the wicket-keeper. 'I don't go as far as that on my holidays!'

On another occasion we snapped up Harold Rhodes, formerly of England, to play for us against the Cross Arrows, the Lord's ground staff team, on the Nursery ground at Lord's. Most of the team assumed that the match would be off because it had rained most of Saturday and was still raining on Sunday morning. The people at Lord's were also pessimistic about the chances of a ball being bowled, but I had no intention of letting slip the only time I was likely to play there.

I spent most of the morning persuading them we should go ahead and then bullied our team into helping to mop up the ground. Eventually it was decided to take an early lunch and play a limited-overs match.

Harold Rhodes' career was in limbo at the time because the authorities considered he had a suspect arm action and he had been no-balled for throwing. My plan was to save him up until his adversary Jack Bailey, later to become secretary of the MCC, came in to bat. But Jack must have rumbled my plot because he declined to come in and declared with only him left to bat just as Harold was marking out the start of his run-up somewhere near the sight-screen.

Even so, I was delighted to claim the wickets of John Murray, the England wicket-keeper, and Middlesex's Harry Latchman (real name Amritt Harrichand), in two balls. Later my brother and I batted out until time, so we claimed an honourable draw with my father there cheering us on. But there was a major disappointment when we were prevented from having our team photograph taken in front of the Lord's pavilion. That is so typical of the hierarchy at Lords.

Whenever we played it suited us to field first. I used to go through the formality of tossing up but, by tradition, the other side batted first. That way we knew what we had to do and we could be sure the match would not end too quickly. There was also a further practical reason. I knew I could not control the boys from breaking loose in the bar if we batted first. Then their fielding would go to pieces.

The problem with a team of jump jockeys is that you can never be sure who is going to be fit to play. Falls and injuries could mean a last minute change in the eleven, but I always managed to have enough players to fill the gaps. It used to infuriate me when we turned up with a full side, only to find that the opposition had mustered nine or ten players. Even worse, I could not abide any of our team turning up late.

This led to a public confrontation with John Buckingham when he arrived after one of our games had started. John was so upset at being reprimanded that he was about to go straight home again and only changed his mind when I promised to give him a bowl. John has always been a keen golfer and I had not realised that he had hitch-hiked through the night from Scotland, where he had been watching the Open at St Andrews.

Later, when John broke his leg, he agreed to my request to umpire for us even though he was in plaster up to his waist. I soon realised I had chosen the wrong man after he turned down several lively appeals while I was bowling. By this time you could see the steam coming out of my ears. I marched past John and gave him a little nudge with the result that he fell off his shooting stick and lay helplessly on the ground. He claims I did not speak to him again until the game ended, but, as usual, we were the best of friends in the bar later.

One night, in the early years of the cricket team, a few of us including Terry Biddlecombe, Michael Scudamore and Stan Mellor sat round at table and decided to form an association to protect the interests of jump jockeys. This was long overdue, for we knew that certain things were wrong and that we badly needed a voice in racing's corridors of power. Jockeys were still treated much like servants in those days. I was elected secretary and duly scribbled down a few notes on the back of a cigarette packet. At once we began taking the Inspector of Courses, Colonel Tony Teacher, to task on a variety of issues. Late in 1969, jump and flat jockeys combined to form an association under the guidance of our first paid secretary, Peter Smith.

My brother Richard was one of several decent cricketers who turned out for the Jockeys XI. Richard was good enough to play regularly for Cheltenham, but his experience at work showed that injuries are not confined to jockeys. His first team debut for Cheltenham was delayed when he broke his right arm polishing the propeller of one of Dowty's aircraft at Staverton. Other regulars included Ian Arthurs, a gifted allrounder, Reg Lomas, course manager at Stratford, Sam Wilson, Bill Comerford, Jim Meads, the photographer, and Bill Warren. Bill could always be relied on to produce a spare player if we were short.

Some weeks as many as six pairs of brothers were available for the team: the Nicholsons, Terry and Tony Biddlecombe, John and Tom Buckingham, Josh and Macer Gifford, Richard and James Evans and Victor and Gerald Dartnall.

It was also handy to be able to call on top class professionals like David Brown, the England and Warwickshire fast bowler, to play for us when they were free, though David always complains that I gave him the stiffest bollocking he ever had in cricket.

David was fielding at slip and dropped a difficult chance off my bowling against the village of Chaddesley Corbett. He thought he had done well to save four runs. I was not so charitable at seeing a key batsman given a second chance and let fly with something along the lines of 'Call yourself a —— pro?'

I disgraced myself the day I played for Michael Scudamore's team against his local side near Hereford. When the umpire turned down several enthusiastic appeals from me in a row I suggested that he have his eyes tested. What I did not know was that he was our host for the evening when the game ended. Though I apologised afterwards, my name did not appear on the team sheet for that game the following year.

On another occasion I kept slipping over when I opened the bowling on a pitch made treacherous by heavy rain earlier in the day. Eventually I stood, hand on hips, and shouted to Jeff King, 'Kingy, get me some sawdust.'

Now Jeff never did like being told what to do. When he replied, 'Which tree would you like me to cut down, you ——?' everyone within hearing collapsed with laughter.

Several of the boys, including Josh Gifford and Jeff King, would complain that I took our cricket matches far too seriously. Josh and I had a terrible row after the Jockeys XI, with him as acting skipper, lost to the England Ladies XI. As I was going to be away I had told him to play our normal game against the girls, to show them no mercy and to be sure to beat them. I seem to remember concluding that if we were going to lose to a bunch of girls I did not want to play cricket any more. So you can imagine how I reacted when he rang to say the girls had won. He had gone soft, not used our best fast bowlers, let them reach a useful total and then, the final ignominy, they had bowled us out. I was fuming.

Within reason I was prepared to use any tactics to win. Once at Exning we looked like losing to Newmarket with a few overs left. So I told my boys John and Philip, aged about eight and ten, to move the boundary markers back. This increased the boundary by as much as fifteen yards in some places and had the desired effect of slowing Newmarket's scoring rate.

One year Henry Cecil, many times champion trainer, turned out for Newmarket, which was a bit of a surprise because no one had ever seen him with a bat in his hand. When he was fielding he seemed to spend most of the time chatting up the prettiest girls on the boundary. I tried to hit a six over his head but he turned round just in time to catch the ball. I was speechless.

Time was running out when we looked likely to beat the Old Test Stars XI on the Cheltenham College ground. The clock was already showing 6.57 p.m. as I walked out to bat and I knew that stumps would be drawn at seven. So I sent someone to stop the clock. That gave us a couple of extra overs and victory off the last ball.

I always enjoyed fielding as well as bowling, and my best catch probably came during dinner at Scotch Corner on the way home from riding in the Scottish Grand National for Neville Crump. A lively hunt ball was in progress at the same hotel. Late in the evening Peter Vaux seized a plate of trifle from a trolley and threw it at our table. Somehow I reached out and caught the plate with the trifle intact. What's more, I resisted the temptation to hurl it straight back at him.

The cricket trip to Barbados in 1983 was one of the most enjoyable holidays of my life, even though Dinah and I did not usually go off in a gang. I was the captain and Oliver Sherwood, the Lambourn trainer, was manager. When I put myself on to bowl in our first game on the Test ground at the Kensington Oval in Bridgetown, my third ball was hit out of the ground!

During our tour of Barbados Dinah took the chance to visit the grave of her father, who had died suddenly in 1964 while on holiday there and was buried in the shadow of the Kensington Oval. When she found his grave she placed an empty champagne bottle on it filled with wildflowers.

Then we moved on to Windward Cricket Club, the only all-white club on the island, where I became involved in a rearguard action at around 148 for 8 with our side still needing another 20-odd runs for victory. By the time I came in to bat the light was already fading. It was difficult to pick out the ball, so I was content to take singles. The opposition did not like this much and brought on a fast bowler who hit me so hard between the eyes that I called him a black bastard even though he was whiter than I was! I was very proud when my son John, who was aged sixteen at the time, scored the winning run.

We were thrashed in our third game by the local police, but it was what happened afterwards that sticks in my memory. When I was in the showers next to one of their players, I could not fail to notice that he had the biggest appendage I had ever seen hanging halfway down to his knees! Talk about big men and little boys. I have never felt so inadequate. I immediately walked out of the shower because I felt so insufficient beside him. We were all in hysterics and our wives were furious at not being allowed in on the joke. The player concerned seemed totally unphased by the ribbing from all and sundry. I suppose he has had to put up with it throughout his life.

I ran the Jockeys cricket team for twenty-seven years and hoped one of my sons would take it over. But it was not to be.

When it came to soccer, nobody tried to play harder than me. I have never been one of those who believed the theory that taking part was always more important than winning. What's the point of competing if you do not try your hardest to win?

I liked to play as a no-nonsense defender. If I missed the ball, I usually took the man out. The result was that I had some pretty violent confrontations over the years. Quite a few professionals gave me a working over when I tackled them a bit too vigorously, but the only person who ever retaliated with a punch was the comedian Bernie Winters, the founder and captain of the TV All Stars XI.

It happened in a charity game against his side at Cheltenham in 1960, the highlights of which were shown on television. Bernie was a big, bustling centre forward and it was my job to keep him quiet, but clearly he felt there was nothing friendly about my play and eventually warned Sam Wilson that he would sort me out if I did not back off.

After I had clobbered him for about the fifth time he caught me flush on the chin with an upper cut and laid me out flat on my back. Now Bernie was a big man, tall and heavy, and I can tell you he packed a decent punch. Sam Wilson immediately jumped on him to stop him hitting me again. Later Bernie wrote to me apologising for his behaviour, which was decent of him in the circumstances.

Dave King, the entertainer, used to call me 'the Octopus' because I caught him with everything I could bring to bear in a challenge. Quite honestly, the way I used to play I am surprised it did not happen more often. But, however fierce the battle on the pitch, I would always buy my opponents a drink in the bar afterwards.

I usually ended up taking more stick than I dished out when

we played against professionals. I remember turning out in a testimonial game against Coventry, whose ex-skipper George Curtis was a notoriously hard man. Now I knew George and his ally John Sillett pretty well. Much later I trained a horse for John. So naturally I had to have a go, but there was only going to be one winner when I tackled George head-on early in the game. I went down as if I had been hit by a runaway bus.

Years later, in 1987, I was proud to be at Wembley, wearing my sky-blue scarf and cap, when Coventry won the FA Cup Final. Our party included Dinah, Dave Dick, together with Ben and Pat Brooks. I had supported Coventry through the bad years, too. I used to watch them a fair bit. We started a wonderful day with an Ascot-type picnic in a car park beside the stadium, and gave our side a hundred per cent as supporters. What fun we had seeing my old friends win the greatest prize in football. Of the three Cup Finals I have attended, this one brings the happiest memories.

But much as I enjoyed watching professionals at the highest level I never did learn to hold back when I played against them. Once, I tried a crude challenge on the late, great Billy Wright, for so long captain of England and Wolves. You might as well have run into a brick wall.

Colin Suggett and two of his Norwich team mates took exception to some of my tackles for Newmarket in a game at Carrow Road. Most of the Norwich team played, but out of position. I remember that Martin Peters, for instance, was in goal.

At half-time Suggett warned Gavin Pritchard-Gordon what they intended to do if I did not ease off but naturally Gavin neglected to pass on the message. Early in the second half I had a violent confrontation with Duncan Forbes, a tall midfield player with a reputation as a hard man. At one point I thought we were going to come to blows.

Shortly after that three of them including Colin Suggett converged on me just as I had the ball at my feet. When the game moved on I was left in a heap in the middle of the pitch. If you put it about as much as I did you had to expect some hammer in return.

Inevitably there were arguments with referees and linesmen. In a charity game near Lambourn I was furious at one of our goals being disallowed unfairly. Things deteriorated further from the moment that the opposition scored from an offside position and the goal was allowed to stand. I was giving the linesman responsible for these errors a piece of my mind when he flung his flag at me and retorted, 'If you want a linesman, do it yourself.'

The day after I rode Vivant in the 1961 Grand National I remember turning out, with my arm in a sling, for the Jockeys XI against a Liverpool side, with Stanley Matthews as referee. Sam Wilson, who played alongside me at the back, had the sense to ask Stanley to sign his programme, which he still has to this day.

All sorts of celebrities used to play in these games including Roy Castle, Sean Connery, Russ Conway, Ronnie Carroll, a very youthful Ronnie Corbett and Tommy Steele. Sean Connery was such a gifted player that he was once invited by Matt Busby, no less, to sign for Manchester United but he turned down the chance in favour of an acting career.

Tommy Steele became a good friend after we played against each other in a charity match at Birmingham, despite a crunching tackle by me that left him crumpled on the ground. Tommy was a handy winger who could play a bit. That day he danced past the left half, beat Dave Dick and then advanced on me with only the goalkeeper to beat.

I hit him head-on, bang, and came away with the ball. The next thing his manager came rushing on to the pitch shouting at me to ease up because Tommy was in a particularly lucrative show the following week! I am told he still remembers the incident.

I always enjoyed trying to corner the BBC's Julian Wilson, who was another fleet-footed winger, in our annual clash against the Racing Press XI. Julian used to appear wearing a natty headband and was quite hard to nail once he was on the run, but I usually managed to leave my calling card before the game was over.

We used to play in front of massive crowds for some of these games. I remember leading out the Jockeys XI before a crowd of 10,000 at the Athletic Ground, Cheltenham one Sunday in October, 1959 against a Showbiz XI which included Dave King and Wally Barnes, the Arsenal and Wales international. Today, some Premier clubs struggle to attract a gate of that size.

The jockeys' showjumping was another lively distraction. I always enjoyed the jockeys' competitions, some of which appeared on *Sportsnight* on BBC TV, introduced in those days by David Coleman, who was quite a racing enthusiast. I knew Alan Oliver pretty well, as he had ridden a bit of racing, and he arranged for me to be tutored by his father Phil before the knock-out competition at the National Equestrian Centre at Stoneleigh.

Phil Oliver must have been a great schoolmaster because he helped me win it three years out of four, though of course I had the advantage of riding some pretty decent horses including Bay Rum and Samson.

In 1970 at Stoneleigh I had the good fortune to partner David Broome's superb old horse Jacopo who, at nineteen and with fifteen years' showjumping behind him, could truly be described as a veteran. But he had bags of pace too, and in an exciting final flew round in a time a fifth of a second quicker than that recorded by Josh Gifford on Foxtrot.

Two years later a field of forty jockeys turned out at Stoneleigh, including Willie Carson and Tony Murray from the flat, and also the rugged point-to-point stalwart Major Guy Cunard. I was one of five jockeys in action at Newton Abbot who flew back to Stoneleigh courtesy of the BBC and, riding Samson, pipped Bill Smith in the final run-off against the clock. I seem to remember there was a £1,000 prize for the winner most years but none of it ever ended up in my hands.

In a similar competition at Hickstead I failed to reach the first fence because the horse I had been nominated to ride took off towards the exit at a rate of knots. When I gave him a crack with the whip we ended up in a heap at the back of the jewellery tent. Having driven 250 miles to take part on my day off, I was livid. It did not help that Douglas Bunn, the supremo of Hickstead, thought it terribly funny. I suspect that he deliberately put me on a dodgy horse, and have not spoken too many words to him since. Even if I do not win I like to compete.

Chepstow tried a bold experiment in 1970 by combining their flat-racing card in September with a showjumping competition for jockeys in the middle of the course. I recall that Ladbrokes had a tent beside the collecting ring and for some reason installed me as favourite on Bay Rum. We took first prize with a clear round.

Ladbrokes then sponsored a jump jockeys' cross-country competition at a hunter trial meeting held at Enfield later in the month. I won that, too, on Bay Rum, and also took second prize on Dixieland.

A few years later I teamed up with pop star Kenny Jones of the New Faces to win a sponsored pairs competition on the opening night of the Olympia International Horse Show. This was a relay event for jockeys and celebrities. Kenny made a quick start over the course on Bed Socks, who belonged to Janette Skelton, stepmother of the 1995 World Cup individual champion showjumper Nick Skelton, and I managed to stay in front. We were each rewarded with a Piaget watch. It was a fun idea with Gerald Harper, Stirling Moss and Meriel Tufnell among the celebrities taking part.

People might think I take my sport too seriously but that is the way I have always been. I am just the same playing dominoes, darts or skittles and make no apology for it. Sport mirrors life and I would rather be a winner than a loser. I love to see youngsters get on, whatever game they play, and just wish some of the sportsmen lucky enough to represent England today showed a bit more fire in battle.

10

Early days at Condicote

The start of the new season in 1960–61 was memorable for a short holiday in Rome where the Olympic Games were taking place. I remember riding a double at Stratford at the beginning of September before rushing to Dover to join my brother Richard, Sam Wilson and his brother Henry, who ran a milk round, for the long drive to Italy where we set up camp on a beach outside Rome for the duration of the Games.

Eddie Harty, who later won the Grand National on Highland Wedding, was riding for Ireland in the three-day event and we called in to see David Broome, who was a key member of our showjumping team. Security around the Olympic village was nothing like it would be today, and David managed to smuggle us in. He also found us tickets for the showjumping finals where, riding Sunsalve, he did so well to take the individual bronze medal for which there were sixty-one competitors from twenty-one nations.

Our seats in the Piazza di Siena in the beautiful gardens of the Villa Borghese gave us a superb view of the tricky course, which proved too much for many horses and riders. David ended the first of the two rounds in joint tenth place on sixteen faults with Dawn Wofford. The local hero Raimondo d'Inzeo was the only one to go clear, but even he had twelve faults in the second round.

David Broome and the hard-pulling Sunsalve excelled in the second round despite sweeping into the stadium with such force that they picked up three faults for circling fence three before jumping it because they were going too fast. Their only other mistake came at the final fence where they incurred four faults by hitting the last pole. A total of seven faults in the second round was enough to ensure a bronze medal for David behind the d'Inzeo brothers, Raimondo and Piero. It was a joy to have been there.

Four days later we took our seats in the Olympic Stadium for the Prix des Nations to decide the Grand Prix jumping team event and found ourselves witnessing a shameful judging error which robbed David Broome and the chestnut Sunsalve of the only clear round of the day. We were sitting exactly opposite the water jump, stretching sixteen feet across, and were in a perfect position to confirm that they cleared the water with a foot to spare. Everyone else thought so too, a view that was confirmed when a score of zero appeared on the board beside the name of Sunsalve at the end of his round. The horse and his rider were warmly applauded by 100,000 spectators as they made a slow exit from the historic stadium.

But regrettably, before the end of the next round, Sunsalve's score was quietly changed from zero to four faults. There was quite a furore when it was announced that he had incurred this penalty at the water, since at no time had the judge raised his flag. Dorian Williams was one of many commentators critical of this slipshod judging. I was furious at the injustice of the way David was treated but there was bleak consolation in the knowledge that it did not cost Great Britain a medal as our team eventually finished out of the first seven.

Apart from that incident we had a tremendous time in Rome and even beat a team of Germans in an impromptu game of five-a-side soccer on the beach. I hit one of them head-on so hard he was knocked out. I think it was at this point that Sam cautioned, 'Steady, Duke. The war has been over for fifteen years.' We had to put him in the sea to revive him.

Throughout that holiday I continued to inject myself in the thigh to help control my asthma. It was not easy because normally I am very squeamish. I have never injected a horse in my life, but really did not have any option about injecting myself if I wanted to continue riding.

On the way home we camped in Paris for a few days at Enghien racecourse, which proved to be an unfortunate choice when rainwater started pouring through the tent late one night. It turned out that we had pitched at the foot of a gully running across the racecourse. While we were in Paris, we made our way to the famous Folies Bergères, which fully lived up to our expectations until an alarm sounded, the fire curtain came down, smoke covered the stage and the whole place cleared, with scantily clad girls rushing in all directions. Everyone else bolted but the four of us stayed resolutely in our seats determined not to miss a thing. When the crisis was over, people started to filter back into the theatre and eventually the show resumed.

I remember reaching home at around three in the morning at the end of a great holiday to find a message that I was riding Burley Dam Star for Jack Peacock in a novices' chase that day at Hereford. The horse must have been fitter than the jockey, because he won well.

I was delighted to be back in England to resume my liaison with Dinah Pugh, who had been my steady girlfriend since my twenty-first birthday party. We used to play tennis at the Prestbury Club and at the Lygon Arms. We also used to go out to dinner most Saturday evenings at Rossley Manor Country Club near Cheltenham, which had the added attraction of a three-piece band, where we liked to dance the night away. I had found that the best way to attract the girls in those days was to dance and I think it is a shame that no one seems to dance properly now. Soon after I left school I began taking lessons in ballroom dancing with Sam Wilson, who worked in the yard. The pair of us would cycle to Sylvester's in Cheltenham for evening lessons once a week. We had a lot of fun over the course of that year but I could never persuade my sons Philip and John to learn to dance when they were in their teens.

After a year going out together we were very much an item and it was decided that I should move into a room at Dinah's parents' house. Now this might seem quite forward for that time, but the truth is that living on top of a hill at Temple Guiting helped reduce the problem of asthma. Although I was supposed to be allergic to cats, this theory was disproved when I was adopted by a scruffy model called Woody-Owl, who took to sleeping on my bed at my new home. Since then we have been surrounded by cats and dogs of all varieties, not forgetting our parrot Clouseau.

Dinah became a racehorse owner for the first time at Towcester on Easter Saturday, 1961. I was rotten with flu that day and should not have been riding but was determined to do so because I was tantalisingly close to fifty winners for the season for the first time. To keep me going, Dinah's father gave me an egg flip, consisting of white of egg and brandy mixed up in a flask to take to the races. After two generous measures I was feeling no pain.

Suitably fortified I won the first race of the day, a selling chase, on Biri, an eight-year-old mare owned and trained by Edward Courage. We jumped off, made all and hacked up, which was a bit of a surprise because her form beforehand was distinctly moderate. As soon as I jumped off Biri in the winner's enclosure I pressed Dinah to buy her because I was convinced she would win another race. Luckily there was very little interest and Biri was knocked down to my father for 200 guineas and became Dinah's property that evening.

After five rides and liberal doses of my extremely welcome pick-me-up there was no way I would have passed a breathalyser test by the end of that afternoon at Towcester. But I survived the day in one piece and left the course in high spirits aware that Biri already had an entry in another selling chase at Chepstow three days later.

We took Biri back to Prestbury and I duly rode her to victory at Chepstow on Easter Tuesday wearing Dinah's colours. This time there was not a single bid at the subsequent auction and so the first prize of £186 helped Dinah recoup almost all her money at the first attempt. After that she simply had to marry me!

In June, 1961 Dinah accepted my proposal of marriage but added that I should formally ask her father, Geoffrey Pugh, who was the chairman and managing director of Atco Motor Mowers in Birmingham. Dinah then departed on holiday leaving me to visit her father, who had played cricket for Warwickshire after becoming the only schoolboy at Rugby to score 1,000 runs in a season.

Usually Geoffrey Pugh was back at home from his office by six in the evening but when I turned up soon after six he had not arrived, so Dinah's mother asked me in and poured me a dry martini. As time passed I accepted a few more cocktails with the result that I was absolutely flying when Dinah's father drove in at around eight in the evening. I rushed outside, pulled open the door of his car and asked if I could marry his daughter before he had a chance to move. Once that was over we then returned to the house and had a few more glasses in celebration.

Since we became engaged we have done everything together. Soon we began our search for a home and in October, 1961 paid

£8,100 for an old farmhouse, three acres and some outbuildings at a remote Cotswold village called Condicote not far from my future in-laws at Temple Guiting. The village was so small it did not even have a pub, and though it boasted a post office then, that closed down later on. My father, who was always very careful with his money, was furious and said we had paid far too much for the place. I suppose it was a bit of a dump but we buckled down and worked flat out to knock it into shape. In those days I was quite a handy carpenter and spent some time making fitted cupboards for all the bedrooms.

It is probably best to draw a veil over my stag night but I do recall the response of my brother Richard when my mother politely inquired why he was crawling up the stairs in the dark in the early hours of the morning.

'It is quieter in the dark,' he declared solemnly, before continuing unsteadily towards his room on all fours.

We were married on Thursday, May 31, 1962, two days before the end of the season, with my brother Richard acting as best man, an angelic-looking Peter Scudamore as pageboy, my nephew James Fanshawe in a pram, and a galaxy of jockeys as ushers. In one of the wedding photos Richard Nicholson is the only person who has never ridden a winner among thirty-six jockeys past and present.

Several jockeys started a bottle-throwing competition into the lake below the marquee. This did not deter Josh Gifford and another brave soul from rowing out into the lake as bottles rained down on them. Terry Biddlecombe, or was it his brother Tony, tried to ride past on a Jersey cow and was unshipped to general hilarity. Jeff King took a nap in a cow byre and lost his false tooth. A month later it was found in the manger and returned to him!

We spent our honeymoon in Torremolinos and then returned to Condicote to continue the task of turning the house and yard into some semblance of order. When we arrived there was not a horse in the village.

One of our first priorities was to acquire endless loads of ancient walling stone, which we broke up by hand and used as hard core in the yard, with D. Nicholson at the helm of the steamroller. We then stoned the entire yard by hand. We also converted the coal shed into two boxes. That was the start. One was for Dinah's hunter, the other for the only racehorse we had on the place. Later we bought one or two broodmares. At first the idea was to graze a few animals for a bit of fun and over the years we kept sheep, cattle, chickens and even pigs. Dinah was the one who did all the work with them.

Once we had returned from honeymoon we tried to buy extra land, too, but at that stage we did not have any plans to train, though we both felt it would be nice to have the odd horse at home. Training developed from there. We soon came to appreciate the appeal of Condicote but our first winter there proved to be the coldest for thirty years. I remember that my parents left our New Year's Eve party shortly after midnight and only just made it back to Prestbury through the blizzard. My sister Josie preferred to wait until the morning before leaving and ended up staying for a month!

The village, set on the roof of the Cotswolds, was cut off from the rest of the world under several feet of snow in places with heavy drifts closing the narrow lanes. There was not a lot of urgency to go anywhere for the good reason that racing was wiped out for eleven weeks from Boxing Day and, apart from a lone meeting at Ayr, did not resume until March 8 at Newbury.

The only way to the main roads was across fields where the snow was not lying quite so deep. Showing commendable initiative, Dinah used to ride her hunter to the nearest market town Stow six miles away and bring back supplies for people in the village in her saddle-bags.

For a while I joined a local council gang clearing the roads at the princely wage of 4 sh. 6d. an hour. I just could not sit around doing nothing, so I volunteered for the job while the bad weather continued.

Since the day we became engaged Dinah and I have been a team, working as one. We discuss everything. Dinah was tireless in those early years; she had some experience of riding in point-to-points, loved her days out hunting and was a tidy work rider when we started training a few years later. She could turn her hand to anything in the yard and was as good a box driver as we have ever employed, though she had to take it easy for the few weeks after our two children Philip and John were born in 1963 and 1966.

Dinah enjoyed rearing young stock on the farm and was thrilled when our Aberdeen Angus heifer won the cup for the champion beast at Andoversford Fat Stock Show in December, 1966. Farming brought its own headaches. We bought some Belted Galloways to graze, then acquired a bull at the Royal Show. The Belted Galloways proved to be as wild as hawks with the result that they took off into the distance the minute we tried to move them from one paddock to another. It would take us all day to round them up and we never did find one.

Later Dinah took the bull to Banbury market and, unaware that he should have been led, caused pandemonium when she lowered the ramp on our truck and let him run loose into a pen. People scattered in all directions; in the end he was sold for beef rather than stud.

We were helped in all our farming pursuits, and in so many other ways, by the Habbitts family, who were something of an institution in the village. You did not need to listen to the weather forecast if Nobby Habbitts was in the area. He could tell you exactly what was coming for the next three weeks. He was a wonderful old countryman and it was our good fortune that he adopted us. You name it, he could turn his hand to any job you asked; his speciality was building dry-stone walls with the loving care of a true craftsman. He and his son Ron took us over from the moment we arrived in Condicote. They helped put everything in order around the yard, stables and house. Later Nobby's grandson Stephen worked for us, too. If you had Nobby on your side playing dominoes in the evenings at the Coach and Horses two miles away, you knew you could not lose.

Lots of our lads lived with the Habbitts family over the years, and in 1967 he moved into a house we had bought in the village for £1,700, and lived there until he died aged eighty-nine in 1991. Nobby was a terrific character who enjoyed every day of his life. How he would have enjoyed seeing Jackdaws Castle emerge from an old stone quarry.

In the first years at Condicote we also started buying prospective young jumpers as foals and yearlings and preparing them for sale at three. It was a satisfying hobby which offered the prospect of a decent profit, but usually we lost more money than we made.

Some of our greatest fun in those days came from showing at local events. We began by showing Biri and her foal in a hopelessly amateur fashion, and gradually learned the ropes through trial and error. It was unusual to show horses that were going on to race because judges tend to like them carrying too much condition, but we won quite a few classes with a yearling filly. We had bought her dam Tell Audrey as an old mare, sent her to be covered by Poaching and named the subsequent foal Caught At It. Later we leased her to Dinah's aunt, Joyce Westray, who put her in training with my father. Caught At It eventually won a race as a three-year-old at Brighton.

Nut Brown, a mare we bought on the advice of my uncle Willie Stephenson, bred us Royal Nutmeg, who was quite successful in the show ring before going racing. Royal Nutmeg, in turn, bred a filly, by St Paddy, called Hazeldean, who was successful at the Royal Show for us before winning races at two and three, trained by Pat Rohan, and then coming back to Condicote to win over hurdles.

We also acquired a tiny filly called Little Primrose, who came in a job lot with Oakprime because she was so small. She turned out to be by Master Owen, from the same family as the Gold Cup winner Silver Buck. We hoped she would develop into a racehorse, but she did not grow big enough. We also tried to sell her without success. Little Primrose was a beautiful mover, became one of the best small mares (under 15.2) of her time and won the Lloyds Bank In Hand Championship at the Horse of the Year Show at Wembley. After the presentations we had to parade Little Primrose and her foal on our own in the spotlight and the foal ran straight out of the ring, with me hanging on to the end of the lead rein.

Over the years we learned some useful tricks of the trade. Margaret Rogers, a keen showing person, taught us how to improve a horse's colour with the assistance of two or three packets of dye. We tried it first, with spectacular results, on a wishy-washy chestnut filly named Little Beaver. After giving the filly a wash and hair rinse, we sponged on the dye liberally until her colour changed to an attractive, rich, natural chestnut. Little Beaver then won at the Royal Show, no less. The dye tended to last the best part of a month. Some breeders use it to good effect before yearling sales.

When we started producing young horses, we fitted a cooker into our horsebox and set off most weekends to show them, and made so many chums during our summers on the circuit. We did it for our own pleasure, because we were not professionals, and developed a system in the ring that always seemed to amuse spectators.

With one eye firmly on the judge, I would lead the foal, following Dinah with the mare. The moment I saw the judge glance in our direction, I would command, 'Walk on.' When his attention drifted elsewhere, I would cry, 'Steady.' So our progress round the ring would be punctuated with a series of barked orders: 'Stop. Go . . . For Christ's sake, go. Go on . . . whoa. Stop.' It must have looked very strange but it seemed to work.

Eventually, in 1972, while I was still riding, I was asked to be a judge too. Although we have now given up showing our own horses because we simply do not have the spare time, I still continue to judge at three or four shows a year, including the Royal at Stoneleigh. The first time I judged ridden horses came at the Royal Dublin Horse Show with the late George Rich, a super character. They certainly expect you to work there. The first day, wearing a hacking jacket, breeches and boots, I rode no less than fifty-eight at a walk, trot, canter and gallop.

By the time I reached our hotel room I could not move. My backside and knees were so raw, the chances of my riding a further fifty the next day seemed remote. Dinah suggested I soaked in the bath for half an hour. After I dried off, she told me to bend forward and hit me on the backside with a double handful of aftershave. I shot round that room so fast Linford Christie would not have caught me. But the treatment worked. I was back in the saddle the next day.

In October, 1970 I was asked by Cynthia Haydon to spend a week riding in a Hackney Quadrille twice a day at the Horse of the Year Show. This proved a serious test of endurance, since riding hackneys at a sitting trot is not very comfortable, and after the show was over I would drive home to Condicote. In addition, I rode at Ascot on the Thursday, and on Friday won the last race at Fakenham on Clay Duck, before flying back to London from Norfolk in time for the evening performance at Wembley.

On the Saturday I flew to Norway to ride Sorrento at only 10st. 2lbs, at Ovrevoll, with firm instructions from trainer Auge Paus not to hit the horse with the whip. I kicked and pushed for all but three miles and just beat Terry Biddlecombe, who was riding Sunny Lad for Robert

Sangster. I had an extremely sore backside by Sunday morning.

A showing judge has to decide which of the horses entered has the best conformation and action as a show hunter. Naturally opinions differ on such matters, and many is the time I have been cornered by an irate owner or breeder demanding to know why I overlooked his or her horse. I soon learned that it pays to remember each horse's characteristics, because you need a ready excuse if people question your judgements. You can offend people so easily. John Dunlop, for instance, took me on in a restaurant in Norfolk one night because he was unhappy with my decision.

Once, after a busy morning judging the in-hand class at the Royal Highland Show, I was taken off by Ken Oliver, the show chairman, for a long, liquid lunch, which ended with three glasses of port because I assumed I had finished for the day. Ken then informed me that I had to judge the overall championship in the afternoon.

Ignoring my protests that I was unfit to carry on, he led me back to the ring, where I challenged George Rich, the ridden judge, to the effect that I would ride his champion, but he would be unable to ride mine, an unbroken two-year-old. After tucking the trousers of my grey suit into my socks, I was legged up on to the ridden horse, in a bit of of a haze, to give a show and discovered it was not the greatest mover as we galloped round. Luckily George agreed and the two-year-old was awarded the ticket. Showing was an interesting pastime. Riding was my living.

In those days, before the advent of motorways, we used to travel to most race meetings in the South-East on the train. I would drive to my local station at Moreton and join up with Terry Biddlecombe, Michael Scudamore and others. We seemed to know all the waiters in the restaurant cars and used to play cards all the way to London and back.

After racing at Folkestone, Plumpton and Wye we would return to London just in time for a visit to Jules' Bar followed by a light meal at Wheeler's before the rush to catch the 8.15 home. One night I remember Terry tossing my new pack of cards out of the window as we reached Moreton. The last he saw of me I was scrambling along the track in the dark desperately trying to retrieve them all. On another occasion after a temporary disagreement Terry threw Michael's car keys into the churchyard when they reached Evesham on the milk train. Michael's wife was not exactly thrilled to be woken by a call from her husband asking her to collect him from the station at two in the morning.

We had a lot of fun at dinners and various functions in London. One night, displaying surprising athleticism considering the amount of drink that had been consumed, I caught a pigeon as we waited for a lift in Hyde Park and placed it on the shoulder of Johnny Lehane, who was asleep in the car.

When he woke up, it flapped its wings so much I thought it was going to fly straight through the roof, so I rescued it from Johnny and took it home all the way to Condicote where it was a fixture for several years. The next morning Mrs Nicholson was not best pleased to discover pigeon droppings all over my dinner jacket.

The moment that foot-and-mouth disease threatened to wipe out racing late in November, 1967, my father took the decision to send a small team of horses down to Cagnes-sur-Mer in the South of France, including Guards Cake, owned by Brough Scott's parents, and Sam Vestey's Cavalry Charge. No one seemed to know how long the ban on racing in England would last and there was quite a rush to smuggle the horses out of the country in the nick of time.

Others who took advantage of this loophole included Tom Jones, Ifor Lewis, Paddy Sleator and his jockey Bobby Coonan. Brough and I travelled to the South of France with one stable lad, but Brough was the only one of the party with passable French. Now six weeks in the South of France in the depths of winter might sound a wonderful idea and it is true that after riding out early each morning we used to play golf or go ice skating. Yet the thing I remember most about that trip was the miserable time on Christmas Day away from home. It was the worst Christmas I have ever endured.

Dinah was at home, although she did manage to come out for a few days over the New Year. The stable yard at Cagnes-sur-Mer was like a morgue on Christmas Day. All of us realised then that we should have returned home. Instead, we spent the day in Monte Carlo with a long lunch and a dip in a hotel swimming pool. We did our best to enjoy the festivities, but I swore then that I would never spend another Christmas Day away from home.

This was the first time I had been in charge of a group of horses; in a sense it was the beginning of my life as a trainer. We worked them each morning on a figure-of-eight track in the centre of Cagnes racecourse and I soon discovered that races in France are run at a different tempo, with the result that it took both Cavalry Charge and me two attempts to learn to adapt.

Somehow I boiled myself down to 9st. 13lbs, my lightest for years, to ride Cavalry Charge to a narrow victory in the Prix le Bouif early in January. It was a great feeling when we won, made even better because Sam Vestey had flown out for the race.

The French press, amused by the appearance of such a tall jump jockey, christened me '*le Plus Grand Jockey du Monde*'.

Our day was complete when Brough finished second on Guards Cake half an hour later. One of the French jockeys based in Cagnes that winter, a genial character called Robert Luriou, was remarkably well connected for a man who had only a handful of rides. That night Robert insisted that we accompany him to a restaurant in the hills above Nice overlooking a tiny bull ring.

Our party, including Brough, Stan Mellor and Sam Vestey, consumed liberal amounts of champagne conjured up by our new friend before he invited us to climb into the ring for a photo call. Now I had no intention of moving far from the bar but the the temptation proved too much for Brough and Stan, who started off riding a donkey. They were still marooned in the ring when a small bull suddenly lumbered towards them. Brough, who fancied himself as El Cordobes, began to wave his red cardigan at it in a drunken fashion while Stan Mellor, showing an instinct born of survival, quickly scrambled up a tree in the middle of the ring.

Though we were laughing until the tears ran down our faces, the joke was wearing a bit thin for Brough, particularly when the bull charged past and splintered the rail behind him. He and Stan ran for their lives and I recall that Sam lost his wallet.

This episode delighted Robert Luriou, who seemed to be at the heart of any intrigue at Cagnes, a fact which might explain how he became the Mafia's link with a jockeys' ring and eventually ended up behind bars.

When racing began again in England in January we would fly back for the weekend, then return to France on the Sunday night. The following year my father repeated the French experiment by sending down some horses to Pau with a couple of stable lads including a very youthful Mouse Morris. This time I determined to stay at home and fly out when required.

On one eventful weekend Brough and I rode in the Great Yorkshire Chase at Doncaster on the Saturday before taking a private plane to Heathrow in time to catch the flight to Paris. We were then involved in an interminable train journey through the heart of France during which we drank far too much cheap red wine. My father met us at Pau station at five in the morning and proceeded to give us a guided tour of the area.

That afternoon we both rode in the Grand Course de Haies de Pau, a valuable handicap hurdle. I was on Cavalry Charge and Brough on Black Justice, a very decent horse trained by Syd Dale. Between us we carved up the French champion jockey Christian Mahe comprehensively, as we headed down the back straight for the final time.

Mahe was very much the local hero. On the racecourse he was a little god, so that when he shouted everyone moved out of his way. The trouble was caused by the lack of a rail on the inside of the course; the only thing to prevent you running out was a large irrigation ditch guarded by a bank.

Brough was more or less in the lead when Mahe tried to force his way up the inside on Eclat, but he shut the door abruptly when I cried out, 'Brough, watch your inner!'

The result of this manoeuvre was that Mahe and Eclat ended up heading for the dyke amid howls of anguish. I do not know to this day how they stood up but in the closing stages they came through to take second place in front of Black Justice with Cavalry Charge fifth.

Mahe rushed towards Brough in the weighing-room, fists balled, shouting angrily, 'Assassin. Assassin,' but Brough has always had the knack of talking his way out of trouble and somehow lived to tell the tale. Later we had a long, liquid lunch with Sam Vestey before starting the journey to England, where we were both due to ride at Worcester the following day.

When we missed our connecting flight at Orly, Brough all but knocked himself out by walking straight into a plate-glass door as we sought a hotel for the night. The door was undamaged but he certainly would not have beaten the count.

By the time we reached Worcester the next day we were both ready for bed, but there was work to do and despite feeling distinctly secondhand, we each managed to win a race. Brough did particularly well to win on Mr Wonderful after the tree of his saddle broke at the third last fence. I remember telling him afterwards that he looked much better jumping the last fence without irons.

11

Mill House

By now I was a reasonably fashionable jockey and had become something of a professional substitute for some of the biggest yards if the first choice was injured or unavailable. I was delighted to ride two winners in a day for Peter Cazalet, and took the valuable Stone's Ginger Wine Chase at Sandown on Rough Tweed in February, 1962. Rough Tweed was trained at Middleham by Neville Crump, who was a legend in his own lifetime even then, a fearless former soldier who spoke his mind in the most colourful language.

The next autumn I won another decent race, the Ansell's Brewery Chase, on Rough Tweed and was thrilled to be asked to ride him in the Hennessy Gold Cup. Crump also ran Springbok, the second favourite, ridden by his stable jockey Gerry Scott, who is now a Jockey Club starter.

Going to the last fence the Crump-trained pair had the race between them. Rough Tweed barely stayed three miles, let alone the extra quarter mile so I crept down the inside in the home straight before taking on Springbok going to the last fence.

Springbok made a hash of the fence while Rough Tweed flew it and soon pinched a two-length lead. But the ground was very soft and, hard as he tried, I could feel Rough Tweed tying up beneath me. He was going so slowly that the last one hundred yards seemed to take for ever and right on the line Springbok squelched past to snatch the prize.

Neville Crump was mad with me afterwards, quite furious. When he calmed down I asked, 'What did I do wrong?'

'You got beat,' he replied. 'If you had held on we would have had a decent present from his owner Colonel Simon Lycett Green. Instead we will get nothing out of Springbok's owner!'

The Schweppes Handicap Hurdle soon became synonymous with controversy. The first year it was run at Liverpool in 1963 I remember lining up on Narratus on the inner beside the winner Rosyth, ridden by Josh Gifford. There were forty-one runners that year, far too many for that tight little track, with the inevitable result that poor Stan Mellor had the most dreadful fall at the second hurdle on Eastern Harvest and suffered numerous facial fractures. Rosyth was trained by Ryan Price, who was rarely out of the headlines in the years that he dominated the race. He won it in four of the first five years, and even lost his licence after Rosyth ran away with the prize again in 1964. There was also a stewards' inquiry after I rode to victory on Elan in 1965.

Elan had won the Gloucestershire Hurdle as a five-year-old but his form in the run-up to the Schweppes the next season was hardly encouraging. Several leading jockeys were well beaten on him, including Dave Dick, Jeff King and Johnny Gilbert. A fortnight before Newbury his trainer, John Sutcliffe junior, rang my father to ask if I was available to ride Elan.

When it came to laying out a horse for a big handicap John was very adept indeed and I seem to recall that he was already preparing the grounds for his defence when he suggested that my father should advise General Sir Randle Feilden to back Elan ante-post for the Schweppes as he was putting blinkers on him for the first time. Perhaps he was influenced by the fact that the General was senior steward of the Jockey Club at the time.

There was a huge punt on the well-handicapped Elan, who started 9–2 favourite. He was always travelling well, took up the running after the third last and came clear to beat Rosyth, who was attempting to complete a hat-trick in the race. The blinkers, although small, had certainly helped.

The stewards immediately summoned Sutcliffe to explain the horse's improvement in form. When I was called in I told the stewards my orders were to be in the first four and keep going. John's explanation was noted, but there was never the slightest danger that we would lose the race, which was just as well since Elan paid for a new barn at Condicote.

One of my proudest days as a jockey came later that month at Lingfield where I rode a double for the Queen Mother over fences on Arch Point and Mel. My father was tickled pink, too, because he had won on a horse owned by the future King Edward VIII at Colwell Park, Malvern before the war.

Earlier in my career I had also ridden once for the Queen over jumps on Augustine, at Kempton. The Queen Mother was a delight to ride for and would give her jockeys the best orders possible. On one occasion I rode Colonia for her, in a novice chase, at Sandown. Aware that I had a decent chance in the Grand National the following week, she suggested, 'You know what to do, David. Just go out, enjoy yourself and look after each other.' It is advice I try to give my own jockeys.

At Folkestone, riding Regal Arch, I beat the Queen Mother's horse Silver Dome into second place in the Fremlins Elephant Chase and then found myself receiving the trophy from her. As she handed me the trophy I mumbled my apologies. She is a terrific ambassador for racing.

I had a brief moment of hope in the 1966 Cheltenham Gold Cup on Snaigow. It happened when Arkle, who seemed certain to win the race for the third year running, partly demolished the fence in front of the stands. It was a mistake that would have finished any other horse, and following close behind, Michael Scudamore, on Dormant, and I both thought this was our chance. Yet, quite extraordinarily, Arkle continued merrily on his way as if nothing had happened and we were soon left in his wake.

Asthma continued to be a problem, but by now I had learned to live with it. For a while as a teenager I thought it had beaten me, but regular injections and later, significantly, the advent of inhalers gave me fresh hope. Being able to take a puff or two before and after a race helped my breathing enormously, but panic still set in when I mislaid the inhaler or needed a refill. Inhalers were and are a vital part of my life.

Once, at Worcester, I sent Sam Wilson into the town in urgent search of a chemist's store to find a refill for me. The chemist explained that he could not hand one over without a prescription but relented when Sam pointed out that his life would not be worth living if he returned to the racecourse without one.

I rode a lot of good horses over the years, including Oxo, who was a smashing chaser, and Larbawn, who later won the Whitbread Gold Cup in successive years. He was usually ridden by Macer Gifford, who was known in the weighing-room as Chief Running Hands because he could not hold anything that pulled. Macer suited Larbawn because he just let him run. Nothing worried Macer, who died tragically young from motor-neurone disease.

The proudest victory of my career came on Mill House in the 1967 Whitbread Gold Cup, which brought compensation for his disappointments in the Gold Cup down the years. Mill House was a colossus, a mighty horse like a top class show hunter, brilliant enough to win the Gold Cup at the age of six. He was just unlucky to be born in the same era as Arkle.

Mill House was a very correct horse with a beautiful, light action. I rode a few for his trainer Fulke Walwyn over the years and was offered the chance on Mill House when his regular rider Willie Robinson was injured and his owner, Bill Gollings, wanted a jockey with long legs.

Initially I rode him schooling at Lambourn and then at Newbury where he banked a fence and continued as if nothing untoward had happened. Mill House was enormously powerful, so massive that he could miss out a jump completely and the fence would have to give. Sometimes when he hit a fence, the timber frame would go as well.

Just to sit on Mill House made you feel good. He had a majesty, that horse, which gave you a feeling on his back of reigning supreme. He was certainly the greatest jumper I had the good fortune to ride. It still excites me to try to find one like him to train.

I remember the first time I rode him at Sandown, because I am convinced it was the day that Arkle broke Mill House's heart. By the time the pair clashed in the Gallagher Gold Cup in November, 1965 it was clear that Arkle was the master. He had beaten Mill House comprehensively in successive Gold Cups and so was set to concede sixteen lbs to his old rival. Another stone would not have made the slightest difference to the outcome.

Fulke Walwyn was insistent that I made every fence count down the far side on the second circuit and we met each one spot on with the result that when we touched down in front over the last fence on the far side I thought that was the end of Arkle.

The next thing Pat Taaffe came sailing past on him as if they had just joined in. As they sprinted clear I could feel the resolve go out of Mill House and he was very weary by the time he crossed the finishing line in third place twenty-four lengths behind Arkle. Poor Fulke knew that day beyond any reasonable doubt that his horse would never beat Arkle again.

I rode Mill House for the second time in the 1967 Gold Cup, as Willie Robinson was injured. He was a 4–1 chance that year, but it was not generally known that he had been suffering from a back problem. Nick Gaselee, who was Fulke Walwyn's assistant at the time, warned me that if I trotted the horse around at the start he risked the chance of being withdrawn because he was lame behind. None the less Mill House travelled well through the race. As we came to the last fence on the first circuit, I looked over to Terry Biddlecombe on Woodland Venture and suggested this might be the moment for the pair of us to end up on the front of the Injured Jockeys' Fund Christmas calendar.

Instead, the horses wiped the smiles from our faces by blundering through the fence. Mill House was still in the lead upsides Woodland Venture until he fell heavily at the final ditch, the seventeenth fence at the top of the hill. He met the fence right but put down instead of picking up and that was that. He was still going well enough at the time. This left the way clear for Terry to gain a popular win on Woodland Venture. Terry and I still argue about who would have won if my horse had not come down.

Champion jockey three times, Terry had superb balance and tremendous strength in the finish, and would probably be permanently warned off for his use of the whip if he was riding today. The race he rode on French Excuse in the Welsh Grand National was out of this world. He gave it everything and passed out in the weighing-room afterwards. He was a wonderful jockey.

When Terry emigrated to Australia, I used to ring him up on Christmas Day, a habit I still maintain now that he is back in this country. I also speak to Josh Gifford every Christmas, too, even though we see each other at the races regularly throughout the winter. I rang him when he spent one Christmas in Nottingham hospital with a broken leg, while he was still riding, and it has continued from there.

I am delighted that Terry returned from Australia, and is very much involved in racing again with his wife Henrietta Knight. He has shown great strength of character in giving up alcohol, which had caused him some problems in his life. He is very strong since his conversion, but does not preach about it. When he returned from Australia I told him my door was always open if he needed any help. He has been to Jackdaws Castle in his role as reporter for Central TV, and my offer to give him a ride in the golden oldies jockeys series still stands if he can do the weight! It is great to see him looking so well.

Although Willie Robinson was unfit to ride Mill House in the 1967 Gold Cup, it was thought that he would recover in time to partner the horse in the Whitbread Gold Cup at Sandown, but three days before the race Fulke Walwyn rang up to see if I was available. At the time I was already booked to ride my father's Buffer for Lord Sefton at Towcester, but my father always tried to help out in this sort of situation and solved the problem by deciding not to run the horse. His loyal attitude has rubbed off on me. I am very keen for my jockeys to ride the best horses within reason.

Ever since he first succumbed to Arkle it seemed that English racegoers had taken Mill House to their hearts in a very special manner. He had returned aged ten as popular as ever from a year on the sidelines after being fired on both forelegs and might well have won a second Gold Cup but for that fall upsides Woodland Venture.

At Sandown he set off with his customary enthusiasm in the Whitbread and pulled his way into the lead as early as the third fence. That was his style, lively, exuberant; he always took you there and seemed to be no more than cantering.

As we passed the stands for the second time in front, going well with one final circuit to complete, I can recall the crowd applauding. John Buckingham's mount San Angelo moved up so close behind that he was clipping my horse's heels so I was forced to turn round and give him some verbal abuse.

Swinging right-handed to the awkward downhill fence I sensed Terry Biddlecombe moving upsides to take me on with the Gold Cup winner Woodland Venture. I asked Mill House for a big jump here but he blundered badly, sending the birch flying in all directions.

Even so he never looked like falling and somehow, unbelievably, made ground in the process, a fact picked up by the course commentator as he marvelled, 'Mill House has gained another length!'

Racing down the back straight Mill House was superb, poetry in motion, answering every question I asked with bold, spectacular fencing that extended his advantage; but conscious that he was carrying 11st. 11lb I took a pull landing over the last on the far side to be sure that he had something left for the final hill. This allowed several horses to queue up behind me waiting to pounce. John Buckingham was the first to appear upsides on San Angelo halfway round the bend.

I cried, 'Steady, Buck. You have trotted up.' If John had pressed on then it is possible Mill House would have remembered Arkle and not finished in the first four. Instead the moment he took a pull I kicked for home as if my life depended on it and they never got back to me.

We gained a length at the Pond fence and another at the second last and were halfway home. Mill House met the last fence slightly wrong but popped over it safely and, although the strength was draining away from his legs on the final hill, he held on grimly from Kapeno by one and a half lengths.

Two yards past the post my horse had stopped to a walk. He was out on his feet. He had given everything a horse could offer and more and was so tired he was the last one to come off the track towards the rhododendron walk. As his breath began to come back so the crowd started to clap. I have never known anything like it. The more they clapped and cheered the quicker the adrenalin surged through him.

By the time Mill House reached the winner's enclosure he walked in as if he was the King of England. It seemed to me that everyone present at Sandown was elated. The whole place erupted. It was the most fantastic feeling, a wonderfully moving occasion I shall never forget.

After I received my trophy from the Queen Mother there was a nice touch when Willie Robinson limped forward on crutches to a great ovation and received Her Majesty's commiserations on missing such a memorable ride. Later, following a glass or two of bubbly, I took Dinah and her mother out to dinner that evening at the Manor House in Moreton-in-the-Marsh, but I was so pumped up I could not eat a thing all night.

I had several decent rides in the Champion Hurdle and should probably have won it in 1965 on the Queen Mother's Worcran, who was little more than a novice. He made a bad mistake at the third last hurdle, lost his position completely and then came round the entire field to snatch third place.

Tokoroa, trained by Fred Rimell, also gave me a good ride in the 1960 Champion Hurdle until falling at the third last. The Rimells were old adversaries going back to the days when Fred and my father shared the jockeys' championship in 1944–45. I can remember Mercy Rimell administering one of the worst

bollockings I have ever received when I was beaten a short head
at Stratford on Sharuk, trained by Fred, in the final stride, by
Ron Vibert on Queen's Copper.

Since the horse started at 20–1 and I had so nearly pinched the
race you might imagine the trainer and his wife would have been
reasonably pleased. Not a bit of it. Mercy tore into me, claiming
that I had thrown the race away by going to the front far too soon.
She was absolutely right, although not many people have spoken
to me in quite that manner. Once I had committed my horse I rode
as if the devil was on my tail, but Sharuk could not quite hang on.

The Rimells must have been furious because it was a good
three years before I was asked to ride for them again. Unfortunately the result was the same. I was beaten by a short head
once more.

Michael Pope, a loyal supporter of my father's apprentices
on the flat, also trained a few jumpers. It was Michael who set
Pat Eddery on the road to stardom with a string of successes
on Alvaro in 1969. Late the following year, at the suggestion
of my father, he called me up to ride Tantalum over fences.

Tantalum had been a decent handicapper over hurdles but
would not jump fences at home for Michael's own jockey, Barry
Davies, who had started on the flat with my parents at Prestbury.
When my father offered my services, Michael retorted, 'But he's
nearly finished!'

Father replied, 'Don't worry about that. He will get the horse
jumping.'

So, late in 1970, I turned up to school Tantalum, a big,
imposing brown gelding with an attractive white blaze on his
face. Though Michael Pope trained at Streatley, he had taken
the horse over to Frank Cundell's schooling grounds near by.
It was a miserable late October morning, cold and wet, and
my spirits were not lifted by Barry's description of Tantalum's
previous reluctance to jump.

It was well known at the time that Michael Pope had a thing
about his horses being hit by the whip; even today he still writes
letters to the newspapers about it. I waited until we were out of
sight of the trainer behind some gorse bushes and gave Tantalum
three sharp cracks on the backside. We then turned back and
led by another horse ridden by Barry Davies, headed towards
a line of three fences with me growling in Tantalum's ear. He
flew all three like a natural.

Pope called out, 'That will do, David.'

'No. I'm going down again,' I replied.

So we hacked behind the gorse once more where I peeled off three further smacks on his backside. As we soared over the schooling fences again the second time, I had a fair idea that Tantalum could become a top class steeplechaser. Windsor was chosen for his debut over fences. In the paddock, Pope, uncertain about my plans, asked me what I was going to do. When I announced that I would qualify Tantalum for the Totalisator Champion Chase at the Cheltenham Festival, he gave me what might best be described as an old-fashioned look.

My only orders were to be sure not to hit the horse with the whip. Since we won unchallenged that was never likely to happen and after two further successes we headed for Cheltenham. Tantalum's odds of 14–1 offered solid testimony of the task before us. He gave an absolute exhibition of jumping that day, close behind the leaders on the inside the whole way, pinged the last where Statfold Monty fell and, even though I took a pull, won easing up by fifteen lengths. We ended a memorable campaign in triumph at Worcester.

The sky really did seem the limit for Tantalum. He won twice more the following season but was killed tragically when he fell and broke a leg in the 1972 Hennessy Gold Cup at Newbury. I was inconsolable as I walked back without the horse.

I had a much happier experience riding a winner at the Cheltenham Festival in the evening of my career for my great friend, Gavin Pritchard-Gordon. A chance meeting at Wolverhampton one day on the flat in 1972 led to an invitation from Gavin to travel up to Newmarket to school a quartet of likely hurdlers including King Pele and Do Justice.

Gavin had just taken over from Harvey Leader and knew my father because he shared a claim with Geoff Barling on Pat Eddery. Father, who was always on the look-out for opportunities for me, suggested that Gavin should run some horses over hurdles and that I should ride them.

Gavin was not really interested in jump racing at this stage but I was so keen I took the trouble to go back three more times in the next fortnight, invariably stayed the night and was always given a royal welcome. The results more than justified our efforts. We had an unforgettable season together.

Do Justice won all four of his races over hurdles and King

Pele gained a narrow victory in the Gloucestershire Hurdle at the 1973 Festival only nine days after making a winning debut over hurdles at Windsor. Gavin and his wife Coral came to stay with us at Condicote and we had a riotous party the night that King Pele won. From what I can remember we were still in the cellar bar at the course several hours after the final race and ended up having dinner in Stow. We left there at about four in the morning, but the party continued unabated at home until it was time for me to ride out first lot.

Gavin claims that my behaviour that night was appalling, but he must have enjoyed himself because he has not missed a Cheltenham with us since. The Festival would not be the same without him. In turn I often stay with Gavin at Newmarket for the Guineas meeting. Once, after a convivial dinner party, his brother Giles decided some time after midnight that he wanted to ride one of the horses. By then, I think, Gavin had gone to bed so, feeling slightly responsible, I offered to help.

We stumbled into the yard and pulled a horse out of the first box we could find. I held on to the head collar, legged up Giles bareback and gave him a couple of turns round the yard before replacing the horse. As we returned to the house Gavin appeared, looking somewhat irate. The next morning, we were dragged out to watch first lot including the horse in question, La Bamba, who all but ran away with his lad at a steady canter. He did, however, come out and win later, so we were forgiven.

I often used to join up with Gavin for a night out in London at the stable lads' boxing championships, which I was always keen for my lads to win. One year William Haggas, now a Newmarket trainer, put out his foot and tripped me up, to the huge amusement of his pals on his table, as I walked towards the ring with one of my fighters.

They say revenge is a dish best enjoyed cold and I can confirm it after sorting Haggas out at Gavin's fortieth birthday party six months later. During dinner I crept up behind him and took a leisurely five minutes to rub a pound of butter into his hair. That wiped the smile from his face for the rest of the evening. As I recall he left early.

I trained both King Pele and Do Justice at Condicote while Gavin concentrated on the flat, but my friendship with him cost me the ride on my father's useful young hurdler Fighting Kate.

She had shown some promise in schooling at home but I had the distinct impression she was not fancied on her debut at Newbury and so elected to ride Gavin's King's Equity, who was a decent horse on the flat. The betting that day suggested I had made the right decision for King's Equity was joint favourite while Fighting Kate, ridden by one of my boys, Robin Dickin, started at 33–1.

This time the bookies' intelligence service was way off the mark, for just as I brought King's Equity through to lead at the last hurdle Fighting Kate swept past to claim the prize. After that I could hardly blame my father for wanting to keep Robin on Fighting Kate, who ended her first season by running well in the Daily Express Triumph Hurdle won by Attivo.

The following season Fighting Kate was unplaced three times in a row before running rather more prominently than my father had intended at Nottingham. As he was not there, I was asked to accompany Robin Dickin at the subsequent inquiry. The moment the film of the race was shown to us I feared the worst, probably a spell on the sidelines for Robin and a hefty punishment for my father for not allowing the horse to run on her merits.

Robin, however, seemed unconcerned and told me not to worry. Asked by the senior steward for an explanation for his notably tender handling of Fighting Kate, Robin replied that the panel had been following the wrong horse. The one they had been pinpointing at the inquiry was ridden by another jockey. We were off the hook.

Less than three weeks later Fighting Kate landed quite a coup for Father in a handicap hurdle at Wincanton on Boxing Day. The rider he had booked for her that day did not impress him in the first race, so he removed his name at the declarations counter, seized the first jockey he could find, who happened to be Nigel Wakley, and gave him the type of instructions we all want to hear: 'Don't win too far.'

Fighting Kate still won by eight lengths. Father had instructed my brother Richard to have the car ready for a lightning getaway immediately after the race. They shot out of the car park, almost before the weigh-in, with Father hanging out of the window to hear whether an inquiry was called into the mare's sudden improvement!

There was no better man to ride for than my father. He kept

his orders simple so that you knew exactly where you stood with him, and if anything was wrong he would say so in that short, sharp, blunt way of his. Then the matter was closed.

I had some tricky moments as a jockey, too. At Devon & Exeter one day I was attacked by a punter after finishing second on a decent horse called Chinese Lacquer. The man kept insisting that I had stopped the horse, who had actually run extremely well under joint top weight. I reported him to the ring steward and demanded a written apology or I would take him to the stewards of the Jockey Club and invite them to warn him off. A week later I received an abject apology from him in the post.

Sometimes there were days which ended in despair. One of the worst came when poor Tobago had to be put down at Cheltenham after another horse jumped into the back of him and broke his hind leg. I jumped off him as soon as the accident happened and waited for the vet to put him out of his misery. Tobago was a lovely horse in every way, talented and willing, a top class hurdler looked after by Tony Murray in his early days as an apprentice with my father. Tony and I were in tears for ages.

I hate the sound of the gun going off. It sends shivers down my spine. I have never been able to come to terms with the injuries and deaths that are an inevitable part of racing. If a horse had to be put down at home, my father would hold it himself, he would always be there; but I have to admit I am not very good at that kind of thing.

I hate being on the spot when one of mine is put down at home. It is so distressing. Things have improved a little bit, because now our horses are put to sleep by injection, whenever possible. We try to do it as humanely as possible, so that they do not suffer any fear or anxiety before the end. They are simply led into the covered ride as if they are going to go on to the horse walker and put down with the greatest care and attention.

On racecourses, when an injury is irreparable, vets are encouraged to use an injection, too, though they are also equipped with a humane killer. The important thing is the speed of the operation; never mind whether the screens are up. There is no need for the public to watch. It is the animal that is suffering and must be dispatched as quickly as possible.

12

The greatest crime in racing

There is one crime in racing that stands head and shoulders above everything else. It is the deliberate attempt to prevent a horse winning by administering drugs. The result is that the lives of both horse and jockey are put at risk, particularly in a race over jumps. That is why I believe that people who dope racehorses should be strung up.

In my time as a jockey I rode three horses that were doped up to the eyeballs to prevent them winning. The first was Blessington Esquire – of all the horses that I ever rode, the one with the greatest potential. Bought out of Willie Head's yard in France he proved to be a cracking hurdler, but I always felt he would be an even better chaser.

Blessington Esquire was an absolute smasher, a fine, big imposing horse with the class, scope and attitude to go right to the top over fences. I really did think he was going to be the business.

We won four of our first five steeplechases together and only just failed to give nine lbs to King's Nephew in a tremendous tussle at Hurst Park in December, 1960. Three months later we returned to the same course to take on the brilliant Irish novice Scottish Memories. There were two other runners, including the future Grand National winner Ayala, but for the purposes of betting this was a match with the pair starting joint favourites at 11–8.

Blessington Esquire was normally a superb jumper but that day he did not take a single fence cleanly. It was as if he was drunk. Things were so bad on the way round that he hit some of the fences with his head. For three miles it was as if he could not see the obstacles in front of him.

People have often asked me why I did not accept the inevitable and pull him up. There is no doubt that is what I should have done, but at times when things are difficult your competitive spirit takes over. Despite a succession of jumping errors we were still in the race with a bit of a chance, so I felt we had to continue. It says much for Blessington Esquire's character that, despite his condition, he still managed to finish second, though well beaten.

It has long been my view that people who dope horses should be made to ride them themselves. I am not being overdramatic when I say that both Blessington Esquire and I could have been killed. That is exactly what happened to The Finn, a decent chaser of Bob Turnell's who was another victim of a doping gang.

Unfortunately the Jockey Club's rules on doping at the time actively discouraged trainers and owners from speaking up. If a horse was found to have been doped for whatever reason, it was the trainer who was held responsible. The rule was there to deter horses being given illegal substances to enhance their performance, but trainers had been punished unfairly when outsiders had tampered with their horses to prevent them winning.

Perhaps this explains the reaction of Blessington Esquire's owner Lord Carnarvon when I assured him as I unsaddled that his horse had been doped. 'Shut up. Don't talk such nonsense,' he commanded with a look that suggested he would like to strangle me.

Despite my protests, the horse's trainer Atty Corbett was pretty reticent, too. Nowadays a dope test would have been a formality but I am sorry to say not a single test or sample was taken from Blessington Esquire.

Although he won more steeplechases, Blessington Esquire was never quite as good again. He broke down twice and had a spell with Fulke Walwyn before Lord Carnarvon gave him to me as a hunter. I am pleased to report that he gave both Dinah and me a lot of pleasure with the Heythrop Hunt. I remember taking him to a meet of the South Hereford Hunt at the Wormelow Tump where a cap was taken in aid of the Injured Jockeys' Fund. Several jockeys turned out including Stan Mellor, Jeff King on Limanali, John Haine, Paddy Cowley, Johnny Lehane and Peter Jones, who is now our postman at Jackdaws Castle. Michael

Scudamore, grounded at the time, was there to support his local hunt. Best of all was the sight of indomitable Tim Brookshaw walking determinedly on crutches, laughing and joking as if he was the fittest man in the world.

In October, 1963, over two and a half years after that fateful afternoon at Hurst Park, it emerged at a notorious trial at Lewes Assizes that Blessington Esquire was one of the first horses doped by a gang who had systematically set out to make a fortune from tampering with racehorses. Six of the gang were sent to prison, including a woman who gained entry to a number of yards by posing as a prospective owner. They also claimed to have doped Pinturischio, one-time favourite for the 1961 Derby.

In 1965 Master Mascus was doped the day that I rode him in the Totalisator Champion Novices' Chase at the Cheltenham Festival. He was a good horse, a quick, accurate jumper and an automatic favourite on the strength of five previous victories over fences that season.

But he felt so lifeless going to the start that I half knew our fate then. When the race began Master Mascus ran like a blind, drunk horse. He did not see a single fence properly. I had learned my lesson at Hurst Park and so pulled him up after he crashed through six fences.

Someone met me on the way back and took the horse from me, but the stewards refused to order a dope test. The horse's trainer, Dave Thom, was furious that they would not do it, though he felt that the slippery ground after a heavy frost might have contributed to his poor jumping.

I was also convinced that Hypur II was got at the day I rode him in November, 1966. We had won easily at Hereford a fortnight earlier but he was completely lifeless when we returned to the course a fortnight later and finished in the rear.

Owned and trained by Hugh Sumner under permit, Hypur II was usually an excellent jumper but he nearly fell several times on the way round and appeared drunk when he came in. I had a fair idea of the culprit that day but once again nothing was done.

Thank goodness the Jockey Club now treat any suspected doping of horses with the severity it demands. Surveillance is much tighter following the débâcle at Doncaster during the 1990 St Leger meeting when two horses were given tranquillisers by an intruder who made his way into the racecourse stables.

Security cameras have since been installed at many course stables.

I also have to record that my father and I suspected for a while that a lad in his yard was giving one or two of his horses some illegal assistance to make them run faster. The cases of Cannobie Lee and Oakleigh Way were proved beyond doubt in my mind when they won on successive days at Cheltenham in April, 1962. Cannobie Lee, as I have explained earlier, was a dodgy old devil who kept a lot for himself. He was not a horse to trust, never really took hold of his bit and was a difficult ride because he had to come with a late run.

That day, we were so concerned that Father stood down by the point on the edge of the lawn where the horses go out on to the course to see if anything was untoward. I nodded my suspicions to him as I trotted past with Cannobie Lee uncharacteristically trying to pull my arms from their sockets.

Normally the horse would not take much interest in a race and was inclined to pull up on me. This time he was always pulling double, was in the lead from the start, drew clear a long way from home and won unchallenged. Later a private dope test arranged by Father showed that Cannobie Lee was full of a banned substance.

Oakleigh Way was a similar sort of ride. You had to adopt exaggerated waiting tactics on him and then try to pop him in front on the line. But at Cheltenham the following day I could not hold one side of him with the result that he was always in contention, led two fences out, ran up the hill like a lion and won easily.

As I came back Father declared, 'That was a funny way of waiting.'

I replied, 'Well, I waited in front.'

We were both sure that Oakleigh Way had been doped to win, too, and believed that the culprit was an elderly lad in the yard who had looked after a Classic winner before the war. He had, we deduced, acquired some powerful medicine, which he had then administered to both horses, who had won in a manner they had never displayed before. My father did not dare take up the matter with the Jockey Club for fear of losing his licence. He knew it would have been the end for him. The stable lad concerned left Father's employment shortly afterwards.

When you are riding over jumps in a tightly packed bunch

of horses, you are aware that you are only one careless stride from disaster. You quickly learn to rely on the good sense and co-operation of your fellow riders. When I started out the senior jockeys swiftly sorted out anyone who stepped out of line. If you were wrong you did not dare argue. We had respect for the senior riders, but attitudes have changed since then and not necessarily for the better.

Inevitably in such a competitive sport there are violent disagreements when two or more jockeys are going for the same gap or fighting for the same position in a race. Most arguments are settled at once and instantly forgotten; others fester until a full-blooded confrontation occurs.

It happened to me twice and to my horror I also carved up my great mate Terry Biddlecombe, who was in his final week as a jockey when I began to tighten him up a bit approaching the second hurdle going away from the stands at Cheltenham. Before any serious damage was done I realised I was in the wrong and pulled off.

The unwritten rule then was that if you were on the inside you were entitled to keep it; if, on the other hand, you were making a run from behind you knew better than to force your way through on the inner unless the one in front was clearly beaten.

At Cheltenham I apologised to Terry afterwards and that was the end of it. But unfortunately that was not the case when I clashed with David Mould and Tim Norman. I fell out with David after he tried to push through on my inside going to the second last in the Lloyd's Bank Champion Novices' Hurdle on the second day of the 1974 Festival.

I had made nearly all the running up to that point on Sasha, and was still lying second when I stopped David, on Blue Shore, coming through with the result that he almost ripped his boot off as he hit the rails going to the elbow of the course. After that Blue Shore shot backwards very quickly before rallying to finish fourth just in front of my horse. I was fully entitled to take the action I did and do not believe for one minute that it cost him the race.

There was a lot of squealing then and afterwards; David had a right go at me when he came back in but I stood my ground. Although Terry Biddlecombe and others in the weighing-room tried to make peace between us we were at loggerheads for the next two days.

David would not even discuss what happened, which was a bit unfortunate when you consider that we were mates and he used to stay with us at Condicote. At the end of the Festival Dinah tried to persuade David to shake hands with me but he resolutely declined. But time is a great healer and I am delighted to say we are now good friends again.

My second argument was with Tim Norman, who won the 1966 Grand National on Anglo. We clashed at Taunton where I was riding a little horse called First Flight in a novice chase. My horse jumped the last fence on the far side in front, then Tim came wide of me on the bend on a great big brute called Kilburn, moved sharply across and turned me sideways. Somehow we got back up and still won while he fell at the second last.

When he returned I called out, 'Cheers, Tim, was it for the horse, the owner, the trainer or me?'

'It was for you,' he replied.

I muttered, 'Thank you,' between clenched teeth. No more was said because that was the way my father had brought me up. I had the chance to return the compliment five years later at Plumpton where my horse was beaten running down the hill for the final time. Going to the third last hurdle we were still on the inside when I heard a voice behind calling urgently, 'Inner, Duke.'

There was no need to look round because I knew that voice. I shut the door and did not miss him. The rails and the wing of the hurdle flew everywhere as he went straight through them. Tim came charging back . . . eventually, literally spitting blood with a tooth hanging out and his eyes blazing, ready to attack me.

I said, 'Shut up, you. Elephants don't forget. Taunton. First Flight. Five years ago. Now sit down.' He did not say another word.

Quite a few years earlier I was the victim of some bunching at the top of the hill at Cheltenham on a horse called Wise Choice in a three-mile hurdle. Four of us raced upsides round the top bend with Wise Choice going the shortest way on the rails, which, in those days, were mainly wooden but also contained the odd bit of steel.

When the horse on the outside ridden by Dave Thom started to come in on the other three, I found myself squeezed up so tightly that I was forced to lift my left leg suddenly to avoid it being crushed as we collided with the running rail. The next thing I was sitting on the ground still on my saddle while Wise Choice galloped off riderless. It transpired that the sharp edge of the rails had sliced through the girths and surcingle, which is there to hold the saddle in place. I did not blame Dave one bit, but he never stopped apologising.

13

Riding and training

In August, 1968 David Nicholson embarked on the next phase of his racing odyssey as a trainer. He began, like many of the best jumping trainers, on a wing and a prayer, with a diverse collection of home-breds, hopefuls and characters, a phrase in racing that tends to cover any number of faults in a horse.

Naturally he gave his small team of horses the very best of care and attention. No expense was spared to ensure their continuing welfare. But there was a problem. Though training jumpers had seemed a logical progression, Nicholson soon discovered that he lacked some of the fundamental knowledge of how to bring horses to a physical peak for the business of racing. That, he now knows, only comes with experience.

Then, as now, he could not have coped without the overwhelming support of his wife Dinah, who skilfully turned her hand to the many and various jobs in the stable yard that must be done to keep the show on the road.

Who, I wondered, was the head lad in those early days?

'I was,' replied Dinah.

'Not true,' countered the Duke. 'I was my own head lad.'

In truth they shared the job with Dinah taking a vital, responsible role, particularly while her husband continued to ride for the next six years.

Dinah and I had been working for years towards the day I started training, but I had no intention of giving up riding for some time. The best way of life is being a jump jockey. I made a living, a good living, and we enjoyed life, but we were not under illusions that my income from riding would make us rich. Three hundred rides in a season was a lot in my day. How times have changed.

Some people told me it was impossible to do the two jobs properly. The more they said it, the more I was determined to prove them wrong. Some might say I was just pig-headed, but I always liked a challenge and believed in putting in 105 per cent. One of my main ambitions was to win the Grand National. It was the biggest challenge. Still is.

At the beginning the plan was to train in a small way, have a few horses and kick on from there. It has all been self-taught and it did not help that I missed out on horse management. One of my father's favourite sayings was good hay, good oats and plenty of work. Whenever I am in trouble, I still go back to those basics.

We started at Condicote with a handful of horses and twenty acres in 1968, charged a training fee of twelve guineas a week and soon moved up to nine horses. Looking back through some bills at the time, I see that we charged £2.50 for a full set of shoes, plus a further £1 for fitting them, and only two shillings and six pence per mile for taking the horses to the races. There was an additional charge to owners of £1 for the use of a nearby indoor school during bad weather. No wonder we did not make any money.

Vultrip, owned by General Feilden, was our first horse. He was a half-brother to the Grand National winner Gay Trip but you would not have guessed it from his cranky behaviour. At first my father trained Vultrip, but when he became so difficult that no one would ride him I asked the General if I could have the chance to sort him out at Condicote. It was Dinah who was given this doubtful pleasure with a bit of hunting thrown in.

The keener I was to take Vultrip, the more everyone told me I could not possibly ride or train him. Naturally this only made me more determined to show them and so Vultrip joined us in the autumn of 1968. He never did win! From the first my father encouraged me to have a few flat horses, for the very sound reason that he feared we would quickly go skint if we relied on jumpers.

Sam Vestey had always promised my father he would send me a horse as soon as I started training and was as good as his word. He has been a loyal friend and owner in every way, has helped out beyond the call of duty when necessary and still has a horse with me today.

We added boxes as we progressed, squeezing in two here and

three there until eventually we ended up with fifty-eight in and around the old farmyard. Each autumn we scratched our heads before deciding where we might manage to fit in another two or three horses. One summer Norton Brookes helped us put up seven new boxes in a paddock. We converted the former milking parlour into several boxes, the hay loft became our tack room, and at various times we kept all sorts of farm animals, too. It was really quite a small yard, so we just had to use every conceivable inch of space and had horses tucked in every corner. We painted all the doors white and black to maintain some semblance of continuity.

In those early months it was very much a case of feeling our way. We bought a few more acres, then rented some adjoining land which gave us the opportunity to canter up steep banks.

Training was quite hit and miss at first because I had only been with my father before going solo. I was a little bit lost when I started, but the arrogance of youth carries you through at that age. I used to be on the phone to my father every day. The trouble is that you think you know how to do it, but actually it took me nearly until March each season to get my horses race fit. They wanted at least three runs in those days. The hardest thing was to avoid the temptation to keep admiring them and saying how well they looked. The truth is that they were invariably too fat and happy!

I realise we started on the cheap at Condicote. That is why we had such severe financial problems there later on. Every penny we ever made was put back into the place, yet we never charged enough for training fees. You always imagine that, if you charge the correct rate, you will frighten away potential owners.

We soon learned to be diplomatic with owners because not all of them are like Sam Vestey, Brigadier Roscoe Harvey and his wife, or my mother-in-law, Doreen Pugh, who were all major supporters in the early days. We called her the flag of convenience because whenever we had a horse that needed an owner she was put in to fill the gap. That way she covered a multitude of sins. Then there were the difficult owners. Dinah could get rid of them pretty sharp and showed two of them the door early on.

I could not have managed without the missus, who has been a loyal wife and an excellent mother, and has always been willing to turn her hand to anything in the yard. For years she was secretary, did all the clipping and veterinary work, kept the medical records on each horse, rode out, repaired the tack and still found time to run the home. In addition Dinah drove the horses everywhere until we employed a full-time travelling head lad. She was also perfectly capable of running the yard. She never stopped working. Naturally we discuss things all the time; she adds a lot of input about the horses but does not interfere in the training and running programmes. I could not stand interfering trainers' wives when I was riding.

Several people promised to send me a horse when I gave up riding. One who did not keep his word was Andrew Wates, now a member of the Jockey Club. He must have forgotten.

My first cherished winner as a trainer was Arctic Coral at Warwick early in January 1969 in a novice hurdle. He had been threatening to pick up a little prize all season but there are times as you start out when you wonder if you will ever train a winner. It was even better to earn a double percentage as his jockey, too. I remember Fred Winter saying, 'Well done, you will not do that again,' which of course was true as there is only one first time.

The only other success that season came at Ludlow with Tiger, ridden by Andy Turnell, because my father insisted on my being on his horse called Irishman. Tiger, the favourite, jumped clumsily early on, and was some way behind with me tracking him. As we set off on the final circuit I remember shouting to Andy, 'Give that horse a kick in the ribs and get a move on'. They then finished with a flourish to catch the leader on the line.

That first season our horses earned the princely sum of £510 for their owners. My ten per cent of that would not have gone very far towards paying the bills, but luckily my earnings from riding kept the show on the road. Riding and training at the same time was hard work. In addition my weight was not helped by having to socialise a fair amount. There were occasions when I had to go out eating and drinking with owners, knowing that I had to ride at a light weight the next day.

At least if I was riding at Bangor I knew I could fiddle the scales with some nifty footwork. I remember weighing in and out there one day at 10st. 5lbs when I was actually eleven stone. Like many jockeys before and since I was caught changing to a heavier, more comfortable saddle after weighing out at

Newbury in the days when you could take the saddle back into the weighing-room. That cost me a fine of £25.

I had been training for only a year when Sam Vestey invited me to select a small team of horses to take to run in Deauville for the month of August while he was playing polo there. We bought three horses cheaply, added a fourth, Tiger, belonging to another owner and had a wonderful time staying in a little apartment just behind the racecourse. The horses, who were stabled at a private château, usually ran at Clairefontaine or Dieppe. Andy Turnell and I rode the jumpers and Lester Piggott, no less, partnered one or two of them on the flat while Freddy Head rode another.

I returned to England a couple of times that month to ride in the West Country and had a narrow escape on the flight from Exeter back to France with Andy in a small plane piloted by Alan Biltcliffe, better known as Bilco, who now flies Willie Carson everywhere.

We had climbed to about one thousand feet when, noticing that the door was not shut properly, I reached across Andy and pushed it open with the intention of slamming it firmly shut. Instead I was nearly dragged through the open door and probably would have disappeared through it but for my seat belt and the gallant efforts of Andy to hang on to me at all costs. It was not until Bilco made an emergency landing back at Exeter that we were able to secure the door properly. We then took off once more for France without further alarm but I heard later than Bilco had an even more frightening experience as he flew back to Gatwick later that evening.

The engine began to vibrate so violently that he thought it was going to stop, particularly when he heard a sharp, sinister crack from the propeller. He dipped down towards a tanker in the Channel in case he had to ditch but then the engine settled down and he was able to limp back to Gatwick where he discovered that the aluminium spinner holding the propeller in place had sheared off. It was a lucky escape for Bilco, who learned that an American pilot had been killed in a similar incident as he was struck by the spinner when it came through the cockpit window. Soon afterwards all spinners on that model were changed.

After I had finished third on Tiger at Dieppe the French trainer Ted Bartholomew, an old friend, firmly pointed out that in France you have to allow horses to pop their hurdles and not keep asking them to stand off. I reschooled the horse at Clairefontaine, then took him back to Dieppe ten days later where he won by six lengths.

At the end of our stay in France we filled up the spacious compartment above the cab of the horsebox with some of the best local wine we could find, then loaded the horses with their noses almost rubbing against the sliding doors masking the hidden cache. Dinah, as usual, drove the horsebox while I brought our lad back in a little Mini.

Unfortunately a customs officer in England asked Dinah to lower the ramp, looked suspiciously inside, then seemed keen to find out about the contents of the compartment above the cab, even though Dinah explained it was used to store hay and tack. Danger was averted when Dinah offered to pull the horses out, provided the official would hold them. He immediately retreated, lifted the ramp back up and waved her through. Five miles inland I met up with her at a prearranged spot and transferred the lad to the horsebox.

My first double as a trainer came early in 1970 on the flat at Liverpool the day before the Grand National. Copper Witch took the opening two-year-old seller and later in the afternoon Ally won the Knowsley Stakes at 100–7. Both were ridden quite beautifully by Pat Eddery, who was still claiming a five lbs allowance at the time.

Pat also won three times on one of my great favourites, Bob, a horse whose dam Siona we bought the night before his birth for £400 from Bob Day. We then passed him to Dinah's aunt, Joyce Westray, who had a tremendous amount of fun with him in the following years. He ran a few times as a two-year-old, won five races at three in 1970 over five furlongs and proved to be blisteringly fast away from the old-style starting gates. He would touch the strands of tape, brush under them and pinch three lengths in the first fifty yards. Woe betide his jockey if he did not lie beneath his mane or he would be swept off by the tapes.

Over the years Bob proved the most superb schoolmaster and gave no less than twenty-two of our boys their first rides on the flat or over hurdles. Although he did not stay two miles over hurdles, he was the ideal horse for introducing young jockeys to the business of race riding. He was only a pony but jumped like a natural and later he enjoyed team chasing and hunting with Dinah before he moved to Newmarket as Bruce Hobbs' hack.

One of my more unusual owners in the early days was Cyril Lovelock, a partner in a haulage firm, who lived in a council house at Didcot in Berkshire that cost him £3 10sh. a week in 1970. Over a few pints at their local Cyril and his pals decided to buy a racehorse and duly paid £700 to Kim Bailey's father Ken for Final Parade. Cyril wrote out the cheque and was then left with the horse when his friends backed out at the last minute. Luckily he had the last laugh, though his wife Dot did not approve of him buying a racehorse, particularly one that had finished in the ruck in three attempts over jumps with Ken Bailey. The truth is that the old horse had no chance of staying two miles over hurdles; he would not have lasted the trip in a horsebox.

Final Parade turned out to be a right little racehorse with an understandable quirk; because he was so long and barely fitted into starting stalls, he came to hate them. He was a hardy old sprinter, the type you could run frequently, and within a few weeks in the summer of 1970 he collected around £1,500 in prize money from three wins and several placed runs. I remember that Pat Eddery won on Final Parade at Bath in July. Cyril was mad about the horse but readily admitted he knew very little about racing, and when he eventually ran out of money, he gave Final Parade to us and I found him what I thought was a good home.

Unfortunately it turned out to be not so suitable and I had to rescue him. I always try to persuade my owners to give their horses a good, caring home when they retire since you then have a certain amount of control over their well-being, which is not the case if the horse is sold.

That summer of 1970, a tremendous run of success on the flat set me thinking about the future. All ten winners had been prepared on a three furlong dirt track at home. Though I liked Condicote, and did not want to leave, I felt it had its limitations for training purposes. What, I wondered, might I achieve elsewhere with decent gallops?

So, late in 1970, I tried to persuade Dinah that it would be in our best interests to move to Newmarket, where the facilities are so much better. Though Dinah did not reject the idea completely, she made it crystal clear that if I did move to Newmarket she would not be coming with me. It was a serious suggestion by me, but after that there did not seem any point in pursuing it. As it turned out, my plans of training more horses on the flat did not take off at all.

By now I knew in my heart that the people who told me I could not ride and train efficiently at the same time were right. To combine both is impossibly hard. We were able to do it for a few years because Dinah drove the horsebox in addition to all her other roles. The box proved a lifeline. I always felt it was the best horse in the yard.

We enjoyed quite a boost when Landing Party arrived from America on June 17, 1971 with instructions from his new owner Thomas G. Tinsley, the president of the Maryland Music Corporation, to aim him at the Grand National. He had bought the horse from his previous owner, Dr Johnny Fisher, on the understanding that he would continue to ride him in his races, including the Grand National.

Since Landing Party had twice won the Maryland Hunt Cup, America's most famous timber race, and lowered the course record held by Jay Trump on the second occasion in April, 1971, this was an exciting addition to the team. Johnny Fisher, a Pennsylvania vet, who was taller than me and rode in metal-framed spectacles, left me in no doubt that Landing Party was a top class horse, the undisputed star of the US jumping scene.

Unfortunately he arrived with a check ligament on both tendons which we had to treat every day. At first he was a bit light in condition after a long journey, so I turned him out to grass for a fortnight. He was then given a week's walking exercise for an hour each day before going out in a paddock for a further hour in the evening. The following week he started trotting.

Landing Party was a handsome horse and a gentleman to handle, except that he had developed the dangerous habit of rushing forward once he had been saddled. Since he was following the same route as Jay Trump, who came from America to win the 1965 Grand National under the expert guidance of Fred Winter, there was some unbelievable hype about him in the papers.

My first priority in trying to qualify Landing Party for Aintree with three runs here tested my patience to the limit, because

In front over hurdles on Battle Hymn.

Show jumping at Ascot on Stainless Steel to raise funds to save the Grand National.

The best of friends. Dinah and What A Buck.

No. We did not fall. Tibidabo found a leg.

No argument this time.

Official starter in Isle of Wight, 1967. From left, John Buckingham, Josh Gifford, Terry Biddlecombe, David McCready, Jeff King, Macer Gifford, Andy Turnell and John Cook.

Jockeys' cricket team. Back row, from left, Peter Dale, Ian Arthurs, Richard Nicholson, James Pugh, Victor Dartnall, Lawrence Walthew, Gerald Dartnall, Stan Mellor. Front row, David Nicholson, Terry Biddlecombe, Johnny Lehane and Josh Gifford.

Trainer and jockey in relaxed mood after the Princess Royal's victory on Cnoc Na Cuille over fences at Worcester.

By Royal appointment. Script by Alastair Down.

A winning team – David Nicholson and Colin Smith.

An aerial photograph of Jackdaws Castle – the brainchild of Colin Smith.

his American victories, while not making him eligible for the Grand National, prevented him running in other conditions races in Britain. For instance I wanted to run him in the Beachley Chase at Chepstow in October but was unable to do so because it was confined to horses that had not won more than two chases. Talk about having your cake and eating it. It was an absurd contradiction and I made quite a fuss at the Jockey Club. Happily this anomaly no longer exists because the winners and placed horses in the Maryland Hunt Cup and other key foreign races are now automatically qualified to run in the Grand National.

From the very start Landing Party seemed extremely slow. The second bit of work he did convinced me of it because he was kicked out of the way by some ordinary horses. I felt that he was not very good, but pressed on in the hope that he might be one of those that do not shine on the gallops. However, my worst fears were confirmed when I pulled him up on his British debut at Chepstow in December. Although he had to carry automatic top weight in testing conditions he had not encountered before, it was also evident to me that he was too slow to lie up with the pace.

Landing Party then finished tailed off on his next outing, ridden by Johnny Fisher, whose hopes of victory in the Grand National were already beginning to seem like an impossible dream. Next time out he gave me a crunching fall when I rode him at Fontwell where he turned a spectacular somersault at the last fence. Photographs of our dramatic exit appeared in just about every daily newspaper in the country. I knew I had been hit hard and the pictures confirmed it. Although I was in quite a state, I eventually rose shakily to my feet before we staggered up the track together, but it was worrying to hear the horse neighing as I led him back. That is never a good sign.

I was not quite knocked out by the fall but suffered delayed concussion the next day while I was looking at some horses to buy. After inspecting several likely types, I was offered a glass of champagne and crashed out without warning. My father always said that anyone with suspected concussion should prove his fitness by trying to ride a bicycle downhill. He knew it was a test that had found out several jockeys who claimed they were all right. Quite simply, if you are concussed you fall straight off.

That fall at Fontwell ended any lingering chance of Landing

Party going to Liverpool. He ran once more for me, at Uttoxeter in March, again performed without distinction and left to join a hunting yard in Leicestershire, where he died shortly afterwards in an accident.

We had an unusual success on the flat with Shinto, thanks to some assistance from Lester and Susan Piggott. The horse, who was previously trained by Jack Clayton, had finished a highly promising eighth, ridden by Lester, in a decent maiden at Newmarket in May the day before he was due to appear in the Tattersalls sales ring. Afterwards I overheard Lester saying the horse was useless, which was certainly not the impression I had gained in the closing stages of the race, so I made up my mind to buy him as a dual-purpose animal. Since I was riding elsewhere the following day, I instructed David Minton to purchase Shinto for me.

'Minty' rang from the sales paddocks to report that Shinto had been sold to Cormack McCormack, on behalf of Susan Piggott, for 2,300 guineas. I was determined to have the horse, asked him to offer Susan an instant profit and a deal was done. Shinto was placed three times for us and when we entered him in a maiden race at Nottingham in July, Lester rang up asking to take the ride.

Dinah is one of Lester's greatest fans and volunteered to take charge at Nottingham. When he shuffled into the paddock, she asked his views on Shinto's chances.

'He will win,' he replied succinctly.

'But we are not very good flat-race trainers,' Dinah responded.

'You can't be any worse than where the horse came from,' countered Lester.

Shinto duly won comfortably and his jockey offered one further piece of advice before disappearing to weigh in: 'Tell that long fellow of a husband not to pick his stick up on this horse,' he declared.

As usual he was spot on in his assessment. Shinto contracted tetanus that first winter at Condicote and, for a while, was at death's door. We were advised that the slightest noise could send him into a muscle spasm, so for a week or more the lads tiptoed around his box unable even to rattle a bucket. Eventually Shinto pulled through and, after an uncertain start over hurdles, won four races in his second season, including two qualifiers for the Coral Golden Hurdle at Cheltenham.

Riding and training at the same time sometimes led to a conflict of interest. Once, at Uttoxeter, riding Afternoon Sun for David Ringer, I had a right old set-to in the finishing straight with one of my own horses called Kingstown, partnered by his owner Norton Brookes, who had been a top-class showjumping rider. Afternoon Sun was just winning the argument until he took a hefty bump on the run-in from Kingstown, who clawed his way into the lead on the line. David Ringer was keen to object, and felt we were sure to be awarded the race in the stewards' room, until I pointed out that I had no intention of complaining to the stewards, since I trained the winner.

14

The last hurrah

Choosing the right moment to retire is one of the hardest decisions jump jockeys have to face. Many know with a grim certainty that they will not find anything in life to compare with the matchless thrill of riding over fences. Filling the void is an enduring problem for so many fine riders.

Some, like John Francome, have the good sense to leave the stage at the very peak of their powers. Others, unable to match his acute sense of timing, stay too long, nerves frayed, tempers short, deceiving themselves that they are good for one last hurrah.

Riding over jumps is inevitably a young man's game. Ancient, battle-weary jockeys, who continue because they know nothing else, discover eventually that sometimes, cruelly, the game gives them up. Rides evaporate, the phone stops ringing and all too often bitterness sets in.

David Nicholson, a jockey for almost a quarter of a century, faced the moment of truth early in 1974.

The season was coming towards its close when I woke up one morning early in April, 1974 and decided I'd had enough of riding. Cheltenham was over for another year. Liverpool, too, although I did not have a ride in the second Grand National won by Red Rum. No one had asked me.

There was a time when I thought I might even go on riding into my forties, partly because my father managed to combine training and riding for fully fifteen years. But the truth is that when I climbed out of bed that morning, I did not fancy going racing at Hereford even for some really good rides.

The thought had been lurking in my mind for a while. Terry

Biddlecombe had tried to persuade me to retire on the same day as him at the Cheltenham Festival a month earlier, but I had not wanted to steal any of his thunder.

When you don't look forward to riding good horses any more, you have had it. Some days I had to force myself to go out and ride. You can always rev yourself up to ride a really good horse, but it had come to the point where I did not enjoy the idea of having to go out for ordinary rides in run-of-the-mill races. Deep down in my heart I knew I had lost my nerve and that it was time to pack it in.

I have seen jockeys try to continue in this situation, people who are not prepared to admit the truth to themselves. They are very wrong. All the time I was riding I was always capable of looking after myself. I had a rough idea of how to nag one round when things were not going right.

The only thing I had ever wanted to be was a jockey and I had the good fortune that my parents encouraged and supported me all the way. When the job is going well you think you can go on for ever. Riding was a marvellous way of earning a living. You would be a fool not to think about the falls, but I never imagined having a really bad one. Eventually, however, the time came when I did not want to ride any more.

Some people said I was not particularly tough. Well, you need an awful lot of luck to survive intact as a jump jockey and all the time I was riding I was never knocked out, though I did suffer from delayed concussion on Landing Party at Fontwell. I also broke a bone in my leg at the final meeting of the season at Stratford. Then there was the time I dislocated my shoulder at the same course. There were plenty of other heavy falls, incurring minor injuries, but I was probably luckier than most.

Memories of those injuries only strengthened my resolve to call it a day on my next winner. It helped that I was due to partner one of my favourites, What A Buck, at Hereford that afternoon. He was as good a jumper as you could ever wish to sit on. I had started over jumps with a win on Fairval and decided that, if What A Buck was successful, I would stop there and then. I was so certain in my mind I told Dinah of my decision while I was shaving. She must have realised I was serious because she brought both our boys to Hereford. My parents were there, too, and Sam Vestey, who owned What A Buck.

Because the novice hurdles were divided, there were eleven

races that day but luckily for me What A Buck was down to run in the second. I changed in my usual position with mixed feelings and walked out to the paddock for the last time to ride What A Buck, who was a well-backed favourite.

I could not have chosen a better ally for my final race after twenty-three years. He jumped well as usual, took a clear lead on the final circuit and just held Andy Turnell's late flourish on Fortina's Palace by half a length. I had kept my plans to myself but told Michael Dickinson I had finished as we pulled up. As I came back to weigh in I put down my saddle and informed the clerk of the course that I had retired.

'But you can't do that,' he spluttered. 'You have a ride in the next race.'

When I explained that my decision was final the stewards held an inquiry before allowing a substitute to take my place. I felt a huge sense of relief, although it had been one of the hardest decisions I have ever had to make and it cost me two winners the next day. I was delighted; I knew I'd had enough.

However, my father, shaken by my sudden decision to retire, was concerned on two counts. What was I going to do and who could he find to replace me as a jockey? I found it easier to calm his fears about the first question than the second one.

That night we had a bit of a party at the Fosse Manor Hotel on the edge of Stow. I had far too much to drink and ended up nursing a large brandy in the bar trying to watch a Cup semi-final replay between Liverpool and Leicester on television. But it is very hard to follow the game when they seem to be playing with two, and sometimes three balls. Once the season was over, there was a big retirement party where I was presented with a china horse in Lord Carnarvon's colours.

It was only my pride that made me give horses a proper ride towards the end, because I was too bloody-minded not to do it. I realised it was not natural, that race riding was becoming too much like hard work. I had become short tempered and was living on my nerves.

The hardest thing in the world is to stop, yet it is much better to walk away too soon rather than too late. Some go on too long. Every jockey has to face up to it one day. There is also pride. I am not a brave person, never have been foolishly brave or fearless. If there is a noise in the house at night, I put my head under the blankets and suggest that Dinah goes downstairs to investigate.

I was certainly not as courageous or tough as some jockeys who gave everything a ride. I did my best to avoid daft horses that were likely to give you a bad time, and while I accepted falls as part of the job, if I could not get one round I would pull it up. So at the end I was quite content to finish reasonably sane and sound with almost 600 winners.

Curiously one of the worst bangs I ever had on my head came sixteen months after I retired from riding. It happened in August, 1975, during a typically lively late dinner at Punch's Hotel after a busy day at the Doncaster sales, where I had been looking for young store horses to buy.

Ken Oliver, who is an institution at the sales, and had enjoyed a few drinks through the evening, as is his custom, was holding court at the dinner table and took exception when I seemed more interested in the conversation of a pretty girl sitting beside me.

'We had better crown the Duke,' he informed the assembled company before striking me forcefully over the head with an empty wine bottle which immediately shattered into hundreds of pieces. I did not see the blow coming and was so shaken with pain and surprise that I pretended nothing had occurred. I thought I knew what had happened, but was hardly in a position to retaliate, so I felt the best thing was to behave as though nothing had taken place.

I do not know how I was not knocked out for I certainly had a severe headache the following day. Ken, who is a great friend, has laughed about it ever since. The next morning, back in his customary role as auctioneer on the rostrum, he knocked down a good-looking Arctic Slave four-year-old gelding to me for 4,800 guineas.

'Sold to the game gentleman standing in the gate,' he informed the watching crowd. 'As game in the day as he is at night.' After that we had to call the horse Game Gentleman.

Throughout the time I was a jockey I used to go to bed with the *Sporting Life* and form book so that if anyone rang up offering me a spare ride I usually knew if it was worth taking. I did not worry about injuries until the end, but the deaths of friends like Roy Dixon, Tony Moule and Ken Boulton affected us all. There is little room for sentimentality in racing but whatever our feelings all the jockeys knew that we had to go on. That was the job.

The championship was such a distant, impossible dream that I never imagined that I could win it. I did finish third in 1964–65 to Terry Biddlecombe with fifty-eight winners. I was also fourth in the list a couple of times, though in 1966–67, the season I rode the most number of winners, sixty-three, I was only fifth.

My father used to say they had more fun riding in his day. Well, they must have had an awful lot of fun. Jockeys are far more serious today, perhaps because there is so much money in the sport. When I was riding there was not a single jump jockey who finished up with any money. They all used to blow it without exception. If the most successful ones saved a bit in the season they soon spent it all in the summer holidays. We all played hard in those days.

Life was certainly a bit more relaxed the season after I gave up riding. Before the close of that year, 1974, we reached a major milestone when Bentley Boy completed my first century of winners as a trainer. It had been a hard six years.

In the years following my retirement I called on Jeff King to ride our best horses, and shared the rest among several promising young boys in the yard. Jeff was an old friend from the weighing-room and countless cricket matches, an absolutely top-class jockey. At one point I tried to retain him for Sam Vestey's horses, but he wanted to remain freelance and promised that he would ride for Sam whenever possible.

Jeff had the talent to be champion jockey, but his opportunities were reduced because he preferred to remain loyal to his mentor Bob Turnell, whose job he shared with Johnny Haine. Strong, determined, stylish and effective, Jeff could really push and roust one along before going for his whip, which cannot be said for some of today's riders, who reach for the stick much too quickly.

It is something of an understatement to say that Jeff could be extremely volatile at times. Tact was not his finest quality. Direct and brutally honest, he had a reputation for speaking his mind, but I knew how to handle him. If things had gone wrong in a race, you had to reach him first before the owners and suggest he talked to them later when he had cooled down.

I loved my years as a jump jockey. It was a very glamorous way to earn a living. To be one of the best jump jockeys going well, there is nothing like it. We had a great life.

15

The perils of betting

Betting does not appeal to me; never has done. I suppose I am a coward when it comes to putting down the money. Unlike some jockeys I did not even bet when I was riding. I imagine people were deterred from ringing me at home for tips by my father's reputation.

I rather liked the story about Scobie Breasley after he had trained his first winner at Epsom. A steward approached his wife May in the winner's enclosure, congratulated her and added that he hoped Scobie had enjoyed a good bet on the horse.

'Oh no,' replied May. 'Scobie has not had a bet since he gave up riding!'

I do wish I had advised my friends to support the four horses I rode at Haydock Park one day in February, 1967. They all won, at 4–1, 13–2, 20–1 and 11–4. That adds up to a 2,952–1 accumulator. I am told that anyone inspired enough to have backed all four in a £1 win Yankee would have collected £5,291. The first race the following day at Haydock brought me swiftly back down to earth. I finished last on Fustina.

I was cured of any potentially serious addiction to betting after backing one of mine, Sky Train, to win at Wetherby in October, 1974. Twelve months earlier I had suggested to Dinah that it would be fun to lay one horse out for a touch each year, with the owner's blessing, to pay for the next holiday.

Sky Train was the first one. He had shown distinct promise in his only race at Chepstow towards the end of the previous season, and a fortnight before Wetherby had run so well at Wincanton that Jeff King had come back insisting, 'This will win when wanted.'

Now I appreciate that this sort of information would seem

like manna from heaven to those who like to bet every day, but the nearer we came to the race at Wetherby the more nervous I was about the whole exercise. On the way up to Yorkshire I resolved to put £100 on Sky Train even though I was acutely aware that, to me, it was a massive amount to place on the result of a horse race. I began to have second thoughts when we reached the course. The best price that I could find about Sky Train was 9–2, but I remember the bookmaker I approached generously laid me £500–£100.

By the time I reached the stands I was in a terrible state of nerves, trembling uncontrollably and turning greener by the second. Sky Train led quite early in the straight and was clear over the final two hurdles, although I could not see a thing through my binoculars because my hands were shaking so much.

As Jeff King came back to the winner's enclosure he took one look at me and asked, 'What on earth is wrong? Are you ill? You look dreadful.'

I did feel ill, too, quite ghastly, and resolved right then never to back one of my horses again. It is a resolution I have not had any trouble keeping, for I can truthfully say I have not had a proper bet since, just a rare, small interest in one of mine ante-post at long odds in something like the Daily Express Triumph Hurdle.

If I was to start backing horses I am sure I would over-train them at home by pressing the button too much to find out. Now all I want to do is to train winners. If my owners want a punt, I try to advise them correctly but I cannot disguise that the whole business of betting does not interest me. Training horses is enough of a gamble without backing them as well.

In the summer of 1974 I had a call out of the blue from Dorothy Squires asking me to take five of her horses from Bob Clay, who was giving up training. It was the start of an interesting partnership. Dorothy was quite a big name in showbusiness at the time, a singer who was rarely out of the headlines and had been married to Roger Moore. She had some decent horses, too, including Esban, who had already won the Scottish Grand National, and Norwegian Flag, a very promising staying chaser.

Norwegian Flag won twice for us that first season and the odds against Miss Squires singing a song of triumph in the winner's enclosure at Aintree shortened appreciably when her horse was beaten narrowly at Sandown by Carroll Street late in March. But a leg injury ended his chance of running at Liverpool. During that time Dorothy provided tickets for us in the front row at the Palladium, but after two years she departed as abruptly as she had appeared, claiming that she could not afford our training fees. Her horses moved to Jenny Pitman and she moved out of our lives. I always try to stay friendly with owners when they take their horses away because racing is full of swings and roundabouts. My father taught me that it makes sense to leave the door open. You never know when an owner might want to return to the fold.

Bargains appear in the most unlikely places. One of my favourite horses, Kildagin, twice winner of the Grand Steeple-chase de Flandres, was originally sold cheaply in Gloucester market. Although he was a thoroughbred, his pedigree was officially unknown and he started his competitive life with Lorna Sutherland, an international event rider who later was better known as Lorna Clarke. But Kildagin pulled too hard, refused to settle and jumped too flat. When his inability to bend his back caused him to fall heavily several times over solid obstacles, Lorna sent him into training with me at Condicote, so that she might ride him on the flat.

Later, after showing some promise over hurdles and fences, Kildagin was sent to Ascot sales, but he failed to raise a bid, much to everyone's relief, for by now he was quite a favourite in the yard and was known to one and all as the Dragon. Back with us he was ridden by Lorna in a flat race but shortly afterwards she passed him on for £2,000 to T. D. 'Boy' Pilkington, who had not owned a winner since before the war and later became Jim Wilson's father-in-law.

Kildagin, though small, was so versatile and willing that he gave his owner some phenomenal fun in the years ahead. Initially he fell with me over fences at Haydock, but later he came second in the Norwegian Grand National, was fourth in the Whitbread Gold Cup the year it was run at Newcastle and twice finished third in the Scottish Grand National. Apart from his first win over fences he was invariably ridden by John Suthern.

In 1974, when Kildagin was at the peak of his powers, we decided to take him to Waregem racecourse, in Belgium, where the Grand Steeplechase offered a variety of cross-country

obstacles including a set of white posts and rails sloped over
eight feet of water, a white wall, an in-and-out brush fence, a
double bank and a water jump whose width was said to depend
on the weather.

Kildagin travelled over on the ferry from Dover to Zeebrugge
late in August and we all lunched so well that 'Boy' Pilkington
took a nap afterwards and might have missed the afternoon's
racing but for a carnival in the street outside his hotel that
woke him up. The crowd was estimated at 20,000 and we were
disturbed to discover that by the time the first steeplechase was
run the water jump had almost doubled in size to twenty-four
feet through the addition of a strategically placed dam. When
I took a further look I noticed that the drainpipe from the loos
appeared to be adding further to the width and substance of
the water.

It was just as well that I gave John Suthern strict instructions to
be prepared for hostile tactics, for as he and Kildagin approached
the water jump on the first circuit one French jockey tried his
best to ensure that they took an early bath. At this stage John
kicked on into the lead on Kildagin, whose previous experience
of eventing helped save vital ground several times. They still
led at the final fence, shook off a late challenge from another
French runner and came home for a famous victory by one and
a half lengths.

Tears of pride flowed down 'Boy' Pilkington's face when the
band began to play 'God Save the Queen' during the presentation
ceremony. It was, in truth, a marvellous victory and our biggest
so far since we had begun training at Condicote. Dinah later
wrote an amusing account of the successful expedition in
Horse and Hound. The following year, aged eleven, Kildagin
returned to Belgium to win the Grand Steeplechase for the
second year running. To this day he is the only English-trained
horse to triumph in the race.

I trained Willie Wumpkins briefly for 'Boy' Pilkington's wife
Jane at the same time as Kildagin, with spectacular lack of
success. He had won the Aldsworth Hurdle at Cheltenham in
1973 for Adrian Maxwell, but had rather lost his form the
following season and I was quite unable to get him right when
he came to me. Willie Wumpkins was so ill at Condicote that
at one point I thought he was going to die. When he recovered,
he returned to the Pilkingtons' home near us at Stow and never

looked back. In the evening of his career, trained very skilfully under permit by Jane, he won the Coral Golden Hurdle Final at the Festival three years in succession between 1979 and 1981, ridden each time by Jim Wilson.

16

The Big Time

Jump racing is one of those emotional sports that can grab you by the throat and send your spirits soaring one moment, and leave you in despair the next. Anyone who assembles a large team of steeplechasers is uncomfortably aware that disaster is but one false step, one unlucky fall away.

David Nicholson began the new season in the early autumn of 1974 full of optimism now that he was able to concentrate fully on the business of training his horses without the distractions brought on by race riding at distant meetings. But a series of crushing reverses over the next five months left him perilously close to turning his back on the sport that had been his life for as long as he could remember.

We had such high hopes that autumn. Almost fifty horses somehow crammed into Condicote, potentially the best team by far that we had put together; but the deaths of five horses within the space of a few weeks brought me to my knees. It did not help that they were all decent animals with the promise of being top class, but the fact is that the death of any horse, however modest, tears me apart.

After O Mandado became the fifth of our horses to die inside two months, in a fall at Leicester on December 30, I came home to Dinah and told her I could not go on; that I was going to give up training because I could not stand the anguish of it all. I said it and I meant it.

When you become attached to a horse – any horse – and the worst happens, it hurts too much. I know jumping by its very nature is a hard business, but you never get used to losing a horse. You feel so responsible and guilty.

Horses are so trusting; they give you everything. They give, give, give.

As usual Dinah pulled me through. She kept me going when I was at my lowest ebb and quietly pointed out that I could not do anything else but train racehorses. She always insists I would be a bloody nuisance if I was not a trainer.

The first horse we lost was King Pele, whom I had ridden to victory in the Gloucestershire Hurdle for Gavin Pritchard-Gordon. Later he came to me to start a new career over fences, but he fell heavily on his debut at Newbury in November, broke a leg and had to be put down. It was a dreadful loss and set the grim pattern of what was to follow.

Tudor Dance, who had won twice the previous season, ran well at Towcester at the end of that month but collapsed and died as he came back to unsaddle. At home we lost another lovely young horse, who reared over backwards and ruptured his spleen.

Then Sky Train, a winner twice in the current season, sliced right through his tendon in the closing stages when all set to take the Olympic Hurdle, at Chepstow, at Christmas. The injury was so severe that he had been put down, to save him from further suffering, by the time I reached the forlorn group with him near the second last hurdle.

Finally O Mandado, an exciting young chaser who had won his previous race over fences ridden by Bob Champion, broke his hind leg at Leicester at the end of December and he, too, was destroyed. I could not wait to see the back of the old year.

At times like this you desperately need a lifeline and it came in the reliable shape of What A Buck, the horse who had given me my last winner as a jockey. Patience is essential for anyone involved in breeding, owning and training potential chasers; you simply cannot hurry them. What A Buck was a typical example. He was already four when I bought him for Sam Vestey the week before his half-brother L'Escargot won the first of his two Cheltenham Gold Cups in 1970. Yet he did not win a race for more than two and a half years. I brought him along steadily and he was usually ridden at home by Dinah.

What A Buck started his racing career over hurdles and eventually won two minor races, but he was always going to be a chaser. At one stage I hoped he would go right to the top and he might have done so but for a number of setbacks; he was hobdayed for a wind infirmity as a six-year-old and then suffered leg trouble the following season. Eventually What A Buck began to fulfil his undoubted potential over fences that difficult winter. After finishing second at Ludlow in November, 1974, he quickly recorded victories in handicaps at Cheltenham, Ludlow and Doncaster.

He came back in December, 1975, to beat Royal Relief and Bula in the SGB Chase at Ascot. A bold-jumping, free-running horse, he usually made the running, won again at Kempton and then completed a hat-trick in the Tote Northern Chase run in a howling gale at Haydock in January, 1976. That was one of his finest moments. After leading all the way he was headed by Cantabet on the run-in, but despite galloping straight into a gale force wind fought back doggedly to snatch the race by a short head. Fearing What A Buck was lame, Jeff King immediately dismounted and led him back but happily the horse was sound when we took the bandages off his legs in his box at home the following morning.

Though I did not realise it at the time, Haydock was the beginning of the end for him. He had a desperately hard race there in the most testing conditions and was never quite so good afterwards. I felt he deserved his chance in the Gold Cup two months later, but the exceptionally firm ground at Cheltenham that year did not suit him at all and Jeff eventually pulled him up.

The following season, aged ten, he ran with great credit to take sixth place in the 1977 Grand National, which will always be remembered for Red Rum's record third victory in the race. Later he suffered further leg trouble and was retired by Sam Vestey.

Sam confided one day that he had written a clause into his will leaving What A Buck to Dinah, who had become very attached to the old horse over the years. When she pointed out that in all probability the horse would die long before his owner, Sam generously agreed to give him to her then and there.

What A Buck was always a superb jumper and fell only twice in his life, once with me on his second run over fences at Kempton and once with Tommy Stack when he sat on him at Condicote shortly before he ran in the Grand National. They turned two somersaults over the little schooling fences. Luckily neither horse nor rider was hurt and a week later Tommy rode to his finest victory on Red Rum at Aintree.

In retirement What A Buck proved to be a treasure, an absolute star. He became a brilliant hunter, was equally adept at hunter trials and showjumping, proved an ideal schoolmaster to lots of our boys, led the schooling for years and eventually became my hack. He was also the making of Princess Anne as a jump jockey when she began riding out at Condicote, and was the first horse she rode over a schooling fence.

During one particularly lively New Year's Eve party at home several showjumpers, including Nick Skelton, Jeff McVean and John and Michael Whitaker, expressed a desire to ride a racehorse at least once in their lives, so I suggested they all turn out the next morning, which proved to be as wet and wild a day as you will ever see in the Cotswolds. Some did not appear, and others did not seem well enough to take to the saddle, but Michael Whitaker rode What A Buck up over our fences in true racing style and still talks about the experience.

What A Buck lived to the age of twenty-two and died in the summer of 1989 cantering up the all-weather gallop leading the young horses, as usual. He had just reached the point where he used to stand with me watching proceedings with his ears pricked when he fell like a stone. We were on holiday in Florida at the time and both burst into tears when we heard the news. Alan King, our assistant trainer, told us that they buried him on the spot, which is the nicest thing they could possibly have done. A headstone now marks his grave.

Sam Vestey proved to be a tremendous ally when a block of three hundred acres came on to the market adjoining our land at Condicote. It was an outstanding chance to try to improve our training facilities. Sam bought the land, sold the middle part straight on and allowed us to turn the remainder into gallops. His generosity did not end there. When we enjoyed a particularly fruitful season for him, he paid for Dinah and me to take a working holiday in New Zealand looking at young store horses.

In 1975, What A Buck proved to be one of the stars of our first open day, held that year on the Sunday before Christmas, after Brian Fanshawe, my brother-in-law, then Master of the Cotswold Hounds, asked us to do something to help the British Field Sports Society's fighting fund. Just over one hundred people turned up and we raised £250. This was probably the first open day of its kind and we have carried on by public demand, although initially the Jockey Club were not very keen on the idea because of their concern for security.

After one more winter open day we decided to switch the date to the summer and it has just mushroomed with the years. In 1993 the attendance topped 10,000 and we were able to hand over £18,000 to be divided between several charities. This brought the total we had raised over almost twenty years to £65,000. The traffic was so heavy in the area that one poor man on his way to Tewkesbury was swept in here and had to pay to get out! In 1994 the figure we made on the day rose for the first time to £20,000.

Dinah is in charge from start to finish. She begins planning the following year's schedule virtually as soon as each open day is over, and puts together a glossy brochure with pictures and background details on all the horses. Every horse on four legs is paraded and people are free to wander around the yard. Dinah lays on falconry displays, terrier racing, a parade of foxhounds and beagles, marquees and several bars including one for those who prefer champagne.

We also construct a grandstand that can hold 2,000 people and have as many as forty trade stands. We charge per head in each car and people behave very well; they seem to respect the place and the amount of rubbish left behind is minimal. Much to our surprise our open day has become a great annual country event. It is part of our lives and almost a fixture in the racing calendar.

We briefly ran our own pheasant shoot at Condicote and invited a few racing friends for the odd day out, including Peter Scudamore, Steve Smith Eccles, Hywel Davies, Ben Brooks, Henry Shouler, David Minton, Gavin Pritchard-Gordon and Dinah's brother, James Pugh. We also invited our old friend Jim Meads along one day to record the occasion in a series of fine photographs. On one occasion, while Steve was relieving himself near a gorse bush between drives, two of the boys fired into the air. Steve was so terrified that he fell straight into the gorse. Once, while some of the guns were assembling outside the house, a wily fox that had been pinching our chickens trotted through the paddock and popped over the wall into the churchyard, where he sat apparently daring us to shoot him.

Our guests had a lot of fun, but we gave up the shoot after a couple of years, basically because I am soft. I find no pleasure in seeing winged birds fluttering to the ground. Now I have two social days a year, one at Gatcombe, the other with Raymond Mould, and am quite relieved that I do not contribute much to the bag. I am such a poor shot that Mark Phillips says that even on days when the rest of the guns are restricted to shooting cock birds only, I can pot at anything because it is unlikely that I will connect.

Early in 1976 I was approached by the BBC to co-operate in a new series called *The Big Time*, which involved making documentaries about amateurs trying their hand in the professional world. It was explained that they wanted to spend a few months following Joan Barrow, a local farmer's wife and keen point-to-point rider, being trained by me at Condicote in preparation for a race against male jockeys.

Richard Pitman first proposed the project at the Heythrop point-to-point where Joan had ridden a winner. Though my views about female riders and amateurs were widely known, I was keen to help even before a fee of £500 was mentioned. It seemed like an excellent opportunity for free publicity for Condicote, but I did not quite expect the depth of coverage that followed in the non-racing pages of national newspapers when the programme was broadcast late that year.

Joan proved to be a terrific sport even though I gave her quite a hard time to ensure that she was a hundred per cent fit by the time of the race. She took me so seriously when I told her to ride her bicycle everywhere without a saddle that she would be seen pedalling furiously around her village day after day. Later I offered exactly the same advice to Princess Anne when she began riding out at Condicote, but that suggestion did not go down quite so well!

We all had a lot of fun during the filming of *The Big Time*, but although Joan rode well, I had quite a battle before managing to persuade the Jockey Club to grant her the necessary amateur jockey's permit. There was a further problem because the BBC needed her to race before a certain date, and the autumn of 1976 coincided with such a long drought that we could not find anywhere to run Jackstones, the horse that had been generously supplied for her by Bob Heathcote.

Luckily there was just sufficient rain on the West Coast of

Scotland late in September to justify my entering Jackstones at the Ayr two-day meeting on both Saturday and Monday, but I made what could have been a crucial blunder by failing to read the small print of the conditions of entry for the second race on Monday, which proved to be for maidens at starting.

Unaware of this I ran Jackstones at Ayr on the Saturday, ridden by Robin Dickin against another of my horses, Sam Vestey's Roley Hill, partnered by Roy Mangan. After Jackstones finished second to Roley Hill one or two people suggested that we stopped Jackstones that day, but the truth is that he was beaten comfortably.

You can imagine the delight of everyone involved with the programme when Joan hacked up on Jackstones on Monday in a long-distance novice hurdle for amateur riders. Esther Rantzen, who was the inspiration behind the show, gave me a big kiss in the unsaddling enclosure as Joan returned after beating the men by no less than thirty lengths. Later she won on the horse again at Chepstow.

The Big Time was a lively, accurate, entertaining and at times revealing insight into what you have to put yourself through to ride in a race. Perhaps there was a touch of *National Velvet* in its portrayal, but at least this story did happen in real life. The *Daily Mail*'s Shaun Usher was one of several television critics amused by the tough line I took with Joan from the start. He noted:

David Nicholson has three abiding dislikes: amateur jockeys, female jockeys and female amateur jockeys. Nicholson, a big man with a face built on Easter Island statue lines, believes, among other things, that the wearing of jodhpurs and professional horsepersonship are inextricably entwined.

'Jeans are wrong, then,' Mrs Barrow suggested with a sheepish glance at her own jeans, evidently expecting some polite, not-to-worry comment.

'Very wrong,' the trainer responded, instantly and stonily.

Even so Usher enjoyed the programme sufficiently to advise *Daily Mail* readers who had missed it to start lobbying for a repeat. I must say that despite my experience with Joan, I still have some reservations about women riding over fences. They are simply not strong enough and are not cut out for it. I am also totally against girls riding in the Grand National. I suppose it is all right if they are going to jolly round and keep out of everyone's way. But if a girl is there to compete, I think every other jockey in the race would want to know where she is every stride along the way.

Naturally Dinah does not altogether agree with my views. She has always been a highly capable rider and took part in the first flat race for girls at Kempton in May, 1972. Dinah has been riding since the age of four, competed in point-to-points when she was young and gained her first success on the flat on Rolus at Haydock in 1972.

If I am lucky enough to be present when one of my jockeys comes back after an early winner in his career I usually say, 'Well done. Now sit up and look like a jockey.' That really takes the wind out of their sails and was my first comment when I reached Dinah as she returned in triumph on Rolus. Female jockeys were quite a novelty in those days and there was a fair bit of publicity after Rolus won.

One of the local papers quoted Dinah as saying, 'I am so pleased women jockeys have been accepted at last. It is long overdue. Once we are out on the course it is a case of every girl for herself and the language is quite choice at times.'

I encouraged Dinah to ride on the flat and was thrilled that she had won a race. She was so fit she lost only an ounce after sitting in the sauna for three hours in an attempt to manage 8st. 6lbs one day at Newbury. She was livid that she could not boil away a couple more pounds.

Dinah thoroughly deserved her chance as an amateur. She has done absolutely everything at home with the horses for years, and I honestly believe I have never seen anyone ride better work in the mornings. She once rode Alverton, who later won the Cheltenham Gold Cup, on the flat at York, and was also second on one of ours, Seed Hay, at Newbury. Years previously she rode old Blessington Esquire in the Newmarket Town Plate, run over four miles over the July course.

Dinah and I have never seen eye to eye over team chasing, which became so popular in the 'seventies. Frankly, I hate the concept of team chasing; of horses being asked to race over what in my opinion are traps. Eventing is another matter. The fences at Badminton are big and stiff but the horses are professionally trained and skilfully ridden. They go round on their own and know what is coming. That is a big difference from galloping round full-tilt on a Sunday afternoon when they do not have a clue what is coming up next on the other side. That is the way horses are badly injured. Although the top teams know just what is required, there are always those competitors whose qualifications leave a bit to be desired.

For a while I was employed as a marshall at the North Cotswold Team Chase. My role, on old What A Buck, was to watch the teams approaching the final third of the course and to stop any horse or rider I felt was not fit enough to continue. It was a job that did not exactly improve my popularity and was certainly not a way to make friends and influence people, even though all participants were warned at the start that if their horses were distressed to a point of exhaustion they would be stopped. Every rider I halted was furiously upset, but usually, when they had cooled down later, they would come up and thank me for what I had done.

Of course some riders tried to ignore me. Then I simply ran them out until they had to stop. No one made it past me; I even put an end to the round of an old Badminton horse who was staggering as if he was completely drunk. His rider, too, was mad with me, but I insisted that he jumped off and led the poor horse back.

Luckily Dinah did not have any desire to ride in races over fences. She accepted my view that I was the main breadwinner in the family and that she should keep her feet firmly on the ground. But she would insist on going off team chasing and nothing I could say would change her mind. So I was not at all sympathetic when she limped home late one Sunday afternoon with a wing down and a dislocated jaw.

After I retired as a jockey I rode Kildagin once in the local hunt's team chasing event as part of a racing team. It was the only occasion I have ever taken part in this sport, and I do not mind admitting that I was frightened out of my life by the experience, which fully confirmed my misgivings about it. I also took up polo for two years. I was taught by the late Hector Barrantes and played on Sam Vestey's ponies in medium-goal matches. I loved the game despite the fact that I never seemed to be in control. The ponies all used to run away with me.

17

The Duke's Academy

The relationship in racing between a young stable lad and a racehorse trainer is still perceived by some observers as curiously Dickensian. The trainer is seen as an unforgiving, authoritarian father figure, demanding absolute obedience. The young lad, hoping fervently to become a jockey, is a foundling required to toe the line on pain of expulsion from the stable.

Even today English and Irish stable lads and lasses can be heard addressing a trainer as if he were a nineteenth-century Knight of the Shires and they a bunch of serfs. But in the best-run yards, as at Jackdaws Castle, it is a system that has stood the test of time.

David Nicholson knows he cannot force respect from those who work for him. It has to be earned. Yet if his manner in the early morning sometimes seems a trifle sharp, you note that in a business with a high turnover of staff, his lads tend to stay in his employ for years.

My father's outstanding success at moulding young jockeys prompted me to try to follow his example. I share his delight at seeing young people get on in life, and within a few years of starting to train at Condicote had assembled some very tidy young jump jockeys including John Suthern, Robin Dickin, Paul Carvill and Allen Webb. My father observed at the time that once the boys had settled in at Condicote they would never leave because I did not pay them enough to afford the fare home!

He had turned down John Suthern as a young lad because the size of his hands and feet indicated that he would become too heavy for the flat. So John came to me after he began to put on weight after two years with Michael Jarvis at Newmarket, rode his first winner on my father's Eloped in 1971, spent many years at Condicote, won no end of races for us and now takes horses out of training for me at his livery yard.

John says now that my military manner was rather intimidating, and if he did not get a bollocking at least once a day then he felt something was wrong. I think he believes that being put straight so frequently was constructive; he certainly learned from the experience. He was a tremendously hard worker and would turn his hand to anything: bale carting, repairing fences, helping out with the animals on the farm and treading-in the gallops.

He often rode a useful little horse called Salad who belonged to a quartet of Manchester United soccer players, Stewart Houston, Alex Forsyth, Lou Macari and Alex Stepney, in partnership with Ben Brooks. Ben owned a half share, the others an eighth each. The name of the horse was taken from the first letter of each player's Christian name with D. Nicholson, of course, bringing up the rear.

It was a slightly uneasy partnership because all Lou and his team mates wanted was a punt. They encouraged me to try to organise a coup with Salad almost every time he ran. Lou, a racing nut, was the horse's self-appointed racing manager. The endless intrigue did not suit Ben, who is one of those ideal owners happy to leave most of the planning to his trainers.

After several promising runs Salad did land a bit of a gamble for the boys, ridden by John Suthern, at Stratford in April, 1979, where he was backed from 16–1 to 11–1. He won next time, too, at Devon & Exeter, where the boys put their money down again. Dinah was in charge that day and remembers Lou arriving at the course in a long, dark, bulky leather jacket which gave the impression that he had put on rather a lot of weight. All the pockets, he indicated, were full of cash he was preparing to put on Salad. We often wondered afterwards how he managed to carry his winnings home after the race.

That autumn Ben broke his race glasses in anger when John Suthern gave the horse a gentle seasonal introduction at Worcester. He felt that Salad would have won with a more positive ride, but peace was restored among the partners when Salad won twice over fences. Lou's liking for a bet put a bit of a strain on our relationship with the inevitable result that we parted company in the end.

John Suthern was one of several jockeys preparing to take part in a lengthy schooling session at Condicote one morning when a huge hot-air balloon drifted into sight barely one hundred yards above the ground. The nearer it approached, the more the horses became upset as they circled uneasily with their riders waiting for instructions. Eventually the unfamiliar, sinister hiss of escaping gas, combined with the sight of this enormous craft in the air hovering menacingly above them, caused the horses to scatter in all directions. Worse, several of them shed their jockeys in their rush to escape this alien beast.

By this time I was incandescent with rage and shouted as loud as I have ever done, 'Why don't you —— off and go and do something useful?' I like to think that the balloonists heard precisely what I said, for the basket immediately shot up into the air and flew away.

Robin Dickin, a farmer's son from Ludlow, arrived at Condicote straight from school, started off on the flat with two quick victories on Bob, stayed with us for ten years and is now a successful trainer. One day, when we were riding in the same race at Kempton, he remembers me hauling him back into the saddle just as he was about to be unseated, and then giving him a bollocking. John and Robin were with us virtually from the start at Condicote and were so shocked when I announced my retirement from the saddle that they say they felt rather as if an old friend had died. Apparently they anticipated my going on for ever. I wish I had shared their confidence.

We used to keep the all-weather gallop at Condicote in shape by pulling a set of light chain harrows over it behind an old tractor. One day, when the tractor would not start, I managed to persuade several of the boys to attach ropes to the chain harrow so that they could drag it along the all-weather by hand.

Robin Dickin, affronted at being press-ganged into action, retorted, 'Who do you think we are? Bleeding Egyptians?'

Paul Carvill, known in the yard as the Pope because he was so religious, was a decent little rider but was held back by injuries caused by a series of bad falls. He was a handy boxer, too, despite losing the top of one of his fingers in the string which secures a horse's head collar during evening stables. When I entered the box where Paul had been working, I found John Suthern scrambling around on the floor on his hands and knees.

'It's all right, Guv'nor. I am just looking for Paul's finger,' cried John by way of explanation! When he found the missing digit and waved it at me in triumph I almost passed out because I am so squeamish and cannot stand the sight of blood. The two boys rushed off to hospital hoping that surgeons might be able to sew Paul's finger back on but that was not possible.

Allen Webb, who was apprenticed to me for five years, was small, but became a very good hurdle race jockey, although I felt he was a bit mechanical over fences. He won several big races including the Grand Annual Chase and the Daily Express Triumph Hurdle, both at the Cheltenham Festival, and the Mecca Hurdle. These days he works as a jockey's valet.

I tried to bring on all the boys to do the job correctly, just as my father had done. Like him I believe in setting standards and expect my jockeys and lads to be presentable at all times. New lads who arrive with long hair very soon learn to have it cut; if not, they are given a helping hand with the electric clippers. It happened to both Jim Wilson and Tom Jenks.

None of the lads at Jackdaws Castle is allowed to lead up a horse at the races unless he is wearing a collar and tie. There are not many yards in the country that still insist on this dress code; another is that of Tom Jones, whose lads are always turned out immaculately. We designed yard ties at Condicote, and later at Jackdaws Castle, and provided them for any of the lads who did not possess a tie. Appearance, in my view, is very important, and so, to this day, I supply tins of polish in the tack room for the staff's riding boots.

I expect all my apprentices, conditional jockeys and amateurs to be polite, tidy, punctual and hardworking in the yard and to be professional in everything they do. In return I give them the chance to be jockeys, try to advise them about the hazards and characteristics of each racecourse and encourage them to keep improving their riding. I prefer them to ride with hands and heels only for as long as possible. My father always said it took a young jockey at least a hundred rides before he knew which way he was going. He was not far wrong!

There cannot be any short cuts with young lads and apprentices. The majority arrive thinking that they will become jockeys and I believe so strongly that they would have a better chance if racing still required a three-year apprenticeship with one trainer. That way it would be the next stage in life from school while you are teaching them. As it is, some young hopefuls flit from one stable to another, partly because there are always trainers who will promise rides but do not deliver.

Boys that have the right attitude are likely to stay anyway, but three years would offer continuity. I make it a rule never to promise anything to anyone when they join me, because I do not believe in offering anything that I will not be able to fulfil. All new staff have to join the queue, although exceptional talent can sometimes jump a place or two.

If a new apprentice is too impatient, he will not last long. From the very start I demand some form of respect to maintain discipline. That is why I have given one or two boys a cuff round the ear in the past. I would do it again, if necessary, even though today's rules of employment can make it tricky.

The old traditional values still apply at Jackdaws Castle. I believe in the correct style; that is, elbows in, heels down and feet fully in the irons. I dread to think what my father would say if he could see Walter Swinburn today riding with just his toes perched in the irons. I imagine he would knock him out of the saddle to prove the point that you cannot be secure riding in that manner. This modern style that so many jockeys adopt on the flat is ridiculous. You don't see Willie Carson or Pat Eddery trying it.

I prefer my recruits to be natural riders. It is in their favour if they come with a background involving Pony Clubs and hunting. I do not mind if they have stayed on at school a little longer. Ideally, boys should continue their education for as long as possible. I remember one lad, who rode a few winners, being told to give a horse a pick of grass for a quarter of an hour. He asked, quite seriously, if that was twenty minutes.

I have always employed younger lads. Jumping is a young man's game, and until the move to Jackdaws Castle I did not have the necessary accommodation for married lads. You soon know the boys who are going to be any good; the slow learners never make up for lost time. I am turning lads down now because I already have a fistful of applications and will not take any more because I feel a sense of loyalty to the ones who are already with me.

We all have to start somewhere and I believe that every lad in racing deserves at least one chance to be a jockey. When it arrives, no course is too distant to send a boy to take that chance, but you never know how a lad will respond. One particular hopeful rode a fair bit of schooling, and looked the part, but when I gave him a ride at Newbury it was a disaster from the word go. I did not regret it for one minute and I am sure he did not either; he had his opportunity to be a jockey for a day and is still with me now.

I like to think that my owners have sufficient confidence in me to take my word for it and give their support when I say that a particular boy deserves a chance. Sam Vestey, for instance, was good enough to give a first ride to Jamie Davies, who later rode with success for David Elsworth and is now head lad to Mick Channon.

Sometimes it is better to begin as an amateur rider and go on that way. It all makes me appreciate how much my father helped me in the early days. In 1993 we bought a horse called Fly by North specifically for the boys to ride soon after we moved to Jackdaws Castle, but unfortunately he broke down after his second race.

One of my earliest amateurs was Norton Brookes. He and his brother Bev were builders and were among my first owners. They helped me put up what we called millionaire's row, a fine line of seven boxes at Condicote.

Jim Wilson joined me as a raw amateur in 1969 on the recommendation of his uncle, Fred Winter. Jim had a reputation for being a bit wild in those days and for some reason Fred felt that I was the right man to straighten him out. He was a fair horseman and became a high-class amateur jockey and an equally good squash player, but I had the devil of a job to control him. He would come in at all hours of the day and night, and when you asked what he might have had for lunch or dinner the reply was invariably the same: 'Ah Jesus, sex, cheese and water biscuits!'

Jim, who married our secretary Melinda Carden, eventually set up an equine swimming pool business at Charlton Kings in Cheltenham and is now a trainer. In 1980 he became one of only a handful of amateurs to be leading rider at the Cheltenham Festival. A year later he rode to glory in the Gold Cup on Little Owl, a horse left to him and his brother Robin by their aunt, Bobby Gundry, the previous year. He was the first amateur jockey to win the Gold Cup since Dick Black, who had been a prisoner-of-war, triumphed on Fortina in 1947.

Another of my secretaries, Jo Beswick, who later married Bob Champion, rode a winner on her own grey Shermoon at Market Rasen in May, 1978 with the help of some nifty sleight of hand by the trainer. Shermoon made all the running in an amateur riders' chase and had drawn clear at the last fence when I spotted something, which I suspected was a pad, come away from the saddle.

I set off down the course at once to collect it, with the intention of returning it to Jo before she weighed in, but was restrained by a steward. So I turned back, darted into the weighing-room, grabbed a one-pound piece of lead from the table and rushed out to greet Jo in the winner's enclosure. As she prepared to jump off Shermoon's back I warned, 'This is cold, don't jump,' and popped the lead down the back of her breeches. It was a bit of a shock for her but at least she weighed in at the correct mark.

Graeme Roe, a top-class athlete in his day, was single-mindedly determined to ride in a race after watching the exploits of Joan Barrow in *The Big Time* on television. Since he was forty at the time, I did everything to try to stop him. I forcibly explained that he was too old, too heavy and too unfit, but nothing I could say was going to prevent him going ahead and he immediately began taking lessons at a local riding school. Later, when he had learned the basics, I agreed to support him.

After Bob had run away with him on the gallops one morning he came back apologising, fully expecting a bollocking, and seemed relieved when I pointed out that Bob had carted better jockeys than him. The success of Saucy Sam, the first horse I bought for him, at Newcastle, backed from 14–1 to 7–1, merely strengthened Graeme's resolve to ride in a race. He finally made his debut in 1978 on his own horse All Bright at Hexham in a race I expected to win with Westberry Lodge, owned by the soccer star Emlyn Hughes and ridden by Jim Wilson. Westberry Lodge finished second and All Bright, rather to my surprise, beat a few home.

I foolishly imagined that this attempt would be the end of Graeme's ambition, but he came back on All Bright grinning from ear to ear asking where I planned to run the horse next. By now his wife Jean had reservations about his new hobby which, regrettably, were well founded. Next time, at Market Rasen, he had the most terrible fall with All Bright. The first thing to hit the ground was his face.

I was sure he would retire there and then, but when he came round in the ambulance room, he mumbled through missing teeth that he intended to race again. That autumn he won a match race on Gur Amir, on the flat at Sandown, for Gavin Pritchard-Gordon, and five years later achieved his elusive first success over jumps on Dom Perignon at Ayr. You had to admire Graeme's resolve because he was not, in all honesty, a natural horseman. It was just that he had far too much courage for his own good.

A vital part of the team in those early days was Bob Hartop. Though he did not ride for me, Bob was a gifted allrounder who could turn his hand to anything to do with livestock. He became our first travelling head lad and spent most of his time on the road. Later he left with our blessing to become a trainer.

Others at Condicote included Mark Lowry, who later rode as a professional in the North, and John Hughes, who escaped from school a year early to become a jockey and won for me on Nom de Guerre. Simon Andrews, the son of the North Cotswold Huntsman, was a bit too heavy to ride under Rules but did very well point-to-pointing. Tony Gateley, who used to look after Kildagin, soon moved on to Germany and led up the 1975 Arc de Triomphe winner Star Appeal still wearing his Condicote tie.

The career of one apprentice, who had a few rides and had better be nameless, ended abruptly when he stabbed a horse in the ribs at evening stables with a four-pronged fork. He tried to deny it, even though you could see the holes in the rug and the wounds on the horse's ribs. I can tell you he was gone from the yard very quickly.

Plenty of lads have come to me with no riding experience at all, notably David 'Scouse' Barker and Xavier Aizpur. 'Scouse' appeared on the doorstep at Condicote one day looking for a job, having walked seven miles from Moreton station. His qualifications, as such, appeared to be no more than a limited knowledge of the donkeys on Southport sands. I liked his smile and gave him a chance. He learned to ride on Merrydown, a grey thirteen-hand pony belonging to Philip and John, and though he was never going to be a Peter Scudamore, he became a very accurate judge of the well-being of any horse he rode. No end of lads started their riding careers on the various ponies that we had for our sons, but eventually Philip and John moved on to older horses including Baghdad Gold, Bob and What A Buck.

Scouse and I used to have daily bets of nothing more than £2 on anything from the Test Match to the Cup Final. It was a very sad day when he decided to return to his native Liverpool after sixteen years with us. The door is always open if he decides to come back.

Xavier Aizpur, the son of the landlord of the Horse and Groom at Bourton-on-the-Hill, started to help out in the yard during his holidays at the age of nine and learned to ride on Baghdad Gold, who was bombproof and was bequeathed to us on his retirement. He was also the first horse that Princess Anne and her daughter Zara rode at home for us. Xavier has long since moved out of the learner stage and will soon be having his first ride under Rules.

Nobody who knew him will ever forget Roy Mangan, who joined us in 1974 after a miserable run of luck as a freelance jockey in the North. He came to me initially just to ride out and mend the tack, a skill he had picked up with Joe Hartigan, but it soon became clear that he was a fine horsemen, too. Over the years he rode quite a few winners for us and enjoyed an outstanding partnership one season with No Defence.

Increasing weight, injuries and a constant battle with asthma made life difficult for Roy, who was a great character and friend, and married our secretary Julia Smith. He was irrepressible and possessed a wicked, almost macabre, sense of humour that displayed itself in the most outrageous pranks.

Early one morning he put a chicken in the car belonging to Nigel Twiston-Davies. It spent most of the day perched on the driving wheel with the result that the driver's seat was covered in droppings by the evening. Another time at a wedding Roy slipped away from the reception to put cow manure on the screens of several cars.

You could never be sure what he would do next. Once he filled a lad's car brimful with old leaves. It was not done maliciously, just out of high spirits. If he came racing with me, I dared not let him drive while I had a nap on the way home or he would wake me up suddenly by blasting the horn or putting the cigarette lighter perilously close to my nose.

One year I ran two in the Scottish Grand National, with Roy on Game Gentleman and John Suthern on Bentley Boy, who had a nasty habit of falling at open ditches. Roy never stopped reminding John of this failing on the long journey from Stow to Scotland where they shared a room in a hotel. At intervals through the night John was woken up by Roy shouting out in his most ghostly voice, 'The ditch . . . the ditch . . . Beware the ditch.' Even when they were down at the start Roy could not refrain from pointing out to John that the open ditches at Ayr seemed particularly large. Sure enough, Bentley Boy came down at the first ditch he jumped, which was only the third fence. A circuit later Roy gave poor John the thumbs-up as he came past on Game Gentleman.

Roy was always cheerful. When it was clear his riding days were over, he set up an efficient tack and saddlery business in Stow, and looked after all our repairs. We were all devastated when he died suddenly from an asthma attack in the summer of 1994. It was one of the saddest days of my life.

I was deeply touched to be asked to make the address at his funeral in Stow, and at first I turned it down because I am hopeless at public speaking. Dinah, as usual, talked me round. It was one of the hardest things I have ever done, yet such was his sense of humour I know he would have been amused at my discomfort. The church was packed to overflowing with standing room only on a lovely summer's day. Julia has coped wonderfully well and another of my old boys, Allen Webb, is helping her to fulfil her desire to keep the business going. With the support of the Injured Jockeys' Fund it is now a trust which also helps train ex-jockeys in the art of saddlery.

18

The Scudamore years

In his eventful career as a racehorse trainer David Nicholson has given countless eager young apprentices, amateurs and dreamers their first crucial rides in public. Close on a hundred of them have gone on to win races. None has matched the deeds or, indeed, the commitment of Peter Scudamore.

Jockeys emerge from the most unlikely backgrounds. Peter Scudamore, record-breaking champion, was born to be a jockey though his mother Mary earnestly hoped his ambitions lay elsewhere. His father Michael Scudamore was one of the finest and bravest jump jockeys of his era, won the 1959 Grand National on Oxo and played a part in the early tuition of David Nicholson as a jockey.

Peter Scudamore's destiny seemed inextricably entwined with that of David Nicholson from the day he acted as a pageboy at his wedding in May, 1962. Even as a small schoolboy he seemed to sense what lay ahead. When he was asked to write an essay looking forward many years to his life in 1990, he began, 'I have been champion jockey for the past five years!'

Reality came crowding in on his first attempt as a jockey in a point-to-point. Eager young Scudamore, already believing himself to be Lester Piggott and John Francome rolled into one, had been devouring books on the theory of race riding and practising his finish. Approaching the last fence he reached for his whip, the horse dived sideways and P. Scudamore was deposited on the ground in front of his parents, grandparents and headmaster.

This exceptional man, though, always learned the lessons of his mistakes. School, at Belmont Abbey, taught him the value of work, concentration and discipline. Bright, articulate and intense he emerged, at eighteen, with two 'A'-levels which could

*have given him a passport to any number of professions, but the
lure of racing proved irresistible.*

*Peter Scudamore arrived in racing with the sudden, blinding
impact of a meteor. In his first whirlwind, frantic years,
hard-bitten old jockeys forecast that he would burn himself
out long before he was thirty. The man entrusted with the task
of nursing the flame of his rare talent was David Nicholson.*

It was Dinah who first spotted Peter riding at Worcester. We
knew Jeff King was coming to the end of the road and we were
quietly looking for a long-term replacement we could bring on
to take his place. Though Peter was an unknown amateur at
the time, and had not even ridden a winner, Dinah was instantly
impressed by the way he rode over a fence and said he was our
man. His presentation at a fence was the initial gift she spotted.
Further inquiries revealed that he had spent six months with my
uncle Willie Stephenson. We also discovered that his mother was
determined he should not become a professional jockey, because
she could not bear the thought of his suffering the sort of bad
fall that ended Michael Scudamore's career.

I think it was Michael who worked out an acceptable
compromise. He asked me if Peter could ride out at Condicote
each morning once he began working for an estate agent near by
at Stow in September, 1978. From the start it was obvious that
Peter did not have the slightest interest in being an estate agent.
He only ever thought of being a jockey, was determined to be successful and within weeks of joining us won twice on Rolyat for
Toby Balding. There were other winners, too, for outside yards.

Peter was a very dashing amateur, much in demand, because
it was clear to everyone that he rode with his foot hard down
on the accelerator. You never had to tell him anything twice. He
rode his first winner for me on Jacko at Worcester in March,
1979, despite hitting the front too soon.

There was a brief hiccup at that year's Festival where Peter,
on Westberry Lodge, fell at the second last in the National Hunt
Chase, bringing down my other runner Lizandon, ridden by
Sandy Cramsie; both were in with a big chance at the time. Peter
won three more races for me before the end of the season. By
then it was clear that his days as an estate agent were numbered,
so I asked him to join me full-time as pupil assistant after the
summer break.

As soon as racing began in August, I broke the habit of a lifetime and had a rare bet on Peter, something like £100 at a long price, about him becoming champion amateur that season. Halfway through November I knew I had lost my money, because by then it was apparent that he was far too talented a jockey to remain an amateur. After he won on Oakprime for the second time, I called a meeting with the Scudamore family and my father joined us for the evening, too. We all had supper in Broadway and decided that Peter should turn professional at once, while he still had the advantage of claiming a weight allowance. His victory on Regal Command the following afternoon at Leicester put him level at the top of the amateurs' table with Geordie Dun, but by then the die was cast.

Two days later he won on his first ride as a professional on Sea Lane, at Worcester, and then completed his first double later in the afternoon on Birshell. The whirlwind was already gathering momentum. Even then Peter wanted to be the best, nothing less, and he made it to the top so quickly through sheer strength of character. From an early stage I felt he possessed the ability, drive and attitude it required to be champion jockey. His ride on Flitgrove, at Nottingham, confirmed it less than a month after he turned professional.

I ran two in the same handicap chase that day. Peter, who was still claiming four lbs, was on Flitgrove, a horse that at times did not appear to struggle very hard, while John Suthern rode Eastern Citizen, the second favourite, who had won last time out. The pair had a ding-dong battle throughout the final mile with Eastern Citizen looking likely to maintain the slender advantage he had held all the way up the straight, until Peter forced Flitgrove in front right on the line in a photo-finish.

Poor John was sick with despair at being caught by the new boy wonder, who was rapidly pushing him back down the pecking order at Condicote. You could hear the dismay in his voice as he blurted out, 'How do you expect me to beat Jesus Christ claiming four pounds?'

The nickname stuck for a short while, too, but happily for Peter it did not last. Even he could not have coped with that. He was totally dedicated to the business of riding winners. It was so throughout his career. At times, he could be obsessive. He never stopped talking about racing and race riding, was always prepared to learn and worked exceptionally hard on his use of the whip in the early days. There was no doubt that he was tough enough, physically and mentally, for the great years that lay ahead.

Peter rode twenty-four winners within two months of turning professional, but his season ended abruptly early in February when he broke his right leg at Haydock. During his enforced absence, Peter received an offer to ride for Fred Rimell the following season, and also became the fourth jockey at Condicote to marry one of our secretaries. I managed to persuade him to stay with me and he married Marilyn Kington, better known as Maz, at Belmont Abbey on May 29, 1980.

That autumn I bought a horse called Broadsword, who was to take both of us to the very brink of glory at the Cheltenham Festival two years running. A big, powerful, good-looking colt by the American stallion Ack Ack, once voted Horse of the Year, he did not race at two and had won only one ordinary maiden race, over fourteen furlongs at Haydock, from seven starts at three for John Dunlop. However, Broadsword had been recommended to Lord Northampton as a potential jumper, so I drove down to inspect him at John's picturesque stables in the shadow of Arundel Castle.

Broadsword turned out to be the worst mover at a walk and trot that I had ever seen, and he was not much better when he cantered. Since I had travelled a long way, I asked John if he minded if I rode the horse myself, tucked my flannels into my socks and cantered him across Arundel Park. After that I had to have him.

Back at Condicote Broadsword proved to be a dreadful box walker and quite hopeless at learning how to jump, as bad a case as I have ever handled. You name it, whatever we put in front of him – tree trunks, poles, hurdles – he crashed straight through the lot of them. By the beginning of October he was starting to look seriously expensive.

At that point Roy Mangan, who continued to ride out for us after he retired as a jockey, volunteered to pop him over some fences. I thought Roy was quite mad, and told him so. With that he jumped on Broadsword and winged over six schooling fences, with a lead horse, to the manner born. Roy came back proclaiming, 'We've cracked it,' but I was still far from convinced and talked 'Spenny' Northampton out of having a bet on him, because of his suspect jumping, when he ran over hurdles for the first time at Kempton on October 17.

Broadsword drifted badly in the market, started at 7–1, jumped well and, ridden by Peter Scudamore, won comfortably. Despite an unexpected defeat at the hands of Lir the next time he ran, he proved to be a natural hurdler and proceeded to win five more races on the bounce including the Finale Junior Hurdle, the Stroud Green Hurdle and the Tolworth Hurdle. After his second success in the Merit Hurdle at Nottingham I forked out £100 at 50–1 to pay for the party if he happened to win the Daily Express Triumph Hurdle at Cheltenham. Broadsword had a superb attitude but by God he wanted some work. I used to jump horses in with him during a gallop, something I have never done before or since.

I had been waiting thirteen years so far for my first winner at the Festival as a trainer and really did believe Broadsword was the one to break my duck. Punters and bookmakers alike obviously shared my view because he started a heavily backed favourite at 7–4. I watched the race from my usual position on the members' lawn, just to the left of the Royal box, perhaps a hundred yards below the finishing line, and the confusion that occurred shortened my life by several years.

Peter, who was also seeking his first Festival win, rode a sensible race, eased Broadsword towards the leaders in the final mile, took an apparently decisive lead at the last hurdle and quickly drew two, possibly three lengths clear as he started the final climb to the winning post. Broadsword was still almost two lengths ahead as he passed me, and galloping strongly.

I turned and ran off the lawn, shouting, 'He's won, he's won,' and rushed down to greet him on the way back until I was stopped by my sister Josie who told me she thought he had been caught by the late run of Baron Blakeney, an unconsidered 66–1 outsider. Spenny Northampton and I were hugging each other by this stage, certain of victory and I assumed Josie had made a mistake. When another number appeared in the frame for the winning horse I was sure the judge had made a mistake, too.

Once I realised I was the one at fault I was shattered, quite speechless. Poor Peter Scudamore was in a terrible state, too. We did not say a thing as he unsaddled in the spot reserved for the second horse. Somehow I found the strength to walk up to say well done to the winning trainer, Martin Pipe, although I had never heard of the man until that moment. No one had then. After that I retired hurt to the bar with a large brandy.

That night Spenny took a party from Condicote out to dinner, but I was too upset to join them. I was numb by the time I reached home and was then bitten by a three-year-old filly as I looked round. She took one lump out of my coat and another out of the top of my knuckle.

Later, when I was able to study the film of the closing stages rationally, it was clear that the loose horse running just ahead of Broadsword was the cause of his downfall. He thought he was beaten. You could almost sense the resolve draining out of him and then Baron Blakeney came out of the blue in the last fifty yards.

Fifteen days later Broadsword put the record straight in emphatic style in the Sean Graham Hurdle at Aintree. This time he won decisively by five lengths from Kolme with Baron Blakeney a further six lengths away third. Time was to show that his best runs were on the flatter courses like Liverpool.

Peter was in tremendous form that season, won forty-two races for me and, going into the final month, was only half a dozen winners behind John Francome. But any thoughts he harboured of becoming champion in his first full campaign as a professional were ended by a nasty fall on Salad at Taunton, early in May, which left him with a fractured skull and perforated eardrum.

Most four-year-old colts are gelded after their first season over hurdles, but Broadsword combined an excellent pedigree with an ideal attitude to racing, so we hoped he might eventually become a jumping stallion. It takes an exceptional five-year-old to win the Champion Hurdle, but I felt he was up to the task. He won at Cheltenham in November, finished third behind Heighlin at Newbury, then reversed the form emphatically with Heighlin in the Tote Treble Hurdle at Cheltenham in January. On that form I felt he was entitled to finish in the first three in the Champion Hurdle, for which he started second favourite at 100–30.

Once again we were to be disappointed at the meeting that matters most. Broadsword did not enjoy the best of runs through the race, was slightly hampered on the final bend but still came through to take second place, seven lengths behind the 40–1 outsider For Auction. We took him to Liverpool again, but this time he fell at the last flight as he was coming to win the Templegate Hurdle.

The meeting that year coincided with Spenny Northampton's birthday and he decided that we should all celebrate in style. He telephoned his secretary in London and asked her to bring a huge tin of the finest Beluga caviar up to Liverpool. When we arrived back at the hotel after racing we all sat around guzzling caviar and drinking champagne.

Despite these reverses at Cheltenham and Aintree, we were enjoying one of our best seasons at Condicote, with the bonus of Peter Scudamore riding like a man possessed. The fifty-one winners Peter rode for me before the end of April proved the foundation of his championship charge which took him into an apparently decisive lead of twenty over the reigning champion John Francome. But he broke his arm at Southwell on April 26 in a fall that brought his season to a premature halt for the third year running.

John Francome told Peter he was prepared to chase all over the country to close the gap in the remaining six weeks of the campaign, but promised that if he did catch him he would stop riding at once so that they could share the title. That is exactly what happened. It was an extraordinarily sporting gesture by John, who acknowledged that he was clearly beaten until Peter broke his arm. Everyone at Condicote was delighted that Peter had achieved his great ambition to be champion jockey though I did wonder if he would have done the same for John Francome if the situation had been reversed.

Broadsword raced for one final season but the Champion Hurdle eluded him once more. Peter made his ground far too quickly on him by rushing him into the lead prematurely at the second last hurdle, and in the end they only just held on for fourth place behind the decisive winner Gaye Brief, trained by Mercy Rimell. Peter was angry with himself afterwards because he knew he had ridden a bad race.

I would have loved to have run Broadsword over fences because he proved to be a natural in a schooling session at home, but Spenny Northampton's advisors would not allow it. Tough, genuine, consistent and undeniably top class he retired to the Elms Stud, on his owner's estate, in Northamptonshire, where he quickly established himself as a leading jumping stallion. Flashing Steel, from his first crop, won the 1995 Irish

Grand National. I have had a lot of fun, and some success, training some of his offspring, including Shamana.

Peter Scudamore proved to be an ideal stable jockey. We had few disagreements over the years, partly because he was not the sort of person who responded well to criticism, so I seldom sought to tell him off. He was always very serious about the business of race riding, but when the pressure was off he could relax and enjoy a joke and was great fun after a glass or two of port. When his wife Maz came to work full-time as my secretary, the four of us became very close and invariably ate out together on a Saturday night, usually at the Horse and Groom at Bourton-on-the-Hill. By then Peter and Maz had their own home, on the outskirts of Condicote, barely a couple of hundred yards from Cotswold House.

Peter had a rare intensity of purpose. You always knew when it was business with him because he became very quiet. Sometimes, before a big race, he would not say a word as we travelled to the races together in the same car. It was just that he preferred to concentrate on the task ahead.

He was professional at all times and sensible about injuries. If he was not fit, he did not ride. There was one notable exception at Ascot and it was my fault. He was on the ground for five minutes after a numbing fall before coming back in the ambulance so concussed that he did not know if it was Wednesday or Saturday. I remember telling him the name of the horse and the racecourse, the date plus other relevant facts, which he was then able to repeat in parrot fashion to the doctor a moment later.

This subterfuge ensured that a red mark was not made in his medical record book so, in theory, he was able to ride in the next race. I was badly in the wrong because you must not take short cuts with other people's health, particularly when there is a possible head injury. I knew that Peter was not right, so persuaded Maz to smuggle him out of the weighing-room and drive him home but halfway there his condition deteriorated, so she sensibly diverted to hospital in Oxford. He was back in action four days later and, luckily, suffered no ill-effects.

The valets who look after all my jockeys know they have my full support to prevent them going out to ride if they are not a hundred per cent after a fall. You must not take any chances after a bang on the head. I was never completely knocked out in a race fall, but rode at least twice with concussion, not even knowing the distance of the race. Happily, today it is much harder for jockeys to hoodwink racecourse doctors.

On another occasion I filled Peter up with some highly effective French painkillers the day after he hurt his shoulder in a bad fall at Doncaster in which the horse was killed. He dislocated the shoulder in another heavy fall that afternoon at Cheltenham, yet such was the power of the painkiller that he did not feel a thing when it was put back in the ambulance room.

Maz used to do a fair bit of driving in those days, and once took Peter and me up to London for a racing dinner. On the way we stopped to pick up Ben Brooks, who had just enjoyed a day's pheasant shooting. Shortly after we set off again, Maz felt something warm and furry moving around near her feet. At first she imagined it was an old slipper or rug, but when we reached Park Lane she discovered that it was an extremely healthy rabbit, which had been put in the car by one of Ben's pals. A transfer was quickly arranged in Hyde Park.

Peter rode forty-seven of our sixty-four winners in 1982–83, but we drew a blank again at the Festival where Broadsword and Goldspun added to our ever-growing list of placed horses at the meeting. Connaught River, previously trained by Michael Stoute at Newmarket, briefly offered promise of developing into a serious candidate for the Daily Express Triumph Hurdle, with a rapid hat-trick, but soon proved to be as tricky a monkey as I have ever trained. One day he refused to move on the gallops until I brought our Daihatsu truck up behind his tail and pushed him along. It developed into a battle of wills between us, with me nudging him along at three to four miles an hour until he accepted that he could not win that particular argument. Michael assured me that Connaught River was a decent horse if I could find the key to him.

There is usually a reason that a horse is ungenuine, perhaps something is hurting, but I never did understand why he behaved so badly. I try to keep the dodgy ones sweet, to humour them, to keep them bright mentally and to bring them to peak fitness without putting them under too much pressure. In the old days I used to send some of my difficult horses hunting; now they are more likely to go off for a hack on their own.

Despite winning three hurdle races in a row as a novice Connaught River was always kinky. The next time he appeared, as an odds-on favourite at Leicester, he ran out with Steve Smith

Eccles after jumping one hurdle. Five days later he tried a similar trick at Sandown and did a U-turn on the top bend with the result that P. Scudamore was deposited on the ground. The cause seemed pretty hopeless but I enjoyed the challenge of training Connaught River and he ended his first season running a highly creditable second to Very Promising at Liverpool. The next autumn he won twice at Newbury before reverting to his old tricks by refusing to race at Worcester.

I hoped fences might be the making of him. Instead he nearly finished me off during a schooling session on a foggy morning. While I replaced the wing of the schooling fence, I sent him down the gallops the wrong way, because he would not consent to take the normal route. I was still adjusting the wing, from the inside, when I sensed two horses taking off behind me. I stood still, more out of fright than anything, and luckily they kept straight or that would have been the end of me. Later, Peter Scudamore somehow persuaded Connaught River to snatch a dead heat in a valuable novice chase at Cheltenham.

In the years that Peter rode for me I always used to school the horses on Sunday mornings. Teaching horses to jump properly is one of the joys of training when it goes well; I believe in starting them off over very small, solid obstacles and giving them lots of practice. On one memorable Sunday Peter and Steve Smith Eccles schooled fifty horses without a single fall or, indeed, serious error. Steve still talks about it. It was quite fabulous to watch. When Steve started schooling for me he rode like a typical Newmarket jockey by taking Palatinate over some tree trunks flat out, like a sprinter. I gave him a right bollocking and after that we were the best of friends. It would have been a challenge to take him on as a youngster.

Brough Scott brought out a book on world racing at this time in which he offered a case of champagne to the first racehorse trainer to exercise his string of horses bareback at a canter. This was just the sort of challenge I relish. I arranged for my friend Bernard Parkin to drive over the next morning to photograph around twenty of the Nicholson team cantering steadily five furlongs up the all-weather without so much as a saddle between them. All the lads had to sit on was a light blanket. We did hand pick the horses and I am delighted to report that they all arrived intact with their riders at the top of the gallop. The bubbly was well earned.

19

On the brink of bankruptcy

In 1984 a financial crisis that had been deepening at Condicote for several years took us to the very brink of bankruptcy. I would not be training today but for the generous support of a group of friends and owners who clubbed together to bail me out at a time when the tax authorities were about to close the business down.

It is fair to say that money is not my motivation; never has been. That is probably the reason I ended up in such a mess in the mid-'eighties. As a jump jockey I learned to enjoy life. We lived hard and played hard without any thought of tomorrow, but these days, more than ever before, a trainer needs to be a businessman, too, and not many of us have had the opportunity to learn business studies.

My experience suggests that hard-faced, short-sighted, bottom-line accountants do not tend to become racehorse trainers. Anyway I did not have the brains or the inclination to stay at school. Racing, not classwork, dominated my life from the day I first rode in a race at Newmarket at the age of twelve.

In all those years at Condicote I did not think of important matters like balancing the books. We started off in 1968 charging £12 a week, plus blacksmith's fees, vet's bills and the cost of transport. When that did not cover our costs, we began charging gallop fees. Even so, we were always behind, losing money each year.

I doubt if I have ever made any money training racehorses; nor have I ever expected to. Some trainers bet to make ends meet but luckily that did not appeal to me, otherwise we would have been in even deeper trouble. As our training operation expanded Dinah and I continued to pour every penny we possessed into improving the facilities at Condicote. If we had any money we spent it on the place. At one point we bought two cottages, plus twenty-five acres which we used for a new gallop. Money was always pretty tight. I remember paying one term's fees for the boys, at Dean Close, in beef.

Not many people realise the expenses of training horses for a living. It is certainly not the path to fortune and fame. If you set out to do things properly, the costs can be prohibitive, and I suspect owners simply do not appreciate the costs we carry. For a start you require an endless supply of tack, saddles, bridles, sheets, rugs, rollers, head collars, martingales, boots, girths, surcingles and so on. I do not believe in owners sending their own favourite rugs and head collars with their horses when they arrive in training, as they tend to be lost or damaged, so they go back in the lorry. Then there are pitchforks, brooms, barrows and various bits of grooming kit. We have always tried to do things properly and not cut corners.

Horses have to be fed, exercised and groomed each day regardless of whether their owners have paid their bills on time. We pay the same wages as flat trainers but the prize money allocation is slanted in favour of the flat, which cannot be right. What's more, jumpers tend to eat more food because they are bigger and older than the horses that run on the flat.

Looking back, I realise that money was always a problem. By the early 'eighties I could no longer disguise the truth that our finances were in desperate trouble. We were going round and round in ever-decreasing circles trying to honour our debts. Some we were able to pay as best we could; other accounts just dropped further and further behind.

We could not have survived without the goodwill of tradespeople, who put their trust in us and continued to supply us with essentials like hay, straw, food and tack despite the depth of our problems. They knew that if I said I would pay someone, then I would do so, however long it took.

Everything was mounting up, with our outstanding tax bills worst of all. The figure we owed in tax, and in particular VAT, came to a frightening amount of money. In hindsight, we should not have let ourselves fall into that position, but when you are concentrating on trying to train winners it is all too easy to put aside vital paperwork. Obviously I brought on my problems through my own inefficiency in not charging realistic training fees from the start.

I suppose I had wrong advice from my accountants, who should have been able to spot the warning signs in time to arrest our decline. But in the end there is only one person to blame for my financial problems and that is me. I made the mistake of burying my head in the sand. Bookwork is not one of my greatest gifts. Frankly, I hate it.

Like most trainers I ran the business on an overdraft. For a long time my bank gave me *carte blanche* if I needed more money, but then it became more difficult to borrow. Basically, I did not have particularly good advice from my bank manager. I clung to the belief that Condicote was worth a fair bit of money, but it was getting to the point where our debts equalled the value of the house, stables and land. To get away from these ever-mounting problems I retreated into my shell and began drinking much too much.

Relations with the bank reached an all-time low when they refused to meet a cheque for the lads' wages one Friday in 1984. Peter Scudamore generously came to the rescue by paying all the lads that time. Soon afterwards I changed banks, but that did not prove to be our salvation. I always hoped that we would get out of trouble, but we ended up deeper in debt than ever, with the new bank bouncing my cheques.

It was a horrible period, because I hate owing anyone. Some people can borrow money and not worry one bit about paying it back. Not I. I was really upset by the knowledge that I was letting others down. All my owners knew about the problem and I sensed that stories were flying around the racecourse.

I was away racing the day that the bailiffs arrived unannounced at Condicote, but Dinah proved more than equal to the threat they posed. Showing an instinct born of survival, she swiftly locked the door and sent them on their way. The VAT authorities were closing down quite a few businesses in the area at the time and I came to dread their knock on the door.

We were all but bankrupt in the autumn of 1984 when I turned to one of my owners, Raymond Mould, a shrewd businessman who had quickly become a trusted friend. I explained to him that we were on the brink of going under, outlined the extent of our debts and admitted that without help we were certain to go pop.

Luckily I asked the right person for advice. Raymond quickly set about trying to salvage the training operation at Condicote. He contacted Michael Ennever, a close friend of his in the City, and Roger Cort, a banker who promised immediate help and suggested that we recruit two more allies who could help out under the Business Expansion Scheme. I then brought in Ben Brooks, one of my most loyal owners, who farmed near Woodstock, and yet another owner Henry Shouler, also an astute businessman.

By this time I owed everybody, so Raymond's first task was to put a few people's minds at rest by settling the most crucial debts. Then he and Michael Ennever concentrated on setting up a company to run Condicote under the aegis of the BES. As I understand it, this scheme offered attractive tax concessions for investors in the higher tax brackets who kept their money in for a minimum of five years.

Once we had the backing of enough people as shareholders I began to believe that we would survive, that the nightmare was over, though we had some difficult years to come. I was so relieved to be rescued that I left all the details to them; they told me what they wanted, and I was in no position to argue.

Dinah and I were touched by their concern for our well-being from the very start. They felt that we should receive a proper wage and insisted that our house at Condicote did not come into the deal. That way, they explained, Dinah and I would at least have a roof over our heads if the business subsequently foundered. Dinah worked tirelessly to keep things afloat by helping in any way she could, including doing all the rug repairs and other menial tasks.

David Nicholson Racing Ltd was formed in November, 1984, with initial capital of £205,000. I was appointed managing director and we asked Ben Brooks to be chairman. If I was going to lose the reins, I knew that he would be a solid supporter. Dinah was elected to the board with Roger Cort, Michael Ennever, Raymond Mould and Henry Shouler, while Raymond's personal assistant Carey Brett-Holt was invariably on hand to take minutes and act as company secretary.

In addition to those already mentioned, the list of supporters who rallied to the cause in our darkest hour and became the original shareholders included David Cripps, Mike Deeley, James Donald, Captain Johnny Macdonald-Buchanan,

Richard Gardiner, Brian Gregory, Brigadier Roscoe Harvey, Ann McEwen, Rodney Maryan Green, Colin Smith, Ian Stungo and Sam Vestey. Anthony Armitage also joined the board later as a replacement for Michael Ennever. We owe them all a huge debt of gratitude.

I made the point of going to see each one in turn and explaining the sorry state of affairs. I could not have continued without their instant help. Had they been unable to bail me out, it was the end of D. Nicholson as a person and a racehorse trainer. They were all marvellous and I just hope that they feel we have repaid their faith in the ensuing years.

We were fortunate to have Henry Shouler as financial controller, though I did not always appreciate it at the time. Henry was such a tough negotiator that Ben dubbed him the Chancellor of the Exchequer. He produced financial forecasts, which he expected me to keep, and used to go through the books with me once a month. Every cheque required both our signatures.

How I wish someone like Henry had been around to supervise my accounts when I started training. He played a major part in safeguarding our future. His success at turning things round at Condicote led to his setting up on his own as a troubleshooter and company doctor helping businesses with financial problems.

The full extent of the debt at Condicote did not emerge until 1986. When the figure was assessed at £248,000, shareholders in the board resolved that the capital be increased, but Dinah and I did not put any money in for the good reason that we did not have any. At the same time the assets of Condicote were valued at £350,000.

Ben Brooks discovered that we had been wasting money in some areas. In short, I had spent far too liberally without any thought for cashflow or profit and loss. Although most of the horses at the time were bedded on straw, some were on paper. Ben found that the paper we used cost £11 per week more than straw for each horse.

I was also taken to task for spending £28,000 in one year on feed supplements sold by my brother-in-law James Pugh. I rather hoped that these would prove to be the vital mixture to make the horses go faster. You always dream of something like that, but of course it never happens. I was on the look-out for a new idea and it was a good additive, but much too expensive. The board quite rightly pointed out that we could not go on spending that sort of money.

Although Ben remains a good friend to this day, he was quite capable of cracking the whip at the quarterly board meetings held at Condicote. The meetings invariably ended up better than I expected, though there were hard words at times, particularly when I was asked to explain some of my spending. It had to be that way and was a small price to pay for staying in business.

Even as late as 1989 the company recorded a loss of £12,000 and a year later, at our annual general meeting, Ben reported an unsatisfactory financial position. He put his foot down and said that after five years he was not prepared to go on writing letters to shareholders telling them that things were about to improve. We then sold off a cottage in the village.

There was also a drama in 1989 when the company found itself facing court action for desecrating an ancient monument close to the stables. We were accused, absurdly in my view, of disturbing the henge by putting up some fencing stakes. The case collapsed as soon as our counsel discovered that the monument in question was not listed.

By 1991 the company reported a small profit of £6,800, which rose appreciably to £50,000 in 1992. That year, when we moved to Jackdaws Castle, the company sold the Old School House, which had been used as the lads' hostel, for £120,000 and most of the gallops for a further £50,000. By 1994 investors in David Nicholson Racing Ltd had been paid about half what they put in, with the promise of a further major dividend now that planning permission has been granted for three barn conversions and two new houses to be built on the site of the old yard.

20

Ending the Festival hoodoo

The early 'eighties were prolific years for David Nicholson. In four seasons between 1980 and 1984 he trained 228 winners. By the autumn of 1984, every box in the yard was full with the promise of others waiting to take their place.

Then, without warning, Nicholson's fortunes nosedived. The stable was becalmed in midwinter when the nightmare of a virus, which haunts every trainer, became a reality at Condicote. It proved to be the start of two ghastly seasons, which, allied with dire financial problems, took the Nicholsons perilously close to having to give up training.

The virus, in a variety of forms, is the scourge of modern racing. Cynics will suggest unkindly that it covers a multitude of excuses for stables whose horses are badly out of form. Trainers who have seen months, sometimes years of hard work wiped out by the ravages of the virus, tell a different, bleaker story. Many have been driven out of business. Others, like David Nicholson, have been left doubting their own sanity.

The 1984–85 season started well enough with the success of Ben Ewen, but November, usually one of our most productive months, yielded only two victories and a mounting catalogue of disappointments. When we added only three further successes in December, we knew beyond any doubt that something was seriously wrong.

At first, of course, we shut our eyes to it and hoped it would go away. I could not accept that it was happening, partly because the horses looked well, but the warning signs were there from quite an early stage of the season. Time and again, Peter Scudamore would come back after a race and say the horses were not right. At first I thought he was talking nonsense because there was no outward sign of the enemy, but subsequent events confirmed his suspicions.

Our own investigations suggested that the problem began the day that I ran three horses, Gambir, Voice of Progress and Burnt Oak at Newbury's three-day mixed meeting in October. The previous day had been devoted to flat racing. We discovered that our horses had used the same boxes on the course that, on the first day, had housed horses from a major flat yard which was riddled with a virus at the time.

There is no doubt in my mind that my three horses picked up the virus from those boxes and brought it back with them to Condicote. Gambir and Voice of Progress both ran well that day but neither of them was as good again. Next time I felt that Voice of Progress had run up to his form in finishing third in the Mackeson Gold Cup, yet Peter insisted that he had not sparkled at all.

Although my horses continued to run poorly, we could not see any outward symptoms of a virus. The fact that they continued to look well merely confused us further. They did not burst blood vessels or have runny noses, but after running well for two thirds of a race they would find nothing in the closing stages.

With only eight winners by Christmas I decided to summon help from the Equine Research Station at Newmarket. They sent down a specialist who took endless tests, swabs and samples, took them away for analysis and eventually announced that nearly all the horses were suffering from an infection on their lungs. A virus, it seems, was causing mucus to cling to the walls of the lungs. We were advised to try to limit the amount of dust in each box and to keep checking to see if the horses' lungs were clean. We have been doing it ever since, because once you have had a virus, it is always there. You learn to live with it.

At least we now knew the cause of our disastrous season, but finding a cure seemed to be beyond the vets. We tried cleaning the horses' lungs out with a liquid wash, and then drawing that off with a vacuum, but that was not the answer. I have to say that our vets were also at a loss during this crisis. This first experience of the virus knocked us for six. The difficulty was knowing how to handle it. We just had to keep battling, and drew some slim comfort from the knowledge that we were not alone, since every trainer has these problems at some time.

I learned the hard way that if you run horses when they are wrong, you can do untold damage. So, in desperation, I shut up shop for three weeks from New Year's Day. The horses were given just half an hour's walking exercise each day to stretch their legs and keep them sane. The sorry truth is that Charter Party's welcome success at Newbury on February 8 was our sole victory in the first two months of 1985.

A virus can stretch loyalties to the limit. Everyone in turn was getting the blame for our lack of success. Owners become unsettled, jockeys uptight at lost opportunites and lads dispirited at losing bonuses and missing the chance of going racing. I can tell you it does not do much for the health of trainers, either.

Very Promising offered a beacon of light in those desperate days, despite the fact that he came to me in circumstances that strained my relationship with Mercy Rimell to the limit. Our families go back such a long way, I can remember going to their children's parties, and I rode quite a lot of winners for her late husband Fred. The trouble had started in January, 1984 when John Maunders, who was a heavy and fearless punter, had moved one of his horses, Eastern Line, to me from Mercy's yard.

Eastern Line then finished with such eye-catching promise in fifth place in the Schweppes Gold Trophy that John decided to go for an old-fashioned touch on him next time at Haydock, early in March. By the time the horses were circling at the start John had turned a ghastly shade of green. When Dinah asked if he was all right he explained that he had just put £15,000 on his horse.

'What's more, if he does not win I am likely to jump off this grandstand,' he confided. Luckily for everyone involved Eastern Line won easily that day at an unrewarding starting price of Evens.

John Maunders then bought Very Promising in a private deal from his friend Bob Mann after the horse finished third in the 1984 Champion Hurdle. The two men came to my chalet on the final day of the Festival and announced, over a drink, that Very Promising would be moving from Mercy Rimell to me. As far as I was aware, no one had told Mercy of their plan, so I suggested Bob Mann should do so at once.

It would be something of an understatement to say that she was hopping mad. There were serious ructions by the end of racing that day. I felt things were brewing up to an out-and-out brawl, but Malcolm Wallace managed to calm things down.

The matter was not very well handled and proved to be embarrassing for everyone. I rang Mercy that evening as soon as I reached home, but was forced to hold the telephone at arm's length. Did I hear some choice language! I got all the blame and the flak, but I was not the cause of the break-up.

Frankly, Mercy was entitled to be upset, especially after the fine race the horse had run in the Champion Hurdle. Anyone would be furious to lose a top-class horse in those circumstances. I tried to explain the situation to her, but to no avail. The next morning I sent my box to collect Very Promising, who then finished second to Dawn Run on his first outing for me in the Sandeman Aintree Hurdle a fortnight later.

It was a long time before Mercy and I spoke again, but I am delighted to say that the rift was eventually healed, and she came to the opening day at Jackdaws Castle in October, 1992. Mercy is now a most enthusiastic member of the Million in Mind syndicate, who enjoyed outstanding success with Mysilv. I imagine it is nice for her, as an ex-trainer, to retain an interest in racing, and I make a point of keeping in touch, discussing running plans and asking what she would do.

Very Promising was placed on his first three runs over hurdles for me in 1984–5, but was finding it hard to win against the best. Although he was not a very big horse, he gave a hundred per cent every time and schooled with sufficient promise for me to try him over fences. He won impressively on his debut at Haydock in December, fell next time and then won well at Newbury, before running another fine race in finishing a close third to Boreen Prince and Buck House in the Arkle Chase.

Considering how ill our horses had been all season they performed with great credit at the 1985 Festival. Goldspun was fourth in the stayers' hurdle, Against the Grain, a 40–1 shot, was beaten only by a length into second place in the Daily Express Triumph Hurdle, and the enigmatic Connaught River ended the meeting with a late run into second place in the Cathcart Chase. Charter Party fell in the Kim Muir when going well but made up for that lapse with a hard-earned victory at Newbury eleven days later.

That summer we painstakingly steam cleaned and painted every box at Condicote in the hope that we could remove all trace of the virus. Everything possible was done to eliminate the chance of any infection lingering in the yard while the horses were turned out. We also added further paddocks and resolved to monitor the health of the horses even more closely in the future.

Early results in the autumn briefly offered some evidence that we had been successful in removing the menace of the wretched virus. How we all wanted to believe it. November was a fruitful month but soon it became clear that many of our horses were still not right. The twenty-two winners I trained in 1985–6 produced only a slight improvement on the wreckage of the previous season, but this time, at least, we managed to pick up a number of major prizes along the way.

Very Promising started the new season in rampant form at Chepstow early in November, 1985, on a day when he, Tickite Boo, French Union and Cottage Run gave me my first four-timer as a trainer. A fortnight later he beat Buck House comprehensively in the H & T Walker Goddess Chase. It was a terrific race, one of those that remain in your mind for the rest of your life. Peter Scudamore concentrated so hard on the job in hand that he did not speak from the time we left Condicote until we pulled into the car park at Ascot. Horse and rider returned to the course in January to take the Embassy Premier Chase Final with a typically gritty display by a short head from Mr Moonraker.

Unfortunately there was not a suitable two and a half mile championship at Cheltenham for Very Promising, because at that distance he was a superstar. He was not quite quick enough against the best over two miles, and did not stay three miles, but he had bags of class and always ran his heart out for you. A trainer cannot ask more than that.

Even so, I had high hopes that Very Promising could win the Queen Mother Champion Chase at the 1986 Festival, but by then it was clear that John Maunders' days as his owner were numbered. John was one of those maddening owners who have a habit of ringing up late at night, sometimes as late as eleven in the evening. Now this might suit some people but it is hardly fair on a trainer who is up at six each morning. You cannot be available all the time.

Early in March John warned me that, because of a tax problem, he needed to sell Very Promising quickly, but made it clear that he wanted the horse to stay at Condicote. One deal to sell him fell through three days before Cheltenham and it was Peter Scudamore who persuaded a friend of his, Paul Green, to buy Very Promising on the eve of the race and leave him with me. The horse rewarded his faith with another fine effort in finishing second to Buck House the next day. As usual Very Promising was running on stoutly at the end of the two miles.

By now my long-held ambition to train a winner at the Cheltenham Festival was close to becoming an obsession. Each year I tried to train with the Festival as the focal point of my programme, but it just did not seem to work. I had no end of placed horses at the meeting; most of my horses ran well there, without being quite good enough, and I did not know what more I had to do to make the winner's enclosure. Another third prize for Against the Grain on the opening day followed by the narrow defeat of Very Promising on the second day merely increased the anguish. It was getting to me after all those barren years, just as it was to my great friend Josh Gifford, who started training in 1970 and was in the same boat.

Solar Cloud was the most unlikely horse to end the drought. I had bought him in Ireland at three as a fun horse for a partnership of four involving Ben Brooks, Henry Shouler, Mike Deeley and Ann McEwen. Inez Norris of the Curragh Bloodstock Agency took us to see the horse, who was trained by Con Collins. We did the deal in September, 1985, just as Solar Cloud was about to be sold to America. He was still a maiden on the flat because he did not try very hard. Although he won for us at Worcester and Kempton over hurdles he used to run about in his races when he hit the front, and undoubtedly kept a bit for himself.

He was, in short, a rascal, would hang badly either way and try anything to avoid having to win. I do not normally like putting blinkers on my horses, but I felt it was worth a try for the big occasion in the Daily Express Triumph Hurdle at Cheltenham. We thought that with luck he might run into a place but with my record at the meeting, and in particular in this race, we could hardly be confident and his starting price of 40–1 was probably a fair reflection of his chance.

By this time I was prepared to try anything to change my luck, so on the third day of the Festival I pulled on a pair of bright red socks given to me that week by Coral and Gavin

Pritchard-Gordon, who were as usual our house guests for the meeting. The events of Thursday, March 13 ensured that I would be wearing red socks every day at the races in the future.

During the build-up to Cheltenham, Peter Scudamore did his level best to switch from Solar Cloud to more fancied runners including Tangognat, a horse he had already ridden to victory twice, and That's Your Lot, a leading contender for John Francome in his first season as a trainer. I did let him off, on occasions, if I felt he had a better chance elsewhere, but this time insisted that he stayed with Solar Cloud. I also gave him strict instructions to challenge as late as possible, so you can imagine what I was thinking when he struck the front a mile from home at the top of the hill.

Scu's stroke of inspiration proved decisive. Quite simply he stole the race. He explained later that the horse was travelling so sweetly that it would have been madness to disappoint him. So he let him run and still had a useful lead at the final flight of hurdles, but all the way up the hill he was waiting for the sound of the others coming to join him.

Standing in my usual position on the members' lawn I watched Solar Cloud jump the last hurdle fully six lengths clear. Beside me Oliver Sherwood cried, 'Yours has won,' but after my previous experience in this race with Broadsword I was not taking anything for granted. Sure enough I spotted a grey, the same colour as Baron Blakeney, coming fast out of the pack. Solar Cloud seemed to take an eternity to cover the last one hundred yards and was all out at the finish to hold on by three quarters of a length from the grey, Brunico. This time, however, I *knew* we had won.

I think that victory was an enormous relief for both Peter and me and it was nice to do it together. We were both over the moon. My lack of success at the Festival down the years had been getting to me and I know Peter was frantic about it too. Solar Cloud's victory proved to be a big turning point in our careers and was also an illustration of what can happen if a jockey and trainer have complete faith in each other. Peter had ridden totally against my orders and won because of it.

Much of the trouble with the English soccer and cricket teams is that they are too stereotyped. Everything they attempt is so predictable; the natural genius has been coached out of them so vigorously that there is no longer room for the players who offer individual flair. When you find someone like Scu with a God-given talent, you must give him a free rein to express himself, up to a point. You will never see a better example of that than his forceful winning ride on Solar Cloud.

Fate is a curious bedfellow. For seventeen long years I had been desperate to win a race at the Festival. At times it seemed as if I had been banging my head against a brick wall. Then suddenly, unexpectedly, Solar Cloud nudged the door open, and less than two hours later Peter and I completed an unforgettable double with the stirring success of Charter Party in the Ritz Club National Hunt Chase.

After the race Princess Anne, who was created the Princess Royal the following June, asked where we would be celebrating that night. When I replied that the party would be at home at Condicote, she volunteered to bring the puddings, but when she returned to Gatcombe Park she discovered that her cook was out for the evening. Undeterred, the Princess set to and made two puddings herself. We had ten to dinner that evening, including Anthony Stroud, who arrived very late and well over the limit, but sobered up remarkably quickly when he saw the Princess at the end of the table.

After Cheltenham the owners of Solar Cloud received a big offer for the horse from Italy. See You Then was bought by an Italian owner at the same time and I advised the four partners to sell Solar Cloud, too, but they preferred to keep him in the hope that he might make up into a Champion Hurdle horse. Unfortunately for them, his already suspect temperament prevented him reproducing the Triumph form, and although they had plenty of fun, he was eventually sold for considerably less.

On the Sunday after the 1986 Cheltenham Festival we drove down to Lambourn for a drink with Fred and Di Winter before going on to lunch with the Sherwoods. Racing, as usual, was the main point of discussion. At one point Fred explained how much he missed John Francome since his retirement eleven months earlier, and asked who I considered to be the best jockey around. Naturally I put forward the strongest possible case for Peter Scudamore but on the way home Dinah pointed out that it might not have been the wisest answer.

During Liverpool week I felt that Peter was not riding at his best and I told him so. I could sense that there was something on his mind, that things were not quite right between us. I had a fair idea what the trouble was, but he would not tell me.

On the night after the Grand National the four of us ended up having dinner as usual in the Horse and Groom at Bourton-on-the-Hill. When I asked Maz if Scu would be riding for me the next season she replied, 'Why?' I then explained my fears that something was in the wind.

The following Tuesday Peter did not ride out for me in the morning and, significantly, was not at the local Heythrop point-to-point, a meeting he liked to attend whenever possible. The next day he came in a little earlier than usual, asked if he could have a word in my office and then told me that he would be riding for Fred Winter in the future.

I was livid. I thought of all the things I had done for Peter and now he had stabbed me in the back. Although it had been in the offing for ten days, I found it hard to accept what he was saying, and swore to myself that he would never ride for me again. Somehow I did not say it out loud or I would have had to stick to it. Even so, once he had left I did not put him up for almost two years.

The truth is that I never thought he would leave. Because we had a very close relationship, we had helped each other along; we both worked hard and progressed because of it. He had achieved his ambition to be champion jockey while riding for me. I still feel that I made Peter champion jockey; and I suppose I believed he would stay with me throughout his career. In short, we were as close as a trainer and jockey can be.

Looking back now, I dread to think what I said to him. I blew a big fuse because I felt completely let down. Peter's parents Mary and Michael were upset, too; when he left me. It would have been a lot easier for everyone if he had come to me and said what was happening, or that he was going to see Fred Winter. I was also upset that the Winters had not had the decency to discuss the situation with me.

I am fiercely loyal to my staff, and expect the same in return, but nothing lasts for ever and as it turned out I could not have kept Peter much longer anyway. No jockey could have resisted Martin Pipe, who was about to change the face of jump racing.

It did not take me very long to decide on the man I wanted

as Peter's replacement. Richard Dunwoody, who was employed chiefly by Tim Forster, had also spent that season helping me out as understudy to Peter. The previous weekend Richard had displayed a maturity beyond his years in delaying his winning challenge on West Tip in the Grand National until halfway up the run-in.

I rang Tim without delay and asked him if I could approach his jockey as mine had gone. Tim could not have been nicer about it, so I was able to speak to Richard later that day at Ascot. He would not be rushed into a decision but eventually accepted my offer.

Since Peter and Maz lived only one hundred yards away, and still worked for me in the weeks that followed, the atmosphere was strained at times. I felt betrayed, principally because things had not been done in the right way; for a brief spell I was very hurt, and everyone knew it, too; but time heals. Today things between us are two hundred per cent.

Peter continued to ride for me until the end of the season under the terms of his contract. After winning the Golden Miller Chase at Cheltenham on Charter Party in April he came back, eyes glowing with delight, and said, 'I will win the Gold Cup on this horse next year.'

I replied stonily, 'There is no chance of that, because you will not be riding him.'

Once the season ended I sent Solar Cloud to run in the French four-year-old Champion Hurdle and made a point of booking Richard Dunwoody to ride him. The Scudamore years at Condicote were at an end.

On the day he retired from race riding in a blaze of publicity at Ascot on April 7, 1993, Peter had accumulated the quite extraordinary total of 1,678 winners in Britain. It is a unique record that bears testimony to his unrelenting, single-minded appetite for success.

For Peter it was a question of endurance. The only man in my day to reach one thousand winners was Stan Mellor. At the time we all thought his total of 1,035 would never be beaten. Wherever he turned, Peter set new horizons. He was champion jockey a record eight times and a complete professional.

21

By Royal Appointment

Horse racing and riding have long played an important part in the lives of the Royal Family. You have to go back to 1671 to find the first record of a monarch riding a winner. It happened on October 12 at Newmarket where King Charles II was triumphant in the Plate. The other competitors were the Duke of Monmouth, Mr Elliot of the Royal Bedchamber and Mr Thomas Thynne, an ancestor of the Marquis of Bath.

In March, 1674, the King again won the Plate. Sir Robert Carr, writing to his colleagues in Whitehall, reported, 'Yesterday His Majesty rode himself three heates and a course, and won the Plate-all fower were hard and ne'er ridden, and I doe assure you the King wonn by good horsemanshipp.'

Rather more recently King Edward VIII rode winners over fences and in a number of point-to-points in his days as the Prince of Wales. His first success came on Rifle Brigade at Great Brington on March 16, 1921. Later he twice won the Welsh Guards Challenge Cup, a steeplechase at Hawthorn Hill, on Pet Dog and his own horse Little Favourite.

Publicity about the frequency of falls he sustained while racing led to questions in Parliament on the wisdom of the Heir to the Throne taking such risks. Courtiers, too, concerned at the number of times he was injured, pressed him to end his days as an amateur jockey. Eventually, on advice from the Prime Minister, the Prince abandoned both hunting and race riding.

The doughty attempts by the Prince of Wales as a steeplechase jockey in the early 'eighties created immense interest. Royal-watchers who had previously restricted their racing to Royal Ascot found themselves despatched to distant country *meetings at Newton Abbot and Ludlow to witness the Prince riding over jumps.*

No one doubted the courage of the Prince, who still rides regularly to hounds. Finding him a suitable horse for the task proved rather more difficult. The closest he came to success from a handful of rides was a second on Allibar in a handicap chase at Ludlow in October, 1980.

Five years later his sister the Princess Royal, already a consummate horsewoman, became the latest member of the family to be a jockey. Inevitably, she turned to David Nicholson for advice.

We were very proud when the Princess Royal began riding out at Condicote in March, 1985 as part of her preparations to ride in a charity race at Epsom. I had offered to help out when she told me of her plans at a dinner party at Gatcombe Park. At first it was a question of concentrating on helping her to become fully fit and adjust her style from eventing to racing.

The Princess is an outstanding horsewoman with a superb record for her country in three-day events; she competed in the Montreal Olympics and took the individual European Championship with a virtuoso performance on Doublet at Burghley in 1971. But race riding, as I have explained earlier, requires a different type of discipline and fitness. One day I suggested she pulled up her leathers shorter than usual before a long, steady canter.

When she pulled up at the end I asked, 'Does that hurt?'

She replied, 'Yes,' so I instructed her to go round again.

The Princess rode out two lots on every day her crowded diary allowed and was always at the yard by 6.50 in the morning even though Gatcombe is a good forty-minute drive by car. We were always wary of marauding photographers at Condicote; these days they have no chance of trespassing at Jackdaws Castle without being spotted.

My next task was to find a suitable horse for her to ride in the Farriers' Invitation Private Sweepstakes over a mile and a half at Epsom on April 23. Against the Grain, a four-year-old colt who was always beautifully mannered, seemed the ideal choice and his owners eventually agreed to my request. We arranged to go to Epsom the day before the race to walk the course with Geoff Lewis, who had won the Derby on Mill Reef. Poor Geoff found

A day's hunting with Peter Jones (left, now my postman on Limonali) and Johnny Lehane. David Nicholson on Blessington Esquire.

My parents and sister Josie on the day of father's retirement, 10 October 1979, with Lord Willoughby de Broke and Captain Miles Gosling (right).

A winning team – Little Primrose and Dinah at Wembley.

With jump racing's finest patron at Sandown.

Philip Nicholson shows his style on Jacko at the Chair at Aintree.

We join the Royal Procession at Ascot in 1987.

Four stages in the development of Jackdaws Castle.

Work was completed in ten months.

Waterloo Boy takes the 1989 Arkle Chase . . .

Charter Party wins the 1988 Cheltenham Gold Cup.

. . . and returns in triumph at Cheltenham again in 1994. We all miss him after his untimely death in August 1995.

Barton Bank holds off Bradbury Star in the 1993 King George VI Chase.

A superb leap at the last fence ensures victory for Viking Flagship (right), in the 1994 Champion Chase.

Three of the best. Kadi (left), Viking Flagship and Putty Road after completing a treble on the same day at the 1995 Festival.

They shall not pass. Mysilv holds on for a famous success in the 1994 Daily Express Triumph Hurdle.

the searching pace set by the Princess Royal a bit too much for his little legs and had to cut the corners to keep up.

Everyone was delighted when Against the Grain and his new rider finished fourth in the Farriers' race. Before dinner at the Old Wool House in Northleach that evening the Princess indicated that she was unlikely to repeat the experience. Four hours later, after an enjoyable evening, she changed her mind and asked if she might continue to ride out at Condicote. It was just the request I wanted to hear, although her hectic annual schedule would inevitably restrict her opportunities to race.

The next step was to ride in another flat race, at Goodwood in the autumn on Little Sloop. There had been such a furore at Epsom that this time I was determined to play down the publicity. As the Goodwood race was for amateur riders, the Princess was required to take a medical before she was granted the necessary licence. I rang the authorities at Weatherbys and requested that they did not publish this fact in the *Racing Calendar*.

Instead Little Sloop's name appeared in the daily newspapers without a jockey in an attempt to confuse the media. But Peter O'Sullevan spotted us walking the course together shortly before racing in the pouring rain and the secret was out. Although Little Sloop finished out of the money, it was apparent that her rider was now bitten by the racing bug.

A fortnight later the Princess gained further valuable experience at Redcar on Lulav, who was down to be ridden by Mrs M. Phillips to put the paparazzi off the scent. There was no doubt that she was fully capable of riding a winner and I was determined to help her do just that. The Princess ended the season with an interesting experience at Chepstow on French Union, who did his best to emulate the well-known cigar advertisement by remaining in the stalls for some seconds when the rest of the runners jumped off.

The next year the Princess Royal finished a close second on one of mine, Snake River, at Warwick. My racing friends, aware that I was short of suitable ammunition for her on the flat, rallied willingly to the cause. Gavin Pritchard-Gordon was quick to offer the ride on Gulfland, a decent, reliable handicapper, in an amateurs' race at Redcar in August.

Positive started a red-hot favourite here but Gulfland, ridden with strength and purpose, caught him inside the final furlong and quickly drew clear for a famous victory. On the way home in the car I remember the triumphant jockey ringing the Queen, who was delighted at the good news, since she had been unaware that her daughter had been riding that day, let alone won. This success was no more than the Princess Royal deserved, because she is thoroughly professional at everything she does. Now, of course, she wanted to ride more winners.

In 1987 another good friend, Michael Stoute, booked her for Ten No Trumps in the televised Dresden Diamond Stakes at Ascot on King George Day. First, the Princess travelled in some secrecy to Newmarket where she rode the horse in a bit of work without a single gallops-watcher knowing she had been in the town.

A few days later she won decisively on Ten No Trumps at Ascot in front of the Queen and Prince Philip. Further successes came in subsequent years at Newmarket on Vayrua, trained by Barry Hills, and in the Queen Mother's Cup at York on Insular, who ran in the colours of his trainer Ian Balding.

There was also a memorable trip in October, 1988 to Nashville, Tennessee, where the Princess agreed to ride in an amateur flat race on the day of the Sport of Kings challenge. The party included Dinah and myself, plus Nicky and Diana Henderson. We flew out by Concorde at ten a.m. to JFK airport in New York, then took an executive jet down to Nashville, where the Princess won the first race on Wood Chisel at two p.m., local time, to the delight of the crowd. A Royal success was warmly received in America and quite a party developed that night.

The next day we flew up to visit Paul Mellon's stud and art gallery before going timber racing in the afternoon. We stayed with Jimmy Wafford that night and then all set out hunting at dawn the next morning. With the help of Concorde we were back at Heathrow by ten o'clock on Sunday night. The entire trip took barely sixty hours. This was the second year we had been on this trip. Each time we stayed at Franklyn with George and Jane Sloan. The previous year George took us all riding round his farm and, because I was only wearing a pair of jeans, I rubbed my legs raw. Luckily the Princess had some suitable medication that she duly administered.

A hectic diary for twelve months of the year prevented the Princess riding on the flat as much as she would have liked. In the circumstances she did extremely well to win six races, and she ended on a triumphant note on Croft Valley at Beverley in 1991.

I suppose it was inevitable that the Princess would turn her attention to steeplechasing. She started off riding old What A Buck at home, thoroughly enjoyed popping him over our schooling fences and could clearly see a stride. The next step was to find a suitable horse for her debut as a jump jockey. Josh Gifford came to the rescue with Cnoc Na Cuille, a safe conveyance, who arrived at Condicote on a month's trial.

Before the new partnership appeared in public, I arranged a private schooling session for them over six racecourse fences at Cheltenham one Sunday morning, accompanied by Richard Dunwoody. After that I had no qualms about allowing the Princess to ride Cnoc Na Cuille in a steeplechase for the first time at Kempton in February, 1987, where they duly completed the course in fourth place. Next, they finished in midfield in the Grand Military Gold Cup at Sandown, won by my son Philip on Burnt Oak.

Since Cnoc Na Cuille seemed to be suited by fast ground I brought him back into training earlier than usual for an autumn campaign in 1987. After finishing a close second on him at Worcester in August, the Princess gained her first victory as a steeplechase rider on Cnoc Na Cuille on the same course the next month in a tight finish with the odds-on favourite Tiger Ted, ridden by Brendan Powell. That was a very proud moment for everyone at Condicote and not many people were aware that the winning jockey had driven the horse to the course herself. We were all on a high that night.

Looking back now, it would have been fun to have had the chance to work with the Princess Royal when she was younger, because she possessed all the qualities to be a very decent amateur but for her duties disrupting her training. She was already in her mid-thirties when she began riding out at Condicote and I must confess I was always a bit uptight during her races, though steeplechasing is probably no more risky than tackling three-day event courses.

I did worry about her safety despite the fact that she was always very good over the obstacles. No one questioned her nerve and the professional jockeys who rode against her did their best to ensure that she enjoyed the experience. Unfortunately, her partnership with Cnoc Na Cuille ended tragically when the horse collapsed and died after they had finished third at Warwick in May, 1988.

The following season the Princess was placed three times on General Joy, a horse bought by the financial group Save and Prosper specifically for her to ride. But he, too, collapsed and died in a race at Chepstow, ridden by Richard Dunwoody. She also finished a creditable seventh on Bobby Kelly in the Midlands Grand National at Uttoxeter. Later, in 1992, Canon Class, leased from her by Bryan Jenks for his grandson Tom to ride, was our first winner trained at Jackdaws Castle.

When her diary allows, the Princess still rides out for us, mostly on the insistence of her daughter Zara, who shows every sign of following in the family's footsteps.

In 1987 someone rang up out of the blue to ask if Dinah and I would like to join the Queen for lunch during Royal Ascot. At first I thought it was a wind-up but a formal invitation duly arrived. We drove up to Windsor Castle in the morning, and were shown round the Mews and stud by the Princess before changing and joining the Royal party for lunch. Then it was time to travel down the course by carriage in the procession accompanied by the Princess Royal and the Duchess of York.

It was quite an experience to drive along the Golden Mile past the enclosures packed with people anxious to catch a glimpse of the Royal Family. Once on the course we were encouraged to spend the day in the Royal Box. At the end of racing our car was taken to the racecourse car park ready for the journey home.

On another occasion, when Dinah and I stayed the night at Windsor Castle as guests of the Princess, the Queen showed us to our apartment. We were also honoured to be invited to a memorable party given by the Queen and the Duke of Edinburgh at Buckingham Palace in December, 1990, to mark the decades of the Queen Mother, Princess Margaret, the Princess Royal and the Duke of York.

In addition we were guests at the wedding of Prince Andrew and Sarah Ferguson. In turn the Princess Royal attended our silver wedding party. She is always quick to put people at ease and our acquaintance has given us a lot of fun and opened a few doors. We were delighted when she was made a member of the Jockey Club.

Emlyn Hughes, who used to have a horse with me, is a fervent royalist. If you hear him speak at dinners and functions, you could be forgiven for believing he was the Queen's personal racing manager. During his spell as team captain on *A Question of Sport* he was asked to name a jockey, in racing silks and crash helmet, plastered in mud.

'I know him,' declared Emlyn with the utmost confidence. 'That is John Reid.' You can imagine his embarrassment when the jockey was identified as the Princess, who only a few weeks earlier had been one of the guests on his team.

Over the years I have tried to knock no end of soldiers into shape for military races, but the case of my son Philip showed a disturbing difference in attitude on the part of the authorities in the treatment of officers and troops. If Philip had been an officer, his CO would have given him up to three months to prepare thoroughly for a traditional race like the Grand Military Gold Cup. This happened with Malcolm Wallace, Algy Smith-Maxwell, Sandy Cramsie and others.

But because my son was a humble bombadier, he was not allowed to ride out at Condicote in the weeks leading up to the race. I had no help at all from his commanding officer. When I made my feelings known on the subject, in no uncertain manner, he just coughed and spluttered. I am unhappy about it to this day, because it seems so unfair that the boys who do so much behind the scenes have little chance of competing in these events. Philip was not in a position to argue. Just like a good soldier he had to obey orders.

During Philip's time in the King's Troop our good friend Malcolm Wallace invited Dinah and me to watch an official salute in Hyde Park. As we walked out of the mess three young soldiers gave us a full salute with eyes left. I doffed my hat, then out of politeness said, 'Carry on, please.' Malcolm was speechless.

Philip and John are keen on all sports, but by their late teens it was clear that they were going to be too heavy to be jockeys. None the less, I was delighted that they both had a little fling over fences. Philip became the first non-commissioned soldier to win the Grand Military Gold Cup, yet he sat on Burnt Oak only once before Sandown. Confined to his barracks in St John's Wood, all he could do was take out an old gun horse, pull up his leathers and chase it along through Wormwood Scrubs as fast as he could.

Burnt Oak was not an easy ride. On his day he was quite likely to take off on the way to the start, so I led him down most of the way at Sandown. With the Princess also in the race, and both the Queen and the Queen Mother present, the build-up was fairly tense. As Dinah legged up the Princess into the saddle the Queen remarked, 'I suppose the trainer has got to deal with the batty horse.'

I am revved up all the time watching my horses run, and soon discovered that when one's own son is going out there to ride it can be hell. I hope I was able to help a little bit, but Philip was more than up to the challenge. Despite his inexperience he rode a beautiful race, made all the running on Burnt Oak at a sensible pace and galloped on strongly to beat Maori Venture by ten lengths. It was one of the proudest days of my life. We were all in tears afterwards.

With the Princess also enjoying a fine ride on Cnoc Na Cuille at Sandown, we all had a high old time that evening at the Queen Mother's annual cocktail party at her home in Windsor Great Park. The form of Burnt Oak's victory was well and truly franked when Maori Venture won the Grand National three weeks later.

I was a nervous wreck in the final hours before Philip rode old Jacko in the Foxhunters' Chase over the National fences at Liverpool. He was mad keen to have a go over the big fences, but the nearer the race came the more we were all having second thoughts. As we picnicked in the car park on the day of the race, I looked at Dinah and said, 'You had better walk the course with Philip.' It was a suggestion she quickly declined.

My heart was sinking as I set off with him. We were just about speaking as we reached the first fence, but after that not a word was said for the rest of the way round. The fences seemed to be growing bigger by the minute and I felt seriously ill. By the time I reached the stands to watch the race I thought I was going to pass out through sheer terror. Waiting there, shaking with fear, I remember thinking, 'What have I done to my son?'

Since Jacko was a tiny little horse, and his jockey was fully six foot one, they were not, in all honesty, ideally matched, but happily my fears proved groundless. Jacko popped over the first two fences, flew the Chair and as they came past me I could see Philip sitting up there neatly, looking totally in control. They finished eighth, and to this day Philip thinks it is one of the greatest things he has ever done.

He did flirt with the idea of coming into racing when he left the Army after six years, but became a policeman instead. Philip and his wife Sarah have given us two grandchildren, Matthew, four, and Zoë, two, and no doubt if they show the inclination they will get all the necessary encouragement to follow the family tradition in racing.

John, who is younger by three years, had a few race rides too, and was also placed on old Jacko. He worked for Cheveley Park Stud for two years, then took a gin and tonic course at the Royal Agricultural College in Cirencester where he won a scholarship to Australia. He spent a year there with the leading trainer Colin Hayes, has his own home Nobby's Cottage in Condicote, manages Colin Smith's stud interests and married Natasha Kelly in September, 1995.

Hundreds of would-be jockeys passed through my hands at Condicote. Some, like Dan Jones, Nigel Coleman, and Gareth Charles-Jones, were just plain unlucky. Dan was a delightful boy, won a race for me, then had to return to the family farm in Shropshire and was paralysed in a Rugby accident.

Nigel Coleman's bright career ended in tragedy, too, in a race fall that left him partially paralysed. Nigel handed his notice in after his first ride on the flat, but I persuaded him to persevere and he won a number of decent races including the Daily Express Triumph Hurdle. Gareth was always cheerful through adversity, and became Stan Mellor's jockey before cancer ended his career.

I could not control some headstrong boys including Mark Pitman, David Bridgwater, Tom Jenks and Mark Rimell. Mark Pitman is now helping his mother Jenny train at Lambourn. David came to me from Susan Piggott, can certainly ride and is not frightened of hard work. He is going to be very good, but he always had his own ideas and used to take me on a bit too much. Eventually I could not stand it any longer, so I told him to find another job. I have never seen anyone ride a bucking broncho at our open day as well as him. No one else lasts more than ten seconds. He stayed in the saddle for two minutes.

I was very disappointed when Tom Jenks left to join Nigel Twiston-Davies despite enjoying a superb season with me. I had great plans to put Tom's name in lights, but he was determined to go, so I helped him on his way sooner than he expected. William Humphreys did quite well until he felt I was holding him back, and told me what to do with my job.

Others, like Peter Niven and Jamie Osborne, slipped through the net. Peter came to me as an overweight amateur. I confess I did not think he was good enough, or that he would manage to lose enough weight, so I did not give him one ride in the season he was with me. One of his less-known feats at Condicote was to mount the stairs of the hostel on his motorbike. Luckily I did not hear about it at the time.

Peter then worked like a Trojan to earn his chance with Mary Reveley and proved me wrong. Good luck to him. We laugh about it now. I thought I had done quite well as a jockey but he has now ridden more winners than me. I have often tried to book him in recent years, and was delighted when he did ride a winner for me at Wetherby on Boxing Day, 1994.

The best prospects often start in racing by helping out while they are still at school. That was the case with Jamie Osborne, who showed no end of promise in his brief spells with me as a teenager during his holidays. Now and then you see an absolute natural like Jamie at an obstacle. I had high hopes for him and was annoyed when he chose to start in the North with Jumbo Wilkinson, and then moved on to Nicky Henderson.

When an international race was held at Cheltenham late in 1992, I had the misfortune to play host to an Australian rider called Jamie Evans, who turned out to be a big-headed little so-and-so. He stayed near by, asked to ride out each morning and had plans to ride here that winter, but he did not last five minutes. The first morning he schooled here he nearly put Richard Dunwoody through the wing. He was, in my opinion, such a moderate jockey that I would not put him up in a race. Whatever you do in life, it always helps if you give a hundred per cent every time.

Quite a few of my old boys are successful trainers now including Nigel Twiston-Davies, my nephew James Fanshawe and Jim Wilson. Nigel joined me as a pupil after working for Fred Rimell, but lasted only one season, principally because he would not concentrate on sorting out his weight. He did ride a winner, at Sandown, but was solely interested in enjoying the good life. Nigel lived in the house with us, which was fine, because he did not seem to be there much of the time. I would not consider promoting him to assistant trainer, because in those days he took nothing seriously at all. How times change. He has been a revelation since he started on his own barely five miles from me at Naunton.

James Fanshawe began to ride out for us while he was still at Stowe school, where he was master of the beagles and a decent athlete. Once we hijacked him from class for the afternoon to boost our cross-country team in a stable lads' competition, and came close to a coup when he finished second.

Although James was a superb horseman, he did remarkably well in point-to-points when you consider that he was much too tall to be a jockey, extremely short-sighted and lived on cheese. He worked like a demon and had a lot of rides as an amateur, was determined to get on and seemed to live in the office during his time at Condicote until he knew the form book and every pedigree inside out.

Later we sent him to Newmarket for a summer to learn about flat racing with Michael Stoute. That was obviously a mistake. The next summer he left for Newmarket again and never returned. I remember remonstrating with Michael for pinching my staff without so much as a word of warning. If he had said something before, I would not have minded. James and I are still the best of friends. It is no surprise that he has done so well.

Coaching so many amateur jockeys through the years was a challenge, even if some of them did drive me to distraction. Malcolm Wallace, now a bigwig at the Jockey Club, was so keen he even lived with us on and off for a year. He was great fun to have about, with a fund of good stories and, I think, regrets that he did not start race riding much earlier. When he gets above himself I remind him that he was the only amateur who did not win the Grand Military Gold Cup on Burnt Oak.

The success of Algy Smith-Maxwell on Brother Geoffrey was little short of a fairytale. He was a very inexperienced rider indeed when he was sent to me by his regiment to sharpen him up three months before the 1989 Grand Military Gold Cup. Could I find something suitable for him to ride?

With time running out, I learned that Brother Geoffrey was for sale, and so sent Algy and Alan King to Chris Thornton's yard to see the horse. Having watched Algy ride him at a canter Chris, sensible fellow, would not let him school, but a deal was done anyway. Brother Geoffrey proved to be the ideal schoolmaster for Algy. In the space of nine days the new pairing finished second together at Worcester, won at Leicester and then lifted the Grand Military Gold Cup with the Princess a close third on Bobby Kelly. Although Algy was not the most natural horseman, he would take in what he was supposed to do and carry it out.

Jack Wingfield Digby, nicknamed 'Biggles' in the yard, was a smashing fellow, who won another military race for me at Sandown on Brigadier Harvey's Springholm. If Jack could get it wrong at home, he did, so I tended to give him the most explicit instructions in the hope of avoiding a drama. This led to a charade that left me speechless with rage. One morning, during a schooling session, I told Jack to follow Richard Dunwoody, who was on a hard puller called Five Corners. My final words to him were along the lines of, 'Whatever Richard jumps, you jump. Wherever he goes, you follow. Is that clear?'

It was just our misfortune that Five Corners took off with Richard that morning after jumping six fences. Round and round the field they galloped, with Jack doggedly in pursuit. Soon Jack was whacking his horse to keep up the chase. Every time Richard looked like reining in Five Corners, his persistent shadow came up behind and set him off again.

So the two continued lapping the field, with the head of Jack's mount sticking as close as possible to Five Corners' tail. My blood pressure was not improved as they scattered the rest of the string. When the two horses finally tired and pulled up, I started to give Jack the biggest bollocking of his life. He listened calmly, then replied, quite seriously, 'But you told me to follow Richard whatever happened.'

I felt I was attempting the impossible when Johnny Weatherby's parents asked me to train a horse for him to ride in hunter chases. It was not an easy task, chiefly because he would not be told. Johnny started off by parting company with his mother's horse Sanballat in their first two races but, despite my reservations, he then won on the horse at Towcester, followed up at Stratford and completed a hat-trick at Worcester. As Johnny rode back, slumped over the saddle and looking exhausted, I told him, as usual, to sharpen up and look the part.

He replied, 'Don't tell *me* what to do . . . I've just ridden you a winner.' Today he is chairman of the family firm Weatherby

& Sons, which used to act as secretariat to the Jockey Club, and now provides certain administrative services to both the Jockey Club and the British Horseracing Board. I am pleased to say that we remain friends and I still train for his mother.

22

A Charter Party

Richard Dunwoody's arrival at Condicote marked a significant upturn in our fortunes after two lean seasons in which we had only managed a total of thirty-nine winners. Even in those early days Richard was a confident young man who was clearly on his way to the top. I had known his mother, Gillian, the daughter of the Epsom trainer Dick Thrale, before she married George Dunwoody.

Richard proved to be a bright, intelligent boy with an easy, pleasing manner and, like Peter Scudamore before him, had gained the benefit of staying on at school longer than most would-be jockeys. Although he was only twenty-two when he joined me he was mature for his years.

He was very, very strong through the thighs, with unusually thick legs for a jockey, and remarkably resilient, despite numerous heavy falls. Richard was excellent at and over a jump, a total professional at everything he tried. Many jockeys I have known have been extremely competitive, but none disliked being beaten quite as much as him.

Our venture to France in midsummer with Solar Cloud ended disappointingly when the horse was badly bitten by mosquitoes prior to the valuable four-year-old hurdle at Auteuil in June. The poor horse was covered in unsightly bumps on his stomach and sides, so it was no wonder that he did not finish in the first six.

That autumn we kicked off in the best possible manner by sharing a four-timer at Stratford in October with Long Engagement, Rouspeter, Little Sloop and Sicilian Passage. Another spirited victory by Very Promising, in the Mackeson Gold Cup, carrying 11st. 13lbs, sealed the partnership early the following month. Right at the end of the year horse and rider gave me my first winner in Ireland in the valuable Black and White Whisky Champion Chase at Leopardstown.

Shopping for horses in Ireland is entertaining and exhausting, whether you are at the sales or on one of those nonstop tours during which you can visit as many as a dozen racing stables in a day, not forgetting some obscure farmyards. You are basically looking for a youngster that just might win a Gold Cup one day. It is an enduring dream which ensures that hundreds of promising young jumpers are sold to English trainers each year.

The horse that was to achieve my long-held ambition to train a Gold Cup winner came from Ireland, too, though it was not immediately apparent from his breeding that he possessed the qualities to triumph in the race that matters above all others at the Cheltenham Festival.

The sire Document, though a half-brother to The Queen's top-class horses Above Suspicion and Doutelle, was virtually unknown, had a crooked leg, later developed a wind infirmity, failed to win a single race and was eventually given away as a stallion. At least the dam Ahoy There did win a bumper race at four, but subsequently was a severe disappointment at stud for her breeders, the Riddell Martins from the heart of Ireland's thoroughbred grasslands in County Meath.

'We decided that she was useless and we felt that Document was useless, too,' Avia Riddell Martin once declared without apparent regret. In 1977 Document, who by now belonged to Billy Filgate, covered Ahoy There free of charge. It was not a union calculated to offer rich promise for the years ahead, more a mating of convenience.

'The result,' says Avia Riddell Martin with endearing candour, 'was Charter Party, the biggest, ugliest camel you have ever seen!'

By the time I set eyes on him at Doncaster sales in May, 1982, Charter Party was a fine, big, if rather plain four-year-old, a good mover without a pedigree. I took a chance that he might be a racehorse and bought him for 8,000 guineas. A couple of days earlier Raymond Mould had asked me to find him two suitable young horses. I returned from Doncaster with Charter Party and bought Connaught River privately.

Shortly afterwards Raymond and Jenny Mould met over dinner in London with one of his business contacts Colin

Smith, a director of Wimpey, and his wife Claire. When the bill was presented to Colin at the end of the evening he found himself facing a demand of 4,000 guineas for a half-share in Charter Party. No wonder he complains that the meal was a bit expensive.

Colin immediately gave his half-share in Charter Party to Claire, who is from Dundalk, and like so many Irish people has a natural affinity with horses. Charter Party was the Smiths' first racehorse and was to change all our lives immeasurably in the years ahead.

Although Colin and Claire lived at Nazeing, in Essex, at the time they were sufficiently keen to drive down to Condicote the next week to inspect their new purchase. Colin has two clear impressions about that first visit. He cannot remember meeting me, which does not say much for my public relations. Worse, he later admitted that it would be difficult to find a racehorse that looked more like a donkey.

Charter Party ran in each owner's name in alternate years, always seemed luckier in Claire Smith's colours and swiftly developed into a useful hurdler. He won a Haig Whisky qualifier at Haydock in January, 1983 and was all set to win the final at Newcastle under 11st. 12lbs, until he stumbled and unseated Peter Scudamore at the final flight. Such was Raymond Mould's fury at this outrageous piece of bad luck that by the time Colin had calmed him down several drinks later they agreed to buy another horse together. That one was destroyed after a couple of runs, but French Union, the first horse owned outright by the Smiths, won numerous races including the 1987 Grand Annual Chase at the Cheltenham Festival. By this time Colin and Claire had settled into a routine of leaving Essex before dawn on Friday mornings and driving up to Condicote in time to watch first lot.

Charter Party won three times over fences in his second season, but training horses is never straightforward and he developed a frustrating habit of making at least one crucial error in each race. He fell on his first visit to the Festival as a seven-year-old in 1985, threw away a winning chance at the course a month later with another blunder and came down again when going well in the 1985 Hennessy Cognac Gold Cup.

It was all so maddening because I was convinced that there was a big prize in him if only I could iron out his clumsy jumping. He was a tough devil. He had to be to retain the desire to win after all the mistakes he had been making. But when the moment arrived and he did gain the reward for his persistence in the Ritz Club Chase in 1986, and then added the Golden Miller Chase a month later, we detected worrying signs of a wind problem at the end of his races. He also developed a touch of leg trouble at the same time. That summer we decided on a hobday operation to help his breathing, and also treated him for a soft palate. Although the operation appeared to be a success, he failed to win a single race the following season which ended with yet another fall at Cheltenham in the 1987 Gold Cup.

That year's race was almost wiped out by a blizzard which descended suddenly on Cheltenham shortly before the horses were due to enter the paddock, and transformed the course into a scene from a Christmas card. Aware of an imminent rise in temperature which promised a rapid thaw, the stewards held their nerve and the race eventually began eighty-one minutes late.

Despite Charter Party's unscheduled departure at the fifth fence, we enjoyed another excellent Festival meeting highlighted by French Union's popular success on the opening day. The next afternoon Very Promising was simply magnificent in defeat in the Queen Mother Champion Chase, in which he finished three lengths in front of Desert Orchid, no less, but failed by a neck to overhaul Pearlyman in a pulsating finish.

In addition, Against the Grain was placed at the Festival for the third year running before going on to beat some decent young chasers, including Playschool, at Aintree. High Plains then ended a satisfactory campaign for us by winning the BMW Champion Novice Hurdle at Punchestown at the end of April. With forty-two winners and two more in Ireland we had doubled the previous season's score and almost put the nightmares of the virus behind us. The show was back on the road.

A further problem, apparently in his feet, gave me sleepless nights when Charter Party returned into training in the autumn of 1987. Intermittent lameness hampered his preparation in the months leading up to the 1988 Gold Cup. We nursed him through the winter, aware that I had to run him sparingly, but he was lame once more after a tremendous victory over David Elsworth's pair Rhyme 'n' Reason and

Desert Orchid in the Gainsborough Chase at Sandown early in February.

We knew something was hurting him somewhere but were unable to pinpoint the cause of the problem. Usually it showed in his slower paces, but once he warmed up he seemed to be sound. We tried everything we could, a magnetopulse, osteopaths and of course our own vets. I was reluctant to X-ray his feet because I feared it might be the end of the line for him. You had to admire the horse's courage because his recurring lameness did not affect his enthusiasm for racing. As an added precaution I did not allow him to trot on the roads.

I became quite excited about his chance in the 1988 Gold Cup when he produced the best piece of work in his life on a visit to Henry Candy's gallops at Kingstone Warren near Lambourn, eight days before the Festival. Ridden by one of my young jockeys, William Humphreys, Charter Party ran right away from the speed specialists Very Promising and Long Engagement over a mile and a quarter. You had to be hopeful after witnessing the ruthless manner in which he ran past these two top-class horses.

The final days before Cheltenham are the hardest for a trainer. You know so many things can go wrong, and you just pray the horses will pull out sound in the morning and that their tendons and joints will be cold to the hand's touch at evening stables. I could never be sure with Charter Party, because he had worried me all season, so on Gold Cup day when, incidentally, he weighed 536 kilos, I decided to be on hand near the start just in case an over-zealous official tried to pull him out at the last minute through lameness. Once the field set off, I watched the race unfold from a position between the last two fences.

It proved to be a Gold Cup full of incident. Playschool, the favourite, ran unaccountably badly and was pulled up, while poor Forgive 'n' Forget, successful three years earlier, broke a hind leg at the top of the hill and had to be put down. Rhyme 'n' Reason, who was to win the Grand National on his next outing, was another casualty as he came down four fences out just as he was making ground.

Running downhill for the final time Charter Party was the sole threat to the leader Cavvies Clown. Careless jumping had cost him dear so many times in the past; now it was his rival Cavvies Clown who blundered so badly at the second last fence that his jockey Simon Sherwood was sent into orbit. Somehow the partnership remained intact, but I do not believe the mistake made any difference to the result. Charter Party and Richard Dunwoody were going to win anyway.

They were level with Cavvies Clown as they came past me, took a slight lead approaching the final fence, jumped it well and galloped on dourly up the hill with me running like the wind through the crowd behind him. At the line Charter Party had won by six lengths.

In precious moments like this you are overwhelmed with a mixture of emotions. I was immediately on a terrific high, yet felt a profound sadness that my father, who had won a Gold Cup on Medoc II all those years ago, was not there to see it. He was one of only a handful of people who had faith in Charter Party when I bought him.

The next few hours passed in a bit of a blur. I remember arriving back at Condicote at the same time as the horse and then inviting all the lads in for a drink before sending them off to the local pub with ample funds. Later that evening the Moulds held a party at their home close to us at Guiting Grange. The guests included the Princess Royal, who has been a loyal supporter through thick and thin. I recall that she was one of the last to leave the celebrations and, as usual, was one of the first to arrive to ride out at Condicote well before seven the next morning.

We spent an anxious few days over Easter after a letter arrived from the Jockey Club warning us that the formalities following Charter Party's post-race dope test had not yet been concluded. This raised sufficient doubts for me to hold an internal inquiry during which lads were questioned and supplies of feed checked. So you can imagine my relief when the Jockey Club rang on the following Tuesday to give the all-clear.

After the Gold Cup, X-rays revealed that Charter Party was suffering from navicular disease, a degenerative condition of the navicular bone in the foot. This disclosure made his stout-hearted victory at Cheltenham all the more remarkable. Our vets recommended a course of treatment with powders to improve the peripheral circulation by diluting the blood, but for a time it seemed that the doughty Charter Party had run his last race. I was very gloomy at first, but detected a significant improvement in the horse's condition when we returned from our summer holiday.

Happily we seemed to have arrested the problem in time. When Charter Party came back into training he was kept in a stable with a rubber cover on the floor. In addition, pads were fitted to his shoes to absorb the concussion caused by his feet striking the ground, though in accordance with suppliers' guidelines, the drugs that helped ease the discomfort of navicular disease had to be halted at least ten days before each of his races.

Charter Party did not win again, but he was in the process of running a big race when he fell at the eleventh fence in the Vincent O'Brien Irish Gold Cup at Leopardstown in February, 1989. We flew over and back to Ireland in the same plane as the horse, which is not the most comfortable way to travel. I was already feeling ill when Carol Dunwoody came back from the flight deck to inform us that an alarm had warned the pilot that the outer windscreen of the plane had broken. I turned white from a combination of cold and terror.

A month later Charter Party defended his crown with distinction by taking third prize behind Desert Orchid in the 1989 Gold Cup. It was his fifth successive appearance at the Festival. His record at this most competitive of race meetings included two victories I will never forget and two falls.

He then ran superbly in taking third place in the Whitbread Gold Cup at Sandown late in April, despite conceding lumps of weight to Brown Windsor and Sam Da Vinci, the pair that finished in front of him. Richard Dunwoody, who always thought the world of the horse, felt that this was almost his finest performance.

Charter Party raced for the final time the following November, damaged a tendon and now lives in retirement with the Moulds. Occasionally he ventures out to attend functions. He was an honoured guest at Richard and Carol Dunwoody's wedding, travelled to Sandown for Aldaniti's twenty-first birthday party, is still a major draw at local church fêtes and opened an Abbeyfield retirement home at Prestbury.

On a quiet day I will sometimes dust off the video of that unforgettable victory at Cheltenham and watch it again. We experience plenty of lows as well as highs in jump racing and there is no better way of cheering myself up. Seeing Charter

Party gallop on up the hill in front in the Gold Cup still gives me a buzz.

I know now that one winner at the Festival can make your season. It does not necessarily mean that your entire campaign is ruined if you miss out. But one winner, any winner at that meeting gives you good cause to remember the season with pride.

23

On owners and horses

There were times in the late 'eighties when you could be forgiven
for thinking that Desert Orchid was the only jumper in training.
Wherever you turned, his photograph was in the papers, but I
beat him twice in the same race at Sandown with a horse called
Long Engagement, who showed plenty of ability at home but
never produced it on the course over hurdles. Peter Scudamore
did not like Long Engagement, who proved to be a natural when
we schooled him over fences, and developed into a cracking
two-mile chaser. Because he was such a good jumper, I started
him off in handicaps to exploit his generous hurdles mark.

Long Engagement defeated Desert Orchid comfortably for
the first time at Sandown in the Tingle Creek Chase in 1987,
in receipt of almost two stone. Two years later, after winning
the Gold Cup in the spring, Desert Orchid seemed to have
become more a national institution than a racehorse. Such was
his prowess that all three horses which took him on in the 1989
Tingle Creek were out of the handicap, but I was hopeful that
we might upset the odds again.

Richard Dunwoody had an arrangement to ride Desert Orchid
that year, so I booked Brendan Powell for my horse. The script
was much the same as two years previously. Desert Orchid led
until the last fence, but could not withstand the late charge
of Long Engagement on the hill. My horse put up a superb
performance, but afterwards all I could hear was the crowd
sympathising with 'poor Dessie'. They totally ignored the
winner, and rushed to acclaim the runner-up; I could have
crowned them. Desert Orchid did not have a divine right to
win every time. Handicaps are there for the precise purpose of
bringing horses together.

On the day of Desert Orchid's Gold Cup, Highland Bud, who belonged to Sheikh Mohammed, came agonisingly close to winning the 1989 Daily Express Triumph Hurdle on exceptionally soft ground, which did not suit him at all. Highland Bud was one of several horses sent to me by the Sheikh through my long association with his racing manager Anthony Stroud. In his days working for the Curragh Bloodstock Agency, Anthony knew every farm in Southern Ireland; to go shopping with him there was an education. He found me no end of horses including Goldspun, My Boy Jack, Burnt Oak, Waterloo Boy and Another Coral.

Later, when he joined Sheikh Mohammed, Anthony, who loves jumping, would send us the odd four-year-old, belonging to the Maktoums, that was not quite good enough to be sold as a stallion at the end of the flat season. Highland Bud won his first two races for us before Cheltenham, and later ran well at Liverpool and Punchestown on unsuitable going.

At that time the racing press reflected widespread but unfounded concern in the sport that the Maktoums might play a serious part in jump racing. Although the speculation was wide of the mark, the unwelcome publicity led directly to the sale of Highland Bud for £100,000 to race in America. I tried desperately hard to keep him in the yard by forming a syndicate that bid up to £90,000, but it was not enough. I was very sorry to lose Highland Bud, who proved to be a superstar in America. Anthony Stroud still regrets that he let him go. It is fun dealing with Anthony, who always stays with us for the Festival meeting at Cheltenham. He is almost part of the furniture.

In subsequent years Anthony sent us several more good four-year-olds including Spring Hay, Kadi, Scrutineer, Winter Forest and Thetford Forest who, carrying the colours of Saeed Manana, won five races for us in 1991–92 including the Sun Alliance Novice Hurdle at the Festival. But tragically he was killed in a fall at Liverpool three weeks later.

Of all the horses I have ever trained, Carobee has come closest to breaking my heart. Here I have a horse of the highest quality, patently good enough to go right to the top over hurdles or fences, but recurring leg trouble has prevented him running in any of the last three seasons. No wonder racehorses can so easily drive owners and trainers to drink.

A fine, big, backward, loose-limbed gelding by King's Ride, Carobee was originally bought by the Ayr trainer John Wilson for 42,000 punts as a three-year-old at the 1990 Derby sale at Fairyhouse. But, try as he might, John could not sell him on. At Christmas that year he asked me if I could find a buyer for the horse. I turned everywhere, too, without success. Some people perhaps suspected that the horse had already been tried at home by John Wilson, but I was confident this was not the case.

Carobee was such a lovely horse that I offered to take him in July and to find an owner, on the condition that John paid me for his keep. Eventually Roger Skan, who had shares in Banker's Gossip, agreed to buy the horse and passed on a quarter share to Rodney Maryan-Green.

Towards the end of the year I ran four in a bumper at Warwick, including Barton Bank, and to my surprise and delight Carobee trotted up with his ears pricked, without knowing he had been in a race. He was beaten into third place, mainly through inexperience, on his debut over hurdles at Towcester, where he was in front halfway up the hill but did not last home. Rocco won from Mighty Mogul. Afterwards I told David Minton that it must have been the best novice hurdle ever run at the course.

Carobee won his four remaining races in such exciting style that we began to believe he was a potential champion. At Chepstow, on ground that was barely raceable, he drew right away from Galaxy High, Valfinet and Mighty Mogul. Michael Stoute, who watched the race on television, rang to say he had never seen a horse win quite like it. Carobee then beat the country's best novices decisively at Liverpool. The ground was officially good to soft there but he jarred himself up that day, so we blistered his legs before turning him out at Condicote for the summer.

We were bid an open cheque for Carobee at the end of that season, but his owners were not interested in selling. Unfortunately he has not run since. It is quite maddening to have a horse of his limitless ability permanently on the sidelines. Potentially he is the best I have ever trained. It has been so frustrating for everyone involved.

He had already schooled ready to race in the autumn of 1992 when we spotted a tiny bit of heat in one of his tendons. It was just a suspicion but you do not take chances with a horse like Carobee, so we stopped at once, injected his tendon and gave him a year's break. Twelve months later we had a similar problem with the other front leg. That was another season gone. The worst part of training horses is ringing owners with the bad news that their horses have gone wrong.

After two years on the sidelines Carobee returned into training once more in the autumn of 1994. Naturally we took things extremely patiently, with our fingers crossed, but all our precautions were in vain. One of his front legs again gave cause for concern, so as a last resort we decided to fire his tendons. Only time will tell if it will work, but there has to be a big doubt after such a long break from racing. Some horses, like Carobee, seem fated never to fulfil their potential.

It is almost as tough for a trainer when good horses are taken away and sent to one of their rivals. It has happened many times to me over the years. I was particularly dismayed to lose two smashing horses, Tickite Boo and Some Machine.

I had bought both of them in Ireland for Bill O'Gorman. Tickite Boo won three races for me in his first season and had the makings of a top-class horse. The pair had just come back into training at the start of the new season in the autumn of 1986 when Bill rang up to tell me that he was moving them to Jimmy Fitzgerald. I could have cried. It was very hard to take, more so since I had no idea why he did it.

The temptation at times like this is to tell the owner concerned to go to hell, but I had learned from my father that there is always another day. If you fall out with an owner there is no going back. I try to heed his advice to maintain good relations and to keep the door open, whatever the provocation.

There are, however, exceptions. My door is firmly closed to Paul Green, whose Very Promising was a wonderful servant until he lost his form in the spring of 1988. When he ran well below par at Cheltenham in April, I advised Paul to retire him on the spot. He had always given one hundred per cent in his races, but although he was only ten, he was not very big, had raced busily for several years and I was concerned that he was losing his nerve over fences and might be injured.

I was delighted when Paul gave Very Promising to me. He has proved to be a superb hack and lead horse in retirement at home. He is a sweet horse, still leads the schooling and is quite capable of taking anything along over four furlongs. Indeed, well into his teens, he led my one and only Group winner Silver Wisp in some of his work in 1994.

I trained three or four horses for Paul Green, including Stepaside Lord, who finished fifth in the Champion Hurdle, and Let Him By. They all won races but two months after Paul gave me Very Promising, he rang up to say he was moving the other pair to Martin Pipe. Obviously he removed his horses because he was not happy. I think it is fair to say that he tended to follow Peter Scudamore, because they are the best of friends. Though I appreciate Paul's gesture in giving me Very Promising, I was very hurt by his actions in removing the other two.

One of my favourite owners was Jim Joel, who died at the ripe old age of ninety-seven in March, 1992. He was the most charming man you could ever wish to deal with, and one of a handful of owners to have won the Derby and Grand National. I rode for Mr Joel years ago but he was already ninety-three when he asked me to train for him in November, 1987 and still planning for the future.

At his request I used to ring him up at eight every Sunday morning, summer and winter, and I cherish the times that Dinah and I were invited to his home Childwick Bury for lunch. My last winner for Mr Joel was Bishops Island at Warwick, shortly before his death. Later, when the horses were sold, Sam Vestey, who had been a great friend, decided to buy Bishops Island.

Perhaps age mellows those who own racehorses. Certainly you could not ask for a better man to train for than Roscoe Harvey, known to all of us as the Brig. He was born in July, 1900, a month before the Queen Mother, and by the time he reached the nineties was rather proud of his claim to be the country's oldest racehorse owner. It was back in 1924 that the Brig first tried to win the Grand Military Gold Cup at Sandown in his days as a Second Lieutenant in the 10th Hussars.

His efforts to do so since then have been interrupted only by war when he had a notably distinguished record with three DSOs, and by a much longer spell when his appointment in 1946 as a stipendiary steward on the flat prevented him from owning racehorses. He was a much-respected official who dispensed justice with a degree of common sense that is sometimes lacking in the authorities today. His wife became one of my first owners when I started training, and enjoyed a great deal of success with a horse called No Defence.

When the Brig retired in 1969 he became one of our owners, too, though he still claims that he only chose me as his trainer as an excuse to see my wife Dinah more frequently. Though he had won races on his own horse Tiger on consecutive days at the Grand Military meeting as long ago as 1927, the Gold Cup had always eluded him, and there were times when he would admit to me that perhaps he had left it too late. Happily we managed to put that right for him in the years ahead.

You know exactly where you stand with the Brig because he always speaks his mind, more often than not with a twinkle in his eye. The mirror in the downstairs bathroom of his house is engraved with the message, 'Yes, Roscoe. You look terrific.'

In the early days at Condicote he often told me I was making a mistake by training and riding at the same time. After a convivial day at Huntingdon, where the Brig's horse Merciless King had won, we had a slight disagreement about who should drive home. As I climbed behind the steering wheel he commented, 'You are not fit to drive because you have had too much to drink.'

I replied, 'No. I am fine. I have only had a couple.'

'In that case it must be me who has had one too many,' he concluded sagely.

The Brig is the most generous of hosts; his pick-me-up cocktail is legendary in the Cotswolds. He pours a generous measure of Cointreau on to a sugar lump, adds a drop of grapefruit juice and tops it up with champagne. He calls it a moonwalk: after a couple you will feel no pain.

Whenever I am shopping in Ireland I always have half an eye open for a suitable horse for the Brig to run in military races. It was for that very reason that I bought Burnt Oak in 1982. He had won several point-to-points and, at six, seemed to have a fair bit of potential. The new owner, however, viewed his latest purchase with less than undisguised enthusiasm.

'When David first showed me Burnt Oak I told him it might win the members' race at the Heythrop point-to-point. He was a common-looking horse but turned out to be a good one,' he recalls.

Burnt Oak was still a maiden over fences here when he ran in the Grand Military Gold Cup in 1983, but the opposition was not strong and he started second favourite behind Ballyross who, I seem to recall, qualified because during the war his owner Anne, Duchess of Westminster, had served as an ambulance driver.

We knew our horse jumped and stayed, and his jockey Colonel Sandy Cramsie was one of the most experienced in the race. We used to called Sandy Cramsie 'Crasher', for reasons that I cannot exactly remember. Burnt Oak led for the last mile, brushed aside the challenge of Brod Munro-Wilson, the self-styled SAS veteran, on Roman General and came home a comfortable winner. It had taken fifty-nine years for the Brig to achieve his lifetime's ambition; you could almost reach out and touch the pride on his face as he received the trophy from the Queen Mother. In subsequent years Burnt Oak twice finished second in this race, ridden on each occasion by Malcolm Wallace, and also, of course, carried my son Philip to victory in 1987.

The Brig is a tremendous character, full of fun. In 1992 I found an exciting new horse for him in Ireland called Travelling Wrong. I bought him from my old friend Padge Berry, who claims that he named the horse after the Brig's famous exploits on the M4 in the 'seventies.

He had been lucky to escape with his life that day from an incident which caught the attention of the national newspapers. He had motored up to London in his Bentley with his great friend 'Babe' Moseley for lunch. On the way home they took the wrong exit from the M4, and in a moment of chilling confusion rejoined the motorway to discover that they were bowling along the fast lane in the wrong direction towards traffic pouring out of London.

The situation demanded military initiative. The Brig chose the boldest possible tactics and drove like the wind. Years later he chuckled frequently as he remembered the drive of a lifetime.

'It was stupid, really, but what would you do? What would anyone have done? We could not slow down and try to turn round because there were too many cars in the middle and slow lanes. Everyone imagined we had enjoyed a particularly good lunch.

'My navigator Babe thought we should turn off when we did, but once we were above the motorway, we realised we had made a mistake. So we turned round and when we came back on the M4 we found ourselves heading the wrong way. I had to be decisive, so I turned on the headlights on the basis that people would not know if we were cops or robbers. The plan was to go like hell until we got off at the next junction about six miles away.

'Luckily we only met two in the fast lane. I think the first fellow jinked off because he thought we were the police. The second one proved more troublesome. He held his ground for a bit until Babe cried anxiously, 'The bloody fool does not know where he is going!'

'Somehow we managed to miss each other and reached the next exit without seeing a police car. It does not take very long when you are travelling at 100 mph. I must have had a good lawyer because I got off without any trouble in court at Maidenhead. When I look back on what happened I sweat a bit more now than I did at the time.'

The Brig could hardly refuse Travelling Wrong, who was a decent point-to-pointer in Ireland, and proved a great success here, winning four times in his first season in 1992–93. The Brig continues to take a keen interest and often pops over from his home near Stow to see his horses, including Relkeel who developed into a top-class hurdler in 1994–95.

During the time that Peter Scudamore rode for me I had been in the habit of schooling the horses on Sunday mornings. Richard Dunwoody's wedding to Carol Abraham in the summer of 1988 eventually changed that routine. Martin Bosley, his best man, suggested during his speech that I should allow the newlyweds a lie-in on Sunday mornings. At first we continued to school on Sundays, but I relented after a few months. I hope it shows I am not immovable in matters of the heart.

We continued our welcome run of success at the Festival in 1990 with Bigsun's victory in the Ritz Club National Hunt Chase. This horse had been a nimble jumper from day one, a fact he advertised as a youngster in a dramatic incident at Haydock when a loose horse forced him headlong towards a wooden running rail. Many jockeys would have panicked, but Peter Scudamore gave him a kick and Bigsun responded by flying over the rails as if he had been doing it all his life. He belonged to the Brig's stepson Johnny Horn.

Earlier in the day at Cheltenham, Ninja, owned by Raymond Mould, added to my ever-growing list of near misses in the Daily Express Triumph Hurdle. Belying his odds of 50–1, Ninja led at the final flight of hurdles and was only just caught in the last few yards by the Irish horse Rare Holiday.

Winning at the Festival had become a welcome habit. After all those barren years we had enjoyed at least one winner at each of the last five Festivals. So it was quite a shock when we failed to add to the score in 1991. I did not have a runner in that year's Arkle, so Richard was free to take the winning ride on Nicky Henderson's exciting young chaser Remittance Man.

Richard is as tough a jockey as I have ever employed, and displayed extraordinary resilience during a bone-crunching series of falls at Aintree in April, 1992. He began the meeting on Thursday with one of the worst falls I have ever seen when Shamana galloped straight on at the first fence. Horse and rider were lucky enough to emerge alive. Richard showed his nerve an hour later with a flawless winning ride, on The Antartex, in the John Hughes Memorial Chase.

The next day he ended up on the floor three more times, and then fared little better on Saturday. His Grand National hopes on Brown Windsor ended abruptly at Becher's Brook, first time, before he suffered yet another crashing fall when my outstanding novice Thetford Forest was killed in the final race of the meeting.

I do not know how Richard came through in one piece. By the end of the day he looked like a man who had just endured ten rounds with Mike Tyson. He could barely walk, let alone talk, and was so shaken, physically and mentally, that the racecourse doctor recommended he should take three weeks off to recharge his batteries.

Six numbing falls like that would put some jockeys off racing for life. The human body can only take so much, but Richard rang me on the Monday and cheerfully announced that he would be fit to resume at Ascot two days later. That is Richard; he soaks up punishment and bounces back quicker than any jockey I have known, with the possible exception of my father.

I barely had two cross words with Richard in all the years he rode for me. When I am not happy about something I believe in speaking out at once, bang. Now and then I will say something at the wrong time, but usually it helps clear the air.

That winter Duntree, a handicap chaser, did not jump well for Richard. They had fallen at Kempton at Christmas, 1992, then parted company again next time, and were on a recovery mission when they came down once more at an open ditch in the closing stages of the Warwick National.

My mood was not improved when the sprawling figure of Duntree contrived to bring down my other runner Peajade. Richard had asked his horse up from an impossible position; he had put Duntree on the floor. I told him he had lost his way on the horse and had ridden like a blind man. Though he won the next race for me on Persian Sword, it took a day or two before relations between us returned to normal.

24

An invitation to Jackdaws Castle

Racehorse owners who have the rare good fortune to come up with an exceptional horse at the first attempt can be forgiven for believing it is all too easy to win. In steeplechasing, as in life, the freshly converted enthusiast is invariably the keenest of all.

Yet it is in the nature of our perilous sport that nothing lasts for ever. The horse that is champion today is all too often lame tomorrow. When reality comes crowding in, and horses are injured or sometimes killed, their owners, who previously enjoyed unrelenting success, sometimes turn away to other pursuits.

Colin Smith's first horse Charter Party eventually won the Cheltenham Gold Cup. His second, Little Rock, had to be put down after running only a few times, but by then he and his wife Claire were drawn as irresistibly to jump racing as moths to a flickering flame.

Smith joined the building company George Wimpey after a brief reversal when he was sent down from Cambridge at the end of his second year for failing one of his six exams in estate management. He stayed with the company for twenty years, and was a director from January, 1979 until he resigned in 1985 to run his own business, chiefly because he preferred to be more in control of his own destiny.

Short, thickset and decisive, he is a tough, no-nonsense businessman with interests in property, golf carts, helicopters, publishing and commercial real estate in America. He is also the proprietor of Jackdaws Castle, which is unquestionably the most expensively produced, modern and practical state-of-the-art jumps training stable ever built in this country.

In May, 1986 his family bought 240 acres of land, including

the site of a disused stone quarry, a few miles away from Condicote on the windswept hill above the Plough Inn at Ford. At the same time he set in motion plans to move there as well by purchasing an old barn together with some farm buildings on the opposite side of the road from the pub, with the idea of converting them into a new home. Despite the lure of seeing their horses more frequently near by at Condicote, his wife Claire was understandably reluctant to move away from her home and friends in Essex.

At that stage Smith was tempted to become a farmer, but in the meantime he brought in consultants to advise on various uses for the land including sheep, goats, corn and even a golf course. Later he acquired more adjacent farmland, which increased the size of the estate at Jackdaws Castle to some 500 acres.

Even he seems genuinely surprised at the turn of events that followed. What began as a whim, as no more than a sketchy idea of perhaps putting in some gallops on fields that were standing idle, soon developed into a full-blown development plan of mega proportions, which traditional trainers of another era simply could not comprehend. On paper, at least, he has turned the old game on its head.

By the summer of 1995 he had poured upwards of £3.5 million into creating a training estate with unrivalled facilities for jumpers. It is a massive investment in a sport which traditionally has never enjoyed the lavish rewards of flat racing. Indeed, since Jackdaws Castle opened for business in October, 1992 it has operated at a loss.

The proprietor, a man who expects his enterprises to be in the black, will tell you that the losses are not sustainable, that matters cannot continue as they are. It is a situation entirely alien to the commercial instincts that have made him such a successful businessman. Already plans are far advanced to convert another part of the estate into a stud, with two resident stallions and up to sixty boxes for mares and foals.

What is beyond dispute is that the move from Condicote to Jackdaws Castle propelled David Nicholson in one giant leap to the top of the training tree. In his first winter there he produced a hundred winners in a season for the first time. By the end of his second season he had become champion trainer, a title he readily retained twelve months later. The Duke in his Castle is even more formidable than before.

Colin Smith began to call in at Condicote more frequently from 1987 while he was monitoring building work on his barn conversion at Ford. Sometimes, after he had looked at the horses, I would join him for lunch at the Plough. On one particular day in September 1987, we wandered outside the pub afterwards, looked up at the barren land and casually mulled over the best use for it.

When he asked if it would be feasible to put in some gallops, I replied that it could be done and started sketching out some possible areas for an all-weather surface in the belief that his daughter Emma might want to train a few point-to-point horses there. That impromptu conversation began a chain of events which set Colin on course to create his own unique racing enterprise.

First, he put in a planning application for change of use of the land from agricultural to gallops. Then we started talking more seriously about setting out a series of grass and all-weather gallops on the farm, whose land climbed steadily uphill away from the pub for fully a mile. You could not have asked for a better place for the purpose and we had the priceless advantage of starting from scratch.

Over the course of several months no less than 5,000 tons of stone were removed from the land. Particular attention was paid to the areas where we wanted to lay gallops. Contractors brought in special machines from Norway which sucked in the first six inches of topsoil into a series of rotating sieves and ejected the stones into a hopper. The process was then repeated before, on the advice of consultants, the area was sown with a blend of eight types of grass considered ideal for gallops on the prevailing soil. Over 1,000 tons of peat were also added to help cushion the surface.

One morning, as we surveyed the work going ahead on the gallops, Colin asked me a second, even more crucial question than the one he had put to me at the Plough. If he built a yard to go with the new gallops, he enquired, would I move there to train? I accepted the offer without hesitation, though Dinah was not so certain of the benefits when we discussed it later. Having lived at Condicote for thirty years, she would have preferred Colin to buy that and set about improving the facilities there.

A move was a long way off at this stage, but I pointed out to

Dinah the advantages of the new place compared to Condicote, where we had one well-worn all-weather surface and cramped accommodation for the lads. In addition, riding on the slippery roads near the village was becoming more dangerous each year as traffic increased in the area.

There was also the vital question of how the board of David Nicholson Racing Ltd would react to my leaving. I was hopeful that they would support the idea, because I felt it gave all the shareholders a chance to get their money back and maybe make a nice profit by selling up and possibly gaining planning permission for the yard at Condicote. Once I had a formal offer, I put it to the board and was delighted and relieved when they gave me their blessing in principle.

First, though, it was necessary to apply to Cotswold District Council for outline consent to build a new yard and suitable housing for the staff. This was turned down initially on the grounds that it would harm an area of outstanding natural beauty. The council also listed several other objections to the original plans, but did suggest that putting the yard in the old quarry was one acceptable solution. We then submitted a detailed planning application which covered all the previous objections. This time the plans were passed, much to the surprise of some locals.

These were exciting times. By now Colin and his family had moved into his new home at Ford and so he was on hand for the day-to-day discussions and planning that are essential in such a massive undertaking. We visited a number of modern yards, including those of Dick Hern, Stan Mellor, Simon Sherwood, Gavin Pritchard-Gordon and also Barry Hills at Manton, in our search for perfection.

Colin is a practical man who enjoys doing things with clinical efficiency. In contrast, he considers that trainers have their own mythological ways and beliefs. So, together, we looked at all sorts of interesting developments at these yards in the hope and belief that we might pick up some bright ideas which we could incorporate into our plans.

He was quite prepared to veto anything he felt was unnecessary or too costly. He does not believe in wasting money needlessly by letting architects run wild without any control. For instance, one of the stables we inspected had a drying room that had reputedly cost £25,000. Colin thought that was excessive and settled for one that cost about a tenth of that figure. Wanting to encourage as much ventilation as possible, he was also against the idea of insulating the boxes, which he felt was perhaps treating the horses as something other than wild animals. We were both keen to try to reduce the things that can go wrong in a stable yard.

I wanted to have windows in all the boxes. Colin countered that all the windows at Condicote were masked by the top doors that we always left open, and were also covered in cobwebs. With hindsight, I have to say that he was right not to put in windows at Jackdaws Castle. He saved as much as £40,000 by rejecting the idea of an equine swimming pool, which can benefit some horses. But you do not train an athlete in a pool, or a swimmer on the track, so it was not the end of the world when he decided against it. Instead, he installed a mechanical horse walker for six horses at one end of a long indoor school.

The spacious boxes, measuring 12′ by 12′, are light and airy, warm in winter, even though we do not close the top doors, and cool in summer, with just the right amount of ventilation. Every other box has a skylight. Most boxes have bars between – I am a great believer in horses needing company, as they are essentially herd animals. We ruled out automatic water because you can never be sure how much a horse is drinking. That type of system can freeze up in cold weather and makes lads lazy.

Dinah raised a few objections at first, mainly because she would have liked the yard to be designed in a different way with our house adjoining it. We were both keen to be close to the yard because we enjoy being able to see what is going on at all times, but it was not a feasible plan, so the house was built slightly away from the yard.

She also had firm ideas about the trainer's house and, to her delight, was allowed to design it herself. There were obviously a few hiccups, but we only had one major disagreement with the architect, over the colour of the windows. He insisted that black was the traditional colour for the Cotswolds, while we, having lived there throughout our lives, disagreed and so painted them white on the inside.

There was a bit of an argument over the name to be carried on the two lorries taking our runners to the races. Colin decided on the new title of Ford Farm Racing. Dinah, in particular, felt that this was not fair to me.

'Does David's name not mean anything?' she asked during the continuing debate. It was a very sensitive issue. Colin was also keen to build more boxes to increase our capacity. I was against the idea on the grounds that eighty jumpers are enough for any one man to train. Putting up more boxes in the main yard would spoil its nature.

All the buildings had to fit into the site of the old quarry, which had been in use until the turn of the century. Initially the hole was not big enough, so we deepened, widened and extended it to twice its original length and added an enormous bank which we have subsequently landscaped. Into this gaping chasm rose two adjoining yards with a total of eighty boxes, a hostel with twenty-three rooms, houses for the trainer, head lad and travelling head lad, several flats and some spacious offices.

There is also a blacksmith's shop, in which we later added two more boxes, a veterinary unit with facilities for a laboratory, if necessary, two tack rooms, a laundry, drying room and one big feed room between the two yards. We also have large barns for storing hay and bales of paper which we shred ourselves for bedding. Heating and hot water for the entire place is supplied by a giant straw burner which devours several big round bales a day.

In addition, there is a large covered school which is employed mainly for breaking in horses. I do not use it for riding out in the winter because I believe that jumpers must be tough, and anyway it is not big enough. If you started sheltering in the school on a wet or cold day, you would stay there all winter. It would be the first downward step to going soft for both horses and lads.

Shortly before building work began at Jackdaws Castle in December, 1991 thieves ransacked our home at Cotswold House in Condicote. I still regard it as the worst morning of my life. When I made my way to the bathroom at around 3.30 that morning, some of the dogs were barking and our old whippet was halfway down the stairs with her ears pricked. Foolishly, I took no notice and returned to bed. Later, at around six, I came downstairs to discover that all our trophies, cups, small antiques and other valuables had gone. It was a nightmare. I stood there completely shaken at what had happened.

Although we invariably left the back door unlocked, the

thieves had drilled a hole in the window of the ground floor room in front of the house, lifted a latch and broken in that way. Everything of value was gone. Only a candlestick remained, though some plated silver was later found in a river on the Oxfordshire border and returned to us. We have still not recovered from the loss of so many things that held tremendous sentimental value. The thieves were probably in the house at the time I woke up, and subsequently robbed our neighbours on the other side of the green. One of our silver spoons was found in the road between us.

At least events at Jackdaws Castle helped take our minds off the robbery. We were all becoming excited at the excellent rate of progress on site. Building was completed in time for the official opening on Monday, October 12, 1992. Most people, I suspect, would have been satisfied with that, but Colin is still striving to improve the superb facilities at Jackdaws Castle.

No less than 100,000 trees have been planted in the last few years. A reservoir holding 750,000 gallons of water was constructed for the express purpose of feeding the pop-up sprinkler system for the gallops, which is controlled by computer. The water is pumped up from a bore-hole going down 900 feet. There is even a helicopter pad.

Though the yard and buildings were not completed until the late autumn of 1992, I was able to rent the three new woodchip all-weather gallops from the middle of 1990. One stretches nine furlongs uphill from its starting point just opposite the Plough. That is mainly employed for steady work. This gallop also runs into a three and a half-furlong loop, at the top of the farm, at an altitude of 1,050 feet, which we use for slower work. The third all-weather gallop, over six and a half furlongs, is for sharper work. They are all harrowed and rolled between lots by our gallops man, Sammy Joynes, who came with me from Condicote.

At first, I used to box the horses to Jackdaws Castle, but later we began hacking over each morning from Condicote through woods and round the edge of fields without having to open a single gate. Since the journey there and back was the best part of eight miles, each lot of horses was out for about two hours every morning. Some people concluded that we were doing well because the horses were required to do more than before. Whatever the reason, our results improved significantly once we began using the gallops at Jackdaws Castle. The first season, in 1990–91, I trained fifty-five winners, the next sixty-three.

Matters were moving along at a furious pace by then, with the result that the board of David Nicholson Racing Ltd asked to meet my prospective employer to determine the date and financial arrangements for the transfer of the trainer, lads and horses to Jackdaws Castle. This crucial meeting was held at Condicote on May 15, 1992, with Ben Brooks, as usual, in the chair. Henry Shouler, Anthony Armitage, Raymond Mould, Harvey Grove, the company accountant, Dinah and I were all there to hear what Colin had to say.

Originally he was willing to take over on August 1, 1992, but he pointed out that building work at Jackdaws Castle would not be completed in time for the horses to move by that date. Equally, the board was anxious to earn some money before the transfer. June and July, being quiet months with most of the horses absent at grass, normally lost around £22,000, while August generated a small profit of £3,000.

Since September, with the yard full, offered a further month of full training fees, we settled for a compromise that the change-over should occur on October 1. Colin also agreed to accept any redundancy liabilities, though events were to show that only one employee, from the office, did not make the move with us to Jackdaws Castle. Colin further agreed to pay, at valuation, for all the tack, grooming kit, lorries and other items we required. The rest would be sold at auction after the move.

One controversial subject remained to be discussed before the arrangements were complete, and it led to a heated debate. Though the board was willing to release me later in the year, they felt justified in asking for a transfer fee for me, as the major asset of David Nicholson Racing Ltd, and put a price on my head of £100,000. The board was, quite properly, trying to be commercial in the negotiations.

This did not please Colin, who made it clear from the outset that he was not prepared to pay any compensation to them as goodwill for my impending departure. A lively argument ensued. There was a fair bit of heat, especially from one or two members of the board. Ben Brooks supported the claim for compensation by pointing out that the company had, at last, started to make a profit after a number of losing years.

Since I was sitting next to Ben, I leaned over and begged him not to spoil my plans to go to Jackdaws Castle. He knew I was concerned that, if the board did not release me, then Colin Smith would find someone else to train at his new establishment.

These were tense moments, but it helped that I was among friends who were also my owners. I explained to the meeting that I was trying to do the best both for myself and David Nicholson Racing Ltd. My departure, I suggested, would give all the shareholders a chance to cash in on their investment. I added that, whatever the board decided, I had made up my mind to go to Jackdaws Castle. I think it was at this stage that I was invited to leave the room.

Eventually sanity prevailed and an agreement was reached which satisfied all parties. I would be free to move in the autumn without any question of compensation for the board. Three days later I sent a letter to all my owners informing them of our plans for the autumn. I told them:

As you may have already heard, we are moving! However, I can now put you in the picture more specifically. Colin Smith, an existing owner here since 1982, is in the process of building a new complex of eighty boxes with all ancillary buildings, such as lads' hostel, head lad's and travelling head lad's bungalows, assistant trainer's flat, offices etc. and trainer's house.

The gallops are already operational, we have been using them for the past two seasons, and schooling facilities are to be constructed. All this has been taking place under constant supervision and recommendation by me and I believe that it will not only be extremely practical and efficient, but equally personal as our present situation.

I shall be employed by Colin Smith to train the horses under the banner of David Nicholson, but he will be responsible for the financial side. All the staff are being taken on, and are very enthusiastic about it.

We plan to move in early October, and as the horses can be ridden from one yard to the other, there should not be much of a settling-in problem.

The establishment here at Condicote will eventually be sold in whatever form is most advantageous to the shareholders of David Nicholson Racing Ltd, and this will probably be in spring, 1993. The company will then be closed.

I concluded the letter by inviting all my owners to visit Jackdaws Castle at the earliest opportunity.

The letter hinted at the financial arrangements that were to change my life considerably. Previous events at Condicote had already confirmed that I was a poor businessman. In the future Colin was going to take care of all finances. He would set and collect the training fees, pay the wages and deal with all the numerous bills and details that used to drive me to distraction in the past. In turn he would pay me a salary, with the promise of bonuses, so freeing me to concentrate on training the horses.

I had no doubts at all, particularly as we knew the gallops worked, but at first Dinah was justifiably concerned at the loss of our independence after years running our own ship. To go from being top of your own tree to a salaried employee is a difficult and emotional step. Dinah was not sure we were doing the right thing, but as always she supported me. I felt that with Colin's commitment, drive and financial backing the place had to work, and I did not want to miss the bus. I had realised from the start of this venture that if I did not accept his offer, someone else might be given the opportunity to train at Jackdaws Castle.

Quite honestly the salary was not my major concern. Money is not my motivation. As long as I have enough to get by, I am quite happy. Eventually we would like to buy a house somewhere in the vicinity where we can spend our retirement.

The great move took place on October 1, 1992. That day we rode fifty-one horses across country in three lots on the journey of four miles from Condicote to Jackdaws Castle. At the same time our horseboxes ferried back and forth bringing all the tack, rugs, sheets and endless supplies of equipment you accumulate over the years for the business of training racehorses. Dinah and I had moved into our new home almost a week earlier, together with seven cats, four dogs and our parrot Clouseau.

On a brisk October morning twelve days after the move, the Princess Royal officially opened Jackdaws Castle with a brief, witty speech before unveiling a plaque beneath the clock tower. There was a big reception for owners old and new, friends, supporters and a large contingent of reporters and TV crews. Everyone had the chance to wander round and inspect our new training base before a long lunch in a vast marquee. A variety of souvenirs and memorabilia for the guests had all disappeared by the end of the afternoon.

The switch from Condicote after so many years was a vast change in my life and I did not know how successful it might be, but I was optimistic. I felt that if I could not train winners with the help of these superb facilities then I might as well pack up. We have so many more options than at Condicote with the result that by the middle of 1995 we had still not used some of the grass gallops laid down several years earlier. They are being left to mature with an eye to the future.

I hoped that the majority of owners would come with me and they did. It was a bonus that every lad came too. They were keen because they had seen how the place was developing, were aware of the potential, and had been encouraged to produce a fair bit of input in the planning process. All the staff rallied round because they were proud to be part of the new yard. We have a tremendous team spirit.

I had been concerned that the horses might become upset as they walked alongside the gallops while others were working on them, and everyone was pleasantly surprised at how they immediately seemed more relaxed in their new home. All they seem to do here is eat, sleep and work. Every one of them thrived after the changeover.

It was such a difference from riding round the roads at Condicote, where the surface was like glass, with the chance of horses turning upside down and hurting themselves and their riders. The fact that I was tense all the time on the roads there probably wound up all the lads, too. We would all be uptight worrying about the next car sweeping round a corner.

In comparison, Jackdaws Castle is heaven. The horses do not go anywhere near the public roads. They are totally switched off. The facilities alone quickly made an enormous difference in attitudes and I discovered, to my surprise, that I did not mind being employed. Really Dinah and I have the best of both worlds, because we are paid and, thank goodness, do not have to worry about the bills. There is a nice bonus scheme built into my contract, too.

Tim Forster, of all people, told me I was mad to be changing course at my stage of life, yet within two years he had done exactly the same thing. As far as I can see, neither of us has any cause for complaint. I was a bit concerned when a canny old farm labourer at Condicote assured me that the quarry would rapidly fill in with snow in winter but, happily, his fears have been groundless so far.

We now rent out our old house at Condicote and I confess that I do not miss the place one bit. Indeed, I do not like going back there because it seems so lifeless. Looking back now I can say that we trained fifty horses at Condicote on little more than a cabbage patch. At the end there was nothing left of the grass gallop, which was only as wide as a piano, in places. Although we were very limited there and it was never easy, somehow we got away with it and trained a fair few winners. We had thirty good years in the village, but we both believe that if a special opportunity arises in life you must grasp it.

At the time of the move Dinah was worried about losing the atmosphere and community spirit of village life, but from the day we arrived we found that Jackdaws Castle was like a village, too, with the result that even she is settled. It also helped that she was able to take lots of cuttings from the garden at Condicote to help create the new one. Swallows and housemartins have been regular visitors from the start and now the wild birds are beginning to find us. For the past three years we have been adopted by a pair of mallard, who generally produce a clutch of ducklings on the reservoir.

Since Colin Smith is tough and I can be volatile we have had the odd disagreement, but basically we work together pretty well. Although he has the ultimate sanction, we have an easy enough relationship. He gives me a free hand with the training, but I make a point of discussing matters with him that might involve finance. In short, Colin takes a big interest in everything that goes on at Jackdaws Castle, without interfering. His wife Claire, too, likes being involved. He will not buy a horse until she has seen it. She undoubtedly has a way with horses.

He enjoys coming out in the early mornings to watch the horses working or schooling and when he is in the country we speak every day. While he is away he will ring me at least once a week, if not more. At the end of each season he calls a meeting with me, our vet, assistant trainer and head lad. We are very much a team.

25

A Maiden Century

We started that first momentous season at Jackdaws Castle with almost thirty empty boxes, despite the welcome arrival of four decent horses owned by Bill and Shirley Robins. I had first met them briefly at Chepstow, on the day Carobee beat their horse Mighty Mogul. We had a chance to chat again when Geoff Lewis, their flat trainer, introduced them at our annual Royal Ascot drinks party in the car park in 1992. Bill Robins then rang me on the Tuesday of Goodwood week, asked if he could see me and came down with Shirley to Condicote that week. They seemed to appreciate the facilities at Jackdaws Castle that were almost completed preparatory to our move.

That night Bill rang again asking me to take four horses which, until then, had been trained by Jenny Pitman. Naturally I was delighted to accept because three of them, Mighty Mogul, Baydon Star and Wonder Man had excellent form. It's funny how racing can go round in full circle. Years before Jenny had been the one to benefit when Dorothy Squires took her team of horses away from me. Now the boot was on the other foot and, although Jenny must have been heartbroken to lose the horses, she took it philosophically and I am glad to say we are still friends.

Richard Dunwoody was in his seventh season with us, though there was a subtle difference to our agreement this time. Concerned at missing the winning ride on Nicky Henderson's Remittance Man at the 1992 Festival because he was required to partner Waterloo Boy, and wanting to have a greater freedom of choice, Richard asked if I would share a joint first claim on his services with Nicky. I agreed, with some reluctance which was later justified.

Canon Class, owned by Bryan Jenks on a lease from the

Princess Royal, proved to be the first winner from our new quarters on October 7, only six days after the move. The horses settled in so much better than I had dared hope that we were in full flow by the middle of the month. Baydon Star was successful at Ascot and proceeded to win four of his next five races while Wonder Man quickly rattled up a hat-trick of victories over fences, but it was Mighty Mogul who offered the greatest promise for the future.

I could not believe the high quality of his homework that autumn. He trotted up at Newbury, before taking advantage of a generous handicap mark in the Tote Silver Trophy at Chepstow early in November. By the end of the year he was one of the favourites for the Champion Hurdle after three more impressive victories in conditions races, including the Waterloo Hurdle at Haydock, which rapidly developed into a farce of which Brian Rix would have been proud.

When the field of four runners turned into the straight on the first circuit, they found the first flight of hurdles dolled off, apparently in error. Aware that the race would be void if the horses continued, Richard did his best to persuade the other jockeys to stop, but they, in turn, thought that he might be pulling a fast one. The result of all this confusion was that the four continued to hack round at a sedate pace and jumped two more flights as I rushed on to the course in front of the stands, waving my arms for them to stop. Eventually they were halted by the course foreman on the top bend having completed over one lap.

Meanwhile I commandeered a Land-Rover and set off urgently towards the point where the dolls and cones had forced the four runners wide of the offending flight. Philip Arkwright, the clerk of the course, appeared at the same time. The jockeys were ordered to restart at a point one hundred yards or so before the crucial hurdle, from which the dolls had now been removed. When the horses set off again Mighty Mogul won easily. It had taken him twelve minutes and nineteen seconds to cover almost four miles, with a lengthy pause at halfway.

Mighty Mogul's reputation soared even higher when he beat the subsequent Champion Hurdler Granville Again by eight lengths, at level weights, in the Bonusprint Christmas Hurdle at Kempton. The sky truly seemed to be the limit for him at this stage but his next run, at Cheltenham, at the end of January brought us cruelly back to earth when Richard pulled him up after an unusually clumsy jump at the third last. Although we could not see anything specifically wrong, it was all too clear that the horse was in a great deal of pain, so we took him straight from the racecourse to our vets at Bourton-on-the-Water. X-rays revealed that Mighty Mogul had broken a bone in his knee.

His season of excellence was already at an end and, since knees are invariably difficult to heal, we realised that he might not race again. When our vets suggested an operation to pin the fractured carpal bone in the knee, Bill Robins flew in a specialist from America the following Friday to carry out the complicated surgery, which involved inserting six screws to repair the damaged bone.

Initial reports on the operation were encouraging, but the moment I was called to the phone at Sandown the next day I feared the worst. Poor Mighty Mogul was dead. The strain of trying to support the damaged limb proved too much, with the result that he suffered further fractures of another bone above the knee on the same leg. There was no alternative but to put him down.

This was a grim blow which hit everyone at Jackdaws Castle. The big horse, with an attractive white blaze on his face and a gentle nature, had touched us all in the few short months he was with us. Bill and Shirley Robins, in particular, were inconsolable, as was Lizzie Millichap, the girl who rode him every morning.

The loss of horses like Mighty Mogul teaches you to appreciate the good moments in jump racing even more, and none came better that winter than the success of Another Coral in the Tripleprint Gold Cup at Cheltenham in December. It took years of patient handling, particularly by his lads and riders, to transform him from a gassy, impatient, sweaty individual into a thoroughly efficient racing machine.

Nine years earlier Mike Deeley had asked me to buy two store foals for him in Ireland, for no more than 10,000 guineas. I remember giving the order to Anthony Stroud, who had just started working for Sheikh Mohammed, with strict instructions not to buy anything by Green Shoon. What happened? He returned from the Fairyhouse sale with a foal by Green Shoon, and another by Deep Run at a total cost of 8,000 guineas. I was not amused. The youngsters spent their early years on Mike's farm near Bicester, and I came to favour Another Coral, the one by Green Shoon, more than Waterloo Boy.

Another Coral took ages to learn to relax. At the start of his first full season in training we boxed him to six race meetings just to educate him. Each time the sweat poured off him. He was one of those highly strung, nervous, buzzy horses that try to rush headlong to the front of the string. That is why he seemed to be pretty fit early on in the season, and did not hold his form too well after Christmas. Genuine and reliable, he won a couple of races each season and was at his peak in 1991 and 1992.

I had been full of hope that he might win the 1991 Mackeson Gold Cup at Cheltenham, until I heard a brass band playing close to the paddock. Aware that another band had caused him to boil over before a race in the past, I sent Dinah to persuade the band leader to cease playing until the race was over, with the promise of a bottle of champagne if he won.

In as good a Mackeson as I have seen, Another Coral just held on by half a length in an enthralling duel with Toranfield, ridden by Adrian Maguire. The band was delighted, too, because they had all backed him and then duly received their champagne.

A year later there was no sign of them when Another Coral finished second to Tipping Tim in the same race. I thought he might reverse the form with Tipping Tim the next month, on better terms, in the Tripleprint Gold Cup and he did so in style. Another Coral was always in the leading four, struck the front two fences out and readily pulled clear of Second Schedual and Tipping Tim on the flat.

It was a fine achievement by the horse to win both major, valuable, late autumn sponsored handicaps at the course in just over twelve months. The previous day I had completed a treble at Cheltenham with Beauchamp Grace, Travelling Wrong and Duntree. The triumph of Another Coral and two others on Saturday brought my tally for the meeting to six in two days.

Almost two months later Another Coral came so close to winning on his first attempt at three miles at Cheltenham that I resolved to run him in the 1993 Gold Cup, which looked quite open that year. But that plan was foiled when he was found to have a bit of heat in one of his forelegs the night before the big race. So, at the eleventh hour, Richard Dunwoody was free to switch to Martin Pipe's Rushing Wild, who finished a close second to Jodami.

In the early stages of his development I did not think that much of Waterloo Boy, who by now belonged to a partnership headed by Mike Deeley. The horse had a pony action and was rather unimpressive. At the time Amanda McDowell, one of our keenest girls, begged me to allow her to ride in a race. Her chance came on Waterloo Boy, who was just beaten in a photo at Ludlow after turning for home twenty-five lengths behind. On his first run over hurdles he shed Jimmy Frost at the first flight, but in the years that followed Waterloo Boy developed into one of the toughest, most genuine and talented horses I have ever trained, despite a wind problem that troubled him later in his career.

Waterloo Boy was anything but a natural when I first popped him over fences at home. I schooled him again and again until he was reasonably proficient, then let him make his debut in a handicap at Worcester because the handicapper would often drop a horse starting over fences to a mark a stone lower than his rating over hurdles. So it proved in this case. Waterloo Boy duly won three handicaps in a row before I put him in a decent novice chase at Cheltenham. He won that, too, although Beech Road was upsides when he fell at the last fence.

Two months later Beech Road won the 1989 Champion Hurdle, at 50–1, on the same day that Waterloo Boy took the Arkle Challenge Trophy from Southern Minstrel with a typically spirited performance. The decisive moment of the race came at the third last fence, where Richard Dunwoody, seeing a very long stride, asked for the impossible, really, and it came off. It was a stroke of genius. Both horse and rider were very brave, and gained a lead of two lengths which was just sufficent to see them home. That was one of my proudest victories.

The following year Waterloo Boy failed by half a length to beat Barnbrook Again in a titanic duel, from three fences out, in the Queen Mother Champion Chase. This was a race that saw two great horses and jockeys at their very best; Richard was truly outstanding on Waterloo Boy. It was a brilliant race, as exciting a finish as you could wish to see, with the crowd on its feet and both owners and trainers happy. But the Cheltenham stewards thought otherwise, and after a lengthy inquiry suspended Richard and Hywel Davies, Barnbrook Again's jockey, for two days for excessive use of the whip.

Their action marred a wonderful race. Afterwards I fully supported Richard Dunwoody's initial desire to appeal. Frankly, I could not wait to go to Portman Square and ask the stewards how a jockey should use a whip, because in my view he had done nothing wrong. Waterloo Boy was fine after the race; he did not have a mark on him. Richard was all set to appeal until Hywel changed his mind at the last minute. I was extremely annoyed and disappointed with Hywel, since his action would have made any appeal by Richard much harder to sustain.

Waterloo Boy never did quite manage to become the champion two-mile chaser. Soon after he finished second in the race again, in 1991, Richard suggested that he was making a noise, which is an indication of a wind infirmity. As the horse 'scoped clear at home, I disagreed with Richard's assessment at first, but subsequent events confirmed his fears. We then sent Waterloo Boy for a hobday operation to Jeffrey Brain, who reported that he gave three whistles as he lapsed into unconsciousness from the anaesthetic. This, apparently, is a sure sign of a wind infirmity.

Happily, the operation seemed to cure the problem for Waterloo Boy, who finished third the following year to Remittance Man at Cheltenham, and in the evening of his career won the Hall of Fame Chase at Cheltenham in January 1994. I was tickled pink and Richard could not speak when he jumped off the old horse's back. It was a wonderful moment, because they had achieved so much together over the years, and it was a spare ride for him after leaving us. Half an hour earlier Richard had ridden his 1,000th winner on Flakey Dove.

That was the seventeenth and last success of Waterloo Boy. I hate to see old horses trailing round in races if there is the slightest chance that there is something wrong with them, and towards the end Waterloo Boy had started to break blood vessels. He might have done so in the Queen Mother Champion Chase in 1993, and certainly burst at home at least once. When it happened again at Wincanton in February, 1994, I was keen to retire him. It is not fair to ask horses to continue to race in these circumstances.

Waterloo Boy remained an important person at Jackdaws Castle in his new role as a lead horse. He spent his winters here and his summers out to grass at Mike Deeley's farm; that way he had the best of both worlds. He never once shirked a battle in eight years as a racehorse, and never actually fell. I have not trained a tougher one and would have trusted him with my life. His greatest qualities were character and soundness; only his guts got him through. What he lacked in ability he more than made up for in attitude.

Waterloo Boy never had a bandage on his legs in his life, and did not miss one season, which is very unusual for a jumper. From forty-six starts he won £334,504, which, I think I am right in saying, was more than any other jumper in training at the time of his last race. The old boy loved life in retirement at Jackdaws Castle, and we were thrilled to have him. He was an enormous help to our budding jockeys. Everyone involved with him was deeply upset when he had to be put down in August, 1995, after breaking a leg in his box.

The horses were in outstanding form all season following our departure from Condicote. On the final Saturday before the Cheltenham Festival I recorded another four-timer spread over three meetings. Springholm and Emperor Buck, both ridden by my amateurs, won at Sandown, Winter Squall landed a valuable hurdle race at Chepstow, ridden by Richard Dunwoody, and young Warren Marston, my promising claiming jockey, was successful on Scrutineer at Wolverhampton.

The 1993 Cheltenham Festival produced one winner for Jackdaws Castle in its first season – Strong Beau, in the Kim Muir Chase, ridden by Tom Jenks – and several near misses. Wonder Man was just caught on the hill by Travado in the Arkle, Shamana, a daughter of Broadsword, was second in the Grand Annual, while Baydon Star and Travelling Wrong each finished third. We also suffered one major reverse. I thought my exciting young chaser Barton Bank was probably the pick of my team at the meeting but he burst a blood vessel before halfway in the Sun Alliance Chase and was quickly pulled up.

One who did not appear at Cheltenham was Viking Flagship, a recent arrival and as bonny a horse as you could ever wish to train. He had started off by running twenty-three times on the flat in Ireland, at two and three, without ever threatening to win a race. Later, he developed into a useful juvenile hurdler with Martin Pipe and was then bought in a private deal by Graham Roach. It took me ages to get him fit at Condicote during our last season there. He arrived as big as a bull, but once he was reasonably straight after two runs, he won a nice prize at Taunton and ran prominently in all the top handicap hurdle races.

If Viking Flagship had come to me twenty years ago I would not have won a race with him. The work he does at Jackdaws Castle is quite phenomenal. I have never known a horse need so much exercise. He often goes out for over an hour on the horse walker first lot, then canters three times, six days a week, second lot. In the evening he goes back on the walker for another hour.

Viking Flagship proved to be a quick, accurate jumper of fences at home and should have been unbeaten in the spring of 1993. He was well clear when falling on his debut at Nottingham in February, then quickly rattled up a hat-trick in novice chases. He had an outstanding chance in the Grand Annual Chase, but I withdrew him at the last moment because the ground was too firm. Encouraged by weather forecasts promising rain, I then sent him up to Liverpool, but again pulled him out when it did not arrive. He was in such robust form after winning with impressive ease at Chepstow that I took him to Ireland for the Punchestown Festival. What a trip we had.

The morning after Viking Flagship trotted up in a £25,000 handicap, he was so fresh he nearly chased me out of his box. Right, I thought, you can run again. Sure enough on Thursday he beat the best Irish novices with ease, and I swear he was a better horse the second time he ran. Though the ground at Punchestown was ideal for Viking Flagship, the weather was unbearably hot.

During the meeting I stayed with Brendan Powell's parents, Benny and Sheila, at their stud a mile and a half from the course. Brendan had arranged to give me a lift there after racing, but somehow, in the confusion, we managed to miss each other. By this time the celebrations had been in full swing for some time, so, still wearing my sheepskin coat, I set off across country in the vague direction of the Powell home. Sweat was pouring off me when I eventually reached the lane leading to the stud. I suppose I must have been a hundred yards from the house when Brendan pulled up beside me, grinning hugely, and offered me a lift.

You learn to expect the unexpected in jump racing but I admit I was a bit surprised when Richard Dunwoody rang me early one Monday morning at the end of March to explain that he had just been released from a night in the cells at Paddington

Green police station in London. He told me that he had been arrested in the early hours for standing up for another jockey, Roger Marley, after a lively night at the Jockeys' Awards dinner, at the Hilton Hotel in Park Lane. He explained what happened, and for me that was the end of the matter. We all had a good laugh about it since both riders were let off with a caution.

Richard is ultra-professional at all times but he is entitled to let his hair down now and then. I was just pleased that he informed me before I heard the news elsewhere. It was typical of him that he issued a public apology for the adverse publicity he had brought on the Awards dinner and his fellow jockeys. The incident did not appear to affect his ability in the saddle, for the next day at Sandown he won a race for me on a horse called, of all things, Musthaveaswig. I thought he rode very well for a man with a hangover.

There were times that winter when Richard's arrangement to split his rides between my horses and those of Nicky Henderson stretched my patience to the limit. Basically, I felt I was number one, but I still did my best to let him off for one of Nicky's when I could. Unfortunately, Nicky thought that he was number one, too. The whole thing started to go wrong when Richard tried to ride too many of Nicky's horses in preference to mine. I did not like playing second fiddle one bit. It was all very messy.

Since we were having easily our best season, I told Richard early in 1993 that in future I would be having my own retained jockey, either him or someone else. I also brought over Charlie Swan from Ireland to ride for me at Kempton and Doncaster when Richard opted to ride for Nicky on those days. I was not prepared to go on as we had been, with Nicky and I having a permanent tug-of-war. It was not fair on the owners or me. If you have seventy or eighty horses you need total commitment from your stable jockey. You cannot be ducking and diving.

Towards the end of the season Richard rode Wont Be Gone Long for Nicky Henderson in the Grand National, which became void after two false starts. Given what happened before and afterwards, it was probably just as well that I did not have a runner in the race that year.

Four days later Peter Scudamore announced his retirement. The news, though not entirely unexpected, started a frantic jockeys' merry-go-round that ended with my losing the services of Richard Dunwoody after seven eventful and increasingly successful years. This time there were no recriminations from me at the manner of my jockey's departure.

As soon as the news broke Richard asked to see Colin and myself, and explained that if Martin Pipe offered him the job he would have to consider it very seriously. I did not think he would go, because he was already certain to be champion for the first time with almost two months of the season still left. He had an extremely good retainer, was riding good horses for me and somehow I could not envisage Richard ending up at Newton Abbot for Martin Pipe on Boxing Day.

There was a tremendous amount of speculation at the time, because everyone assumed Richard's was one of the names in the frame for Pipe's job. The other two main candidates seemed to be Adrian Maguire and the Irish champion Charlie Swan. As the days passed without any decision, Richard said he had not been approached by Martin Pipe and I believed him, but there came a point when I decided I was not going to be left behind in the game of musical chairs.

At this stage I hardly knew Adrian Maguire, but I admired his riding. The first time I noticed him was when he won three races in a day at Sandown, which he subsequently lost because of a muddle over the allowance he was claiming at the time. It was obvious that he was exceptional on a horse going to and over a fence. First, I sounded out one of his mentors Tom O'Mahoney. Then, at Cheltenham in April, I had the briefest of conversations with Adrian. I asked 'Yes?' and he replied 'Yes.' That was all we said at the time.

Colin Smith and I then decided that we needed to make firm plans for the following season. We were not prepared to wait any longer for Martin Pipe. I told Richard that we wanted to know his answer after the Punchestown meeting in Ireland, which concluded on April 29. At the same time Adrian and I confirmed our brief conversation at Cheltenham. Early the next week, after riding at Newton Abbot for Martin Pipe, Richard rang to say that he had been to see David Pipe, Martin's father, on the way back from Devon, and would be joining them the next season. I remember that his parents were unhappy at his choice and his wife Carol was in tears.

Naturally I was extremely sorry to lose him. I think it was a very difficult decision for him to make, and he had done his best to keep me informed of developments. In the end I think he felt he had to go to Martin Pipe to be certain of becoming champion again. Quantity of winners rather than quality was the decisive factor. Jumping is now a numbers game. I suspect Richard was terrified that, if he turned down Martin Pipe's job, Adrian Maguire would take it and probably the championship as well.

I immediately made formal contact with Adrian and prior to our end-of-season party we had a short meeting to finalise details of the retainer. He proved to be a delight to work with, entirely straightforward in every way. If I asked him to go to ride at Timbuktoo, he would do so without question, irrespective of what might be happening elsewhere. He is invariably cheerful, completely professional, has a wicked sense of humour and a natural way with animals. The moment he walks into our house, the cats and dogs are all over him.

By early May nearly all my horses were already out at grass enjoying a well-earned break, and for a while it seemed we would be stuck in the nervous 'nineties, but a raid on Perth ensured that I finally reached my first century of winners in a season. Sandybraes took my score to ninety-nine during the evening, and the following day, May 13, the victory of Stylus, ridden by Richard Dunwoody, made our total one hundred, plus two in Ireland. It was entirely fitting that Colin Smith was present at Perth to witness this historic landmark for his own yard.

We could not have asked for a better start at Jackdaws Castle, for I readily confess I was thinking in terms of fifty winners. The beauty of the place is that you can do what you want, when you want, how you want. The move from Condicote has given me peace of mind and a new, exciting challenge. Our results that first season offered conclusive evidence that Colin's vision of an ultra-modern, highly efficient training complex had truly become reality. The facilities are second to none.

26

Champion trainer

Adrian Maguire set off in sparkling form in his first season at Jackdaws Castle. With the help of his highly efficient agent Dave Roberts, and a hatful of early winners supplied by John White, he soon established a big lead over Richard Dunwoody. Adrian reached fifty on October 25, 1993 and one hundred two months later. His startling strike rate put my modest efforts as a jockey to shame. It used to take me all season to ride fifty winners. Adrian's first success for me that season came on Belstone Fox at Southwell, early in October. The show was on the road.

While I was riding we used to give top priority to the traditional dinner for the champion jockey. For years it was held on the Friday night of the November meeting at the Queen's Hotel in Cheltenham. After a few starchy speeches from senior members of the Steeplechase Company, the champion then had to reply. Betting on the length of his address was always brisk. Several lasted barely a minute, though in later years John Francome introduced a new level of speaking with his easy delivery and risqué jokes.

Once the formal part of the dinner was over we would really start to let our hair down. Often we rearranged the tables and chairs to form an obstacle race. One year I remember heading for home without any shoes; other years I did not remember much at all the next morning. In those days the dinner was strictly an all-male function, while the wives and girlfriends ate in a separate room.

More recently the dinner has developed into the Champion Jockey's Ball and is now held at the racecourse. I was very proud that Richard Dunwoody became champion in his final year with me in 1993, and extremely disappointed that he decided to give the ball a miss. It would have been unthinkable in my day. By the time he was due to receive his award in November, 1993, he was on his way by Concorde to America to ride in the Colonial Cup.

I appreciate that jockeys have to earn a living, but sometimes you have to make a stand in life. I told Richard he should have been present, however lucrative the ride in America. What's more, if he had still been my jockey, I would have made it very hard for him to slip away. A number of my owners clubbed together to book two tables at the dinner to support him, and they too were disappointed that he did not show up. I think he was the first champion to do this, and I very much hope he has not started a trend. I made my views on his behaviour very clear in my column in the *Racing Post* on the day of the dinner.

That evening Carol Dunwoody put me firmly back in my box in a witty acceptance speech on behalf of her husband. She explained that I had drummed into Richard time and again that he should always put work above pleasure. 'And,' she added pointedly as she turned to me, 'Richard has gone to America to work.' The applause that greeted her remarks suggested she had plenty of support.

Richard Dunwoody was back in plenty of time to ride for me the following weekend at Aintree, where the failure of Meleagris to start led to a heated and widely publicised exchange between the starter Simon Morant and myself. Though the horse is not easy, we have learned now to humour him. The key is to keep him on the go at the start, with me or my representative just behind him, ready to lead him in. At Aintree I sent Alan King to the start with Meleagris, who became upset, began kicking out at the running rails and disappeared backwards from the start line.

By the time Alan tried to bring him forward again, Simon had let the others go. The occasion clearly got to Simon Morant that day. There was a new mechanism in force at the Grand National start, and later a bomb scare caused a delay. As a result he did not give the horse much of a chance. Significantly, Meleagris started in every other race that season and since.

I was furious at the decision to withdraw the horse, lost my cool and told Simon, rather unkindly, that he was not fit to start white mice. I also demanded to see the stewards to register a formal complaint, but they took no action. A week later, at

Leicester, I apologised to Simon and shook his hand. There was an amusing postscript to this story at Christmas. Among Simon's pile of presents was a box of chocolate white mice from another trainer. By a curious coincidence I also received a similar gift from the owner of Meleagris. While I was riding, jockeys had enormous respect for starters and vice versa. Unfortunately today's jockeys do not have much confidence in some starters.

Triple Witching gave Shirley Robins her third successive victory in the valuable Tote Silver Trophy at Chepstow early in November, on his first outing for two years. I had planned to run him in a novice chase at Worcester, but the ground was too firm, so I took advantage of his generous handicap mark over hurdles. He then won impressively at Newbury.

When Triple Witching first joined us, he proved to be the most terrible box walker, would not relax, and became so wound up that I introduced him to a sheep called Jasper. The pair were soon inseparable, and Triple Witching was transformed in his stable. While the horse was out at exercise, Jasper was free to roam the yard, and even helped to keep the grass mown.

This was the first year since our marriage that Dinah did not ride out each morning. We had been a bit concerned when she nearly blacked out while judging at the Jersey Show in the summer. The same thing happened when she started riding on our return from Jersey. Our doctor was sufficiently worried to put Dinah on a heart monitor for twenty-four hours. After further tests she was put on Beta Blockers, which seem to have sorted the problem out.

Barton Bank returned into training without any sign of the problem that had afflicted him at Cheltenham in the spring. He was originally bought by David Minton for Jenny Mould for 24,000 guineas, largely because he was such an attractive, athletic walker. But when he first came to me as a four-year-old, he was so bad tempered he would kick horses and humans alike without any provocation, declined to go through gates and, if he felt so inclined, refused to walk on or off the gallops.

He was, in short, a difficult so-and-so, but eventually became the victim of his own bad behaviour when he reared over backwards and smashed the top of his withers. It was a career-threatening injury which could have affected his co-ordination, and the nature of the damage may well have contributed to his erratic jumping in later years.

Barton Bank missed a year as a result, and was much better behaved when he came back, though he will still kick at another horse. He made a belated debut in the bumper won by Carobee at Warwick in November, 1992, and finished just behind the placed horses. He then won a minor race on his debut over hurdles, ridden by Robert Bellamy, in dreadful ground and improved through the season to such purpose that, starting at 20–1, he beat my much more fancied runner Bishops Island in a decent race over three miles at Liverpool. I have a photograph at home showing Richard Dunwoody on Bishops Island, looking across at Carl Llewellyn at the last hurdle as if to say, 'What the hell are you doing here?'

I had one of my rare disagreements with Raymond Mould over this race. I wanted to use Robert Bellamy again. He insisted on booking Carl Llewellyn. This did not please me, because I believe you should be loyal to your jockeys, but I gave in on this occasion since Raymond was clearly not in the mood to argue.

The next season the signs were not immediately promising when I turned Barton Bank's attention to fences, for he was not the most natural jumper at home. Carl Llewellyn gravely assured me that the horse lacked scope after schooling him over three small fences. I replied, 'Really. Go down, do it again, and let him stride along this time.'

We soon learned that you had to be definite on Barton Bank at his fences. He won four times in impressive fashion that season, fell three out at Kempton with the race at his mercy and then broke a blood vessel after only a circuit at the 1993 Festival.

The following autumn Adrian spent a lot of time schooling Barton Bank on his own over our biggest fences. In the end the horse was doing it the way his jockey wanted. They kicked off together with a stunning victory from the front in the Charlie Hall Chase at Wetherby, then beat Cab on Target in a match at Sandown and crowned it all with an unforgettable success in the King George VI Tripleprint Chase on Boxing Day.

I was so taken by Adrian's positive riding that I told reporters at Kempton he was the best jockey I had ever seen. His aggression and courage ensured victory in a tight finish with Bradbury Star. The pair were locked together on the run-in, but I felt that Barton Bank was always holding the challenger.

I left the course in the happiest of moods, which lasted until I received a call on my return home informing me that the stewards had banned Adrian, and Bradbury Star's jockey Declan Murphy, for two days for excessive use of the whip. Frankly, I was furious at their action. It was comical. Adrian had given the horse a fabulous ride, survived a bad blunder at the fourth last, and left a bit up his sleeve for the run-in. If you have to be critical you can say that Adrian was a bit untidy from the last, but that was hardly sufficient cause for banning him.

It was ridiculous to discipline the two jockeys after such an epic finish. Neither horse was marked. I subsequently spoke to a lot of professional racing people, and not one of them saw anything wrong with the riding of either jockey. Declan Murphy, sensible fellow, later appealed successfully against his suspension. In hindsight, I made a mistake in not encouraging Adrian to appeal as well.

Barton Bank's superb performance catapulted him right to the forefront of the betting for the Gold Cup. I decided to give him a long break and bring him fresh to Cheltenham without another race. But a week before the Festival he burst a blood vessel badly at home during routine exercise, in the presence of television crews and reporters. It was devastating for everyone connected with the horse. We had all been convinced the Gold Cup was his for the taking. Now his season was at an end.

We had assembled a strong team that year including the doughty filly Mysilv, who belonged to David Minton's Million in Mind syndicate. It is not widely known that I am the only trainer who is also a shareholder. I took the view that I should support Minty because he has always supported me, and planned to hand over my subscription at Towcester in December, 1993, on the day of Relkeel's debut over hurdles.

When I could not find Minty, I asked my friend Dave Dick, another shareholder, to pass on the money for me. Dave replied, 'Why don't you put it all on Relkeel first?' The membership fee at the time was £1,250, and Relkeel won at 7–1, but I do not regret declining the suggestion. Since I have a fit if I put £10 on a horse, it was not even an option.

Both my mother and brother are members of Million in Mind, too, along with Mercy Rimell, Brough Scott, John Oaksey and many other friends. That season a total of 160 shareholders owned eight horses running in our colours, four on the flat and four over jumps. The results in the coming months ensured that we all enjoyed a healthy dividend.

The previous season Million in Mind had a lot of fun with a filly called Beauchamp Grace, who won four races over hurdles for me and started favourite for the Daily Express Triumph Hurdle. I like training fillies, so was delighted when David Minton sent me Mysilv as our next candidate for the Triumph. Now if you listen to David for long enough, he will claim responsibility for buying just about every Triumph winner in the last twenty years. The truth is that he has been involved with at least half a dozen, and Mysilv would soon add to his impressive tally.

She had been high on David's shopping list for some time before he bought her for 27,000 guineas at Newmarket, late in October, 1993, the day after she had run at Redcar, and immediately felt he was mad to have paid so much. When she arrived here she proved to be a weaver, which is usually a sign of nerves. We solved that little problem by putting her in a stable which allowed her an excellent view of proceedings in the yard and helped her to relax.

On her first morning Mysilv popped over twenty-seven little tree trunks like a natural. Later she worked decently, so it was not a surprise when she hacked up by thirty lengths at Kempton on her debut. In the next few months Mysilv won four more races on the bounce, culminating in the Adonis Hurdle at Kempton. I took a bit of a chance running her there, because she had aggravated a minor cut on a hind leg in her previous race at Newbury, despite wearing boots as a precaution.

The day after Newbury, a lump came up on the same area which required constant treatment, but I was encouraged that she did not once take a lame step. Only three horses were declared for the Adonis Hurdle and two of them were mine, Mysilv and Winter Forest. There was the added attraction of a £50,000 bonus if the winner subsequently took the Triumph Hurdle. Wearing a bandage to protect the sore spot on her leg, Mysilv won in a canter by thirty lengths from Winter Forest.

Adrian's marvellous season turned sour at Warwick on January 15. He started the day almost forty winners ahead of Richard Dunwoody and the pair fought out a rousing finish in a televised novice chase, which was to have the most serious repercussions in the following weeks.

No sooner had Richard, on Castle Diamond, beaten Adrian, on Ramstar, by a short head, than the stewards called an inquiry during which Adrian was asked to explain his forceful use of the whip on his mount. Many observers felt he was in danger of an automatic suspension, but the stewards, correctly in my view, accepted his explanation that he was only waving his whip in the closing stages without making contact. That should have been the end of the matter.

Half an hour after Ramstar's defeat, I ran two in the Victor Chandler Chase, transferred at the last minute from Ascot, which was waterlogged. Adrian chose to ride Waterloo Boy, as he had been working much better at home than Viking Flagship, who was partnered by Richard Dunwoody. Viking Flagship appeared to be well beaten two fences out, but Richard gave him the ride of a lifetime to catch Egypt Mill Prince on the flat. Waterloo Boy, running a rare bad race, finished tailed off in fourth place.

The later victory of Moorcroft Boy in the Warwick National offered Adrian some consolation for an otherwise miserable afternoon. Previously a hunter chaser, Moorcroft Boy was developing into a serious Grand National candidate, and had already won over four miles at Cheltenham with any amount in hand.

Unfortunately the Warwick meeting was dominated by the Ramstar affair, which was then inflamed by one of the Jockey Club's stipendiary stewards involved in the inquiry. The next day I was inundated with calls from the press, who, to a man, seemed to believe that Adrian had been let off lightly. Worse, one of them informed me that the official concerned was complaining about the stewards' failure to take action against Adrian.

I was dismayed by this turn of events because it is not a stipe's position to be chatting to the press about such matters. Rightly or wrongly, the Warwick stewards felt that Adrian did not deserve to be punished. Crucially, when Ramstar's owner Ron Gladwin came round to see his horse the next day, there was not a mark on him. Ramstar had eaten up and seemed as fresh as paint. After looking at the film of the finish repeatedly, I defy anyone to say how often Adrian hit the horse. This did not deter some journalists from claiming he had struck Ramstar as many as twenty-six times.

On Monday morning Anthony Mildmay-White, the chairman of the Jockey Club's disciplinary committee, announced that the case would be reviewed at Portman Square. I felt the Jockey Club's hand had been forced by the press. Fuelled by the comments of one stipe, the newspapers had whipped up such a controversy that the disciplinary committee had to be seen to do something. After this I knew that Adrian would have no chance at Portman Square.

He had already fallen foul of the stewards twice earlier in the season, at Cheltenham where he was given a caution, and at Kempton. Worse was to come. Before the Warwick inquiry was reopened, he picked up a four-day ban for careless riding at Folkestone. Just over a week later he was belatedly suspended for a further six days for the Warwick incident. I was left fuming at the injustice of what I was convinced was trial by the press. I resented the personal abuse given to my jockey in the papers and did my best to protect him from the unfair criticism.

This whole business of the whip makes me hot under the collar. When the authorities first tackled the subject they had a point. A lot of jockeys copied Lester Piggott's high-actioned, overarm style, without matching his strength or effectiveness. Once a jockey starts winding up a horse in this manner it takes time to break the habit. Peter Scudamore, Richard Dunwoody and Adrian Maguire have all done it in the past. As they all rode for me I suppose I have to take some of the blame; but I certainly did not encourage it. Since then they have all tried hard to conform to the new rules. Now we see polish, restraint and strength, yet they are still being punished.

The decision to suspend Michael Kinane after a truly brilliant ride on Grand Lodge at Royal Ascot in June, 1994, merely confirmed the absurdity of the present rules. He should have been praised for the skilful, and above all correct use of the whip, which ensured the narrowest of victories in a Group One race. Instead he was reprimanded like a naughty schoolboy.

I have had enough ups and downs with the stewards on this topic already but I do know, beyond doubt, that they had their daggers out for both Adrian Maguire and Richard Dunwoody. These are two of the finest, most committed, and dynamic jockeys the sport has ever seen.

Shortly after Warwick, I joined Toby Balding and Peter Cundell in a delegation from the Trainers' Federation to discuss the whole vexed subject at Portman Square with Anthony Mildmay-White and the then senior stipe. At the time I felt that we were making some progress.

The stewards' obsession with the whip is unfortunate for the image of racing. The rules are also too fussy; changes have been made to satisfy the viewing public. I think most people who go racing are more than happy with the way Adrian rides. They know Adrian would never abuse a horse. He is a caring young man who loves animals and is the quickest I know to pull a horse up if he is not happy with it. However, he is also paid to win races.

There are still grey areas that need putting right. For a start it would help if people who understood how to use a whip were on more stewards' panels. At least Michael Pope has always been consistent in his opposition. Others, including some commentators who should know better, have simply jumped on the bandwagon. The fact is that there are many worse problems in the sport, such as horses being asked to race on rock-hard ground.

I have been in racing all my life and have a fair idea of what is right. The whip is there to encourage, not hurt, and is an essential piece of a jockey's equipment. Used correctly with the arm kept low and close to the body, it is often the only way to extract that last effort at the end of a race. Obviously some horses will do their utmost without a smack, but most will pull out just a little bit more with some encouragement.

Most whips nowadays are covered with thick felt to eliminate skin damage, an excellent innovation brought in by the late Roy Mangan. Although an untidy rider may appear to be over-using his stick, it is unlikely that much pain will be inflicted with this type of whip.

I hate the abuse of any animal and do not allow my lads to carry whips at home unless they are schooling. Every jockey should be capable of kicking and pushing throughout a race without having to resort to it. One of the prime exponents of this art is Willie Carson, but sadly there are rather too many lazy riders who pick up their sticks because the alternative is too much like hard work.

Racehorses in general have a superb life and most of them,

being naturally competitive, love their work. Like leading athletes, they live in the best of hotels, have the best food and constant, caring attention. In return they race probably no more than ten times a season and, again like athletes, have the odd hard race. There are not many horses that worry too much about five or six smacks at the end of a race and the ones that do will soon be given another job in life.

Earlier in the season I had intended to use Richard Dunwoody on one or two of mine if Adrian was at another meeting. When it happened, it was clear that Adrian was unhappy with this development, which, he explained, was hardly helping his cause while he chased all over the country trying to keep ahead of Richard in the jockeys' championship. At first I relented, but when Adrian was suspended I felt I had no option but to turn to Richard once more. He was unquestionably the best available; that is what my owners expect and deserve. I also pointed out to Adrian's agent Dave Roberts that I had booked Peter Scudamore in the past while Richard was out of action.

With Adrian on the sidelines, and Martin Pipe's horses back in form, Richard Dunwoody rapidly reduced the gap between them, until a moment of madness on March 1 at Nottingham so nearly ended his chance of retaining the title. Richard was in front on Raggerty approaching the second last in a selling hurdle when Adrian came through to challenge on Mr Geneaology.

What followed defied belief. Richard looked across, spotted his great rival on the only apparent danger, and then proceeded to swerve sharply left and ride him off the course. As a result Mr Geneaology was forced out just as he reached the wing of the hurdle. Raggerty won unchallenged but, inevitably, lost the race at the subsequent inquiry, at which Richard was suspended for fourteen days for intentional interference. I think that was quite lenient because he could not have complained if he had been given a month. It was totally out of character for Richard to behave in that manner; he is not like that. He has never been a dirty rider, but at the time, I suspect, the constant battle with Adrian was getting to him.

This ban left Richard inactive during the Cheltenham Festival, which in 1994 was yet again a meeting of mixed emotions for me. On Tuesday Baydon Star ran well to claim second place in the Arkle. The next day Viking Flagship won the Queen Mother Champion Chase with Adrian Maguire riding like a demon, helping to force the pace down the inside the whole way. It was as good a race as we saw all season, a stirring display of courage and determination by horse and rider.

I watched the closing stages unfold from a point beside the last hurdle where I sometimes seek solitude, away from the crowds, with just my binoculars for company. As three horses galloped past me, more or less in line, with Viking Flagship perhaps half a length down, I remember thinking that if Adrian asked him up there, he had to be very brave. Sure enough, the horse stood off so far you could not believe he would reach the fence. All I saw was his front feet come up. I turned to watch them race away and was nearly mown down by the riderless Remittance Man. I sensed him coming, stood still and he brushed past me. Had I moved I would have been history. I just recovered in time to see Viking Flagship hold on tenaciously, by a neck, from Travado.

I was elated to win this prestigious race after going close in it so many times. Though I have been training a long time it still means so much to me to win any race, but this was extra special. Somehow I managed to make it back to the winner's enclosure, where I gave an interview to BBC television, before I was overcome with emotion and sought refuge, on my own, in the little tea room beside the weighing-room.

I did not know what to do. One moment I felt like crying; the next I thought I was going to be sick. For a while I was speechless, so overwhelmed that I did not emerge until after the next race. A security alert had delayed the presentation, but eventually I made my way to the Royal Box with Graham Roach, who proudly received his trophy from the Queen Mother.

Shortly before the 1994 Festival over ninety members of Million in Mind did their level best to drink us out of house and home on a Sunday visit to see Mysilv. Stocks were running dangerously low before they left to continue their day out with lunch at the Plough in Ford. In my father's day owners were not encouraged to call on their trainer on a Sunday; now we are open to all and sundry. My parents did not keep any alcohol at home; you could say I am making up for them!

Aware of Adrian's concern about risking Mysilv on fast going, I had spent the final week before the Festival praying that the ground did not dry out too much for her before the Daily Express Triumph Hurdle. Really, she had to run, whatever the conditions, because the terms of the syndicate dictated that she would be going to the sales in May. By Thursday, the ground was plenty fast enough for her but at least the nagging minor injury on her hind leg had healed. Mysilv was the least affected by all the build-up. She seemed to spend most of the time asleep in her box.

Once again I watched from my position down by the last hurdle. This time I could see that Mysilv had the race in the bag as she set off up the hill with a useful lead. Afterwards I was engulfed in the winner's enclosure by well over a hundred jubilant shareholders. The scenes around the horse were unbelievable. People who owned one hair of Mysilv's tail were crying with happiness as if they had just won the Grand National. That is the beauty of syndicates.

It was a wonderful occasion and a personal triumph for David Minton, whose brainchild had given a chance for so many people who love racing to have a share in a decent horse at a realistic price. As he walked back in with Mysilv, Minty gave me a smacking great kiss. I hope that is not the reason a beaming smile remained on his face for days. The Princess Royal joined in the party in the winner's enclosure and appeared equally elated.

Jump racing has a habit of bringing you down to earth. Just over half an hour later Triple Witching took a horrid fall in the Stayers' Hurdle. Luckily horse and rider were unscathed but the following month we had a disaster when Baydon Star broke his back in a fall at Ayr. This was fate at her most cruel for all of us, especially the Robins, who had only just come to terms with the loss of Mighty Mogul. It briefly left them wondering if they should pull out of jumping altogether. Baydon Star, who was ridden throughout the previous season by Dinah, was very much a favourite in the yard and a horse with huge potential. He was such a gentleman you could take him up to bed with you.

At Liverpool Moorcroft Boy came desperately close to achieving my ambition to win the Grand National. On ground so testing that only six completed the course, he was always handy, led two out, but tired on the run-in and was eventually well beaten in third place behind Miinnehoma, who was ridden with super coolness by Richard Dunwoody.

When the going is as deep as it was at Liverpool, I tell all my jockeys that they must push their horses right out to the line. By doing just that on Kadi and Corner Boy on Friday,

Adrian won two races narrowly for me that others might have lost. On Saturday, in the opening race, he virtually lifted the Irish-trained For Reg past the leader Land Afar on the run-in. It was further evidence of his single-minded will to win, but the stewards took exception and suspended him, yet again, for two days for excessive use of the whip. It was yet again a questionable decision, because if he had eased up for one moment, For Reg would not have won.

In April Minty laid on an open day for all the Million in Mind shareholders at Tattersalls sales paddocks in Newmarket. Mysilv was paraded with their other horses before I was presented with the Finale Trophy, an equine statue, by now adorned in her colours, which she won at Chepstow.

By this stage we all knew that soon she might be leaving Jackdaws Castle for ever. We talked about putting together a team to buy her back when she appeared at the Doncaster sales in May, and Minty did go up to 130,000 guineas at the auction. I thought she might make as much as 125,000, and won £100 in a side bet with Mick Easterby, who was sure that she would be coming back to me. We were all shaken as the bidding soared past 150,000 guineas.

Eventually Mysilv was knocked down to Charlie Egerton on behalf of another syndicate, Elite Racing, for 155,000 guineas, a world record price for a jumper at public auction. Many of our shareholders at the sale were in tears as she was led away. It was an emotional time because she had given us such a wonderful season.

I was very sad to lose Mysilv, too, both as her trainer and as a shareholder. She is a lovely mare, but sometimes in this business you have to harden your heart and be philosophical. It would not have been right to continue bidding beyond our means. We know now that Mysilv has done her new connections proud, and I am genuinely delighted for them. But it is never easy for a five-year-old taking on older horses, and even harder when you have to do it from the front. At the price offered we had to let Mysilv go.

April, 1994 was notable for my first Group winner on the flat with Silver Wisp, who had finished third in the 1992 Derby, trained by Geoff Lewis. It came in the Group Two Madagans Jockey Club Stakes at Newmarket's Guineas meeting. Bill and Shirley Robins had sent the horse to me at the end of the previous flat season, but try as I might I could not get him right. One day he seemed lame in his off hind; the next he was wrong in his near hind. There was a problem somewhere; it showed when he was cantering in the way that he seemed almost hunched in his quarters. I realised that he was in considerable discomfort, on and off, but tests and X-rays failed to locate the problem.

There seemed two options open to us: to sell Silver Wisp abroad as a stallion, or to geld him. The Robins agreed to the second course and we took the opportunity to hobday him at the same time. As soon as the operation was over Silver Wisp was a different horse. I did consider training him for a hurdle race at Liverpool, but ran out of time, so chose to have a crack on the flat instead. We booked Pat Eddery for his first run at Pontefract, and flew up to Yorkshire with him in his own plane. All the way there Pat said he would challenge very late on Silver Wisp, but in the end he was in front too soon and was just pipped on the line by Alderbrook, who was to make a dramatic impact on jumping the following spring.

At Newmarket Pat switched to the French-trained favourite Apple Tree, so I engaged Michael Hills to ride Silver Wisp, who was ignored in the betting at 20–1. The pair fought out an exciting finish, with Silver Wisp prevailing by a head. I was tickled pink to win such a big prize on the racecourse where I had begun as a jockey forty-three years earlier.

The Hardwicke Stakes at Royal Ascot now beckoned. Dinah and I have been regulars at this meeting for years and always have a huge daily picnic in the trainers' car park. These invariably continue after racing long into the evening. Conscious that Michael Stoute, Ian Balding and Guy Harwood had all enjoyed success at Cheltenham, I was delighted to be going to the best flat meeting of the year with a serious contender.

Unfortunately Silver Wisp lost his chance when he hurt himself coming out of the stalls. He is a serious horse, and has shown immense promise over hurdles at home, but he tweaked a suspensory ligament just before he was going to run over hurdles in the autumn of 1994. The injury has been pin-fired and he has been given plenty of time.

Our double at the Cheltenham Festival on top of another solid season of results had given me a timely boost in my bid to become champion trainer for the first time, but the triumph of Miinnehoma at Aintree helped his trainer Martin

Pipe markedly reduce the gap. By the end of April I had all but run out of ammunition at a time when Adrian, too, needed every assistance if he was to catch Richard Dunwoody in their enthralling duel for the jockeys' title. The last few weeks of the season tested both our nerves to the full.

Late in May, I left with Dinah for a fortnight's holiday uncertain if I would return as champion trainer. The last month was proving the hardest of all. I had been struggling to find runners since Liverpool, and by this stage the fate of the championship was out of my hands. It was just a question of whether Martin Pipe could win enough prize money to catch me. People kept telling me I would hold on, but I do not take things for granted and the championship was never far from my thoughts while we were away.

You never know when you should take a break but we usually manage to snatch a couple of weeks' holiday during the summer. When the boys were small we would drive to the Brittany coast and stay in self-catering cottages. We have also taken canal boat holidays in the Camargue and later down the river Charente, which runs through the brandy towns of Cognac and Jammac, so naturally we had to visit as many of the distilleries as we could. One day, after mooring just outside Cognac, we found ourselves cycling past an impressive riverside estate, which we learned was the home of M. Killian Hennessy. On the way back to the boat we cheekily pedalled down the drive to call on M. Hennessy who, realising we were racing people, arranged a personal tour for us round the House of Hennessy the next day.

We have also spent many holidays on the island of Corsica but the latest craze is Africa. For the last two years we have been on a horse-riding safari in Botswana. It sounds a bit like a busman's holiday, but we both found it a wonderful adventure. Except for the camp staff, you do not see a soul for the entire time you are there; just animals and miles of the Okavango Delta. Best of all, there is no telephone. We enjoyed our trip so much last year that we persuaded no end of friends to follow suit.

On our return from Botswana early in June, 1994 we discovered that I had held on from Martin Pipe by a margin of just over £34,000. Eighty-one horses from Jackdaws Castle won eighty-one races, and earned £754,069 in win and place money. I had never thought in terms of being champion trainer, and certainly did not expect to be that season, since I did not imagine for one minute that I had the necessary firepower. We started off with a lot of backward horses who offered promise, more in the long-term. A century of winners was a beginning the previous year; it showed what we could do at Jackdaws Castle. My first championship in our second season there was a team effort and another feather in the cap of Colin Smith. I hope there are more to come.

Adrian Maguire was not quite so fortunate in his valiant attempt to become champion jockey. Richard Dunwoody finally caught him on May 14, and then quickly pulled nine clear with a flurry of winners. Adrian all but closed the gap with a superhuman effort in the final days, but Richard held on to win, with 197 winners to Adrian's 194. Theirs was surely one of the longest-running duels in sport. The result was tough on Adrian. No other jump jockey has won so many races and not become champion in the process. But time is on his side; his day will come.

In our first season together, he proved to be the most tremendous asset. If you are lucky to employ a rare, precious talent like him, you sense it might be unwise to try to alter him. The best, instinctive sportsmen like Adrian do not need much coaching. He has learned from his mistakes and the proof is in the results. It would have been wrong to change him just as it would have been unwise to tinker with a player of David Gower's class. Natural brilliance has to be nurtured and directed forwards, not coached out as is so often the case in sport today.

It is a delight to have Adrian riding for me. He leaves nothing to chance, is positive in everything he does, seems to have tunnel vision and is focused on one thing, on knowing what he must do to win. I rode against some great jockeys including Fred Winter, Bryan Marshall, Stan Mellor, Terry Biddlecombe, Josh Gifford, David Mould, Jeff King, John Haine and Bill Rees. Adrian is as good as any I have seen, but I would not want to put one above all the others. I just hope he stays with me for many more years.

27

The Duke's Way

My biggest problem in the early autumn of 1994 was finding enough room for all the horses on their way back to Jackdaws Castle. I was not complaining. It is the best possible problem for a trainer to have. With a bit of juggling we managed to increase our capacity to eighty-eight boxes.

Given the choice, I like my horses to come back into training in July so that they can have ninety days' work before they are ready to appear on the racecourse. My uncle Willie Stephenson always said that July was the month jump races would be won. I learned from my father to encourage my owners to feed their horses a bowl of oats at both ends of the day while they are out at grass in the summer. That way, he said, they would always come back in much harder, with their guts already accustomed to a little solid food. The last thing you want is for them to be overweight and soft, which is liable to happen if they stay out too long.

Owners who have the facilities naturally like to keep their horses at home for as long as possible, and some get them semi-fit before sending them back into training. I have thought for a long time now that, unless there is a clinical need for complete rest, every horse would be better off receiving daily light exercise during his summer break to keep his muscles in trim. It would surprise a great many people to know just how many horses develop leg problems in the field through lack of muscle support. How many human athletes completely let their bodies go for two or three months a year?

Happily, road work no longer forms part of our early season routine since our move. We had to do it at Condicote but now, with 500 acres at our disposal, the horses stay on site. It is a relief not to have to go out on the roads. The horses start off with fourteen days walking around the tracks. The fatter ones also go on the horse walker in the mornings, and sometimes evenings as well. This is followed by a further fourteen days of intermittent trotting on the all-weather gallops.

The next step is to start long, extremely steady canters. As the weeks go by the horses build up to two to three canters a day. At the same time we gradually increase their hard feed, which revolves round good hay and oats. After sixty days I start to increase the tempo of work. If it is possible I like my horses to be ready to run by the end of October. That is when jumping starts properly, if there has been enough rain to soften the going sufficiently at racecourses. Over the years I have had no luck running horses early on. You learn from bitter experience that, when the official going is said to be good to firm in the autumn, it is usually more firm than good and your horses come back from the races jarred up. So my season is geared from mid-October to the end of April.

This routine is fundamentally different to the way I trained in the early days at Condicote. Then my horses used to need two or three runs before they were fit; sometimes they were not ready to win a race until after Christmas. It takes time to change your habits, but I do give them all considerably more work now. I often wish that I had spent some time working for another trainer, apart from my father, before I started on my own. My methods have been almost entirely self-taught. It was a question of trial and error, particularly in the early days. Now it is fair to say that most of mine are fit enough to win first time out, if they are good enough.

Michael Dickinson was the man who changed the game in his unrelenting desire to make his horses fitter than those of his rivals. You had the impression that he did a lot of long, steady work with his horses. The results in his heyday were phenomenal. He seemed to be on a different planet.

Martin Pipe does it the other way, and has proved to be even more successful than Michael Dickinson. Trainers from the past would not believe the sheer volume of his triumphs in the last ten years. Martin leaves no stone unturned in his pursuit of winners because he is determined to stay ahead of the pack. His regime, based on short sharp work, seems to have been copied in the last few years by almost every trainer in the country.

Trainers at Lambourn, in particular, appear to be convinced of the virtues of interval training. But as Tim Forster enquired one day at Cheltenham last winter, what is the interval between one canter and the next? Horses have always been trained at intervals, I think it is just different speeds and intervals nowadays.

We have experimented, too, in the vain hope that we can find a new mixture that makes the horses run faster. Unfortunately there is no such thing. A few years ago, on the recommendation of three nutritionists, I had a supplement made up to complement my own feed programme. This is added in powder form to the horses' feed, and appears to be beneficial.

I also put a drop of cider vinegar in the drinking water of horses that are prone to break blood vessels or become set fast. It is an old remedy that is supposed to help thin the blood, and is certainly effective in some cases. Other trials were not successful. I fed the horses lots of carbohydrates for a while, but that did not prove to be the answer.

I always seem to revert to my father's tried and trusted routine of giving horses good hay, good oats and plenty of work. For more than twenty years I have used hay grown by the Hutsbys, a traditional hunting and point-to-pointing family from Ettington in Warwickshire. They grow their own mixture of racehorse hay and used to supply Ryan Price and Fred Winter in years gone by. Fred Hutsby is with me now as an amateur.

I do not feed cubes or nuts, chiefly because I do not know what is in them. In the past salesmen used to badger me to try various types of nuts, but they eventually realised that they were wasting their time and mine. My horses eat up to fourteen lbs of high protein naked oats a day, plus additional vitamins, minerals and fibre considered necessary by the nutritionists.

We have a Jackdaws Castle routine now. The horses canter six days a week. Work mornings are on Wednesdays and Saturdays when they have two warm-up canters before being asked to do something more strenuous. There was a time in the early days when I was definitely looking at my horses rather than training them. Over the past ten years I have increased considerably the amount of work I ask the horses to do, particularly since we started using the all-weather gallops at Jackdaws Castle in 1990.

In contrast, at Condicote I could not work the horses as

quickly as I wished as there was a dip along the fastest stretch of the all-weather gallop that could put undue strain on their tendons at too great a speed. Here the gallops are all uphill, which puts less strain on their legs.

There has also been a significant change in the type of horse I try to buy. Having ridden the great Mill House, I was inclined to be on the look-out for big store horses like him, that might develop into decent chasers one day. Many is the enjoyable day I have spent with my friend Padge Berry in Ireland looking at likely young jumpers. We had plenty of success, too, but a lot of patience was needed as they were invariably slow to mature. I still buy horses from Padge but more of the ready-made variety.

I have to admit an early prejudice against the idea of training horses that had come from the flat. However, by 1981, the year Broadsword was a four-year-old, we were beginning to take on more of these precocious youngsters. Some were cast-offs; others, like Broadsword, clearly had ability. The penny dropped when he came along. Now I love training three-year-olds; I have never had so many of them. They do not need the work of the traditional chasing types, just plenty of schooling.

In the summer of 1995 I had more orders to buy horses than ever before. I buy a good many through David Minton, a bloodstock agent who has been a friend since the days I was riding. I hope Minty will forgive me for suggesting that he is not exactly built on athletic lines. You would not believe it now, but he was once a useful sportsman and used to ride out with me occasionally. One morning he jumped off in a narrow lane when his saddle slipped and was unable to vault back into the saddle. Did I give him some stick. There we were, struggling to heave him on to the horse's back, while the rest of the string disintegrated in mirth.

I speak to Minty seven days a week and also stay in constant touch with Aiden Murphy, who, though he lives in England, has his finger firmly on the pulse of Irish point-to-points. He is over there every weekend and is an excellent spotter of horses for me. It was Aiden's company Whitson Bloodstock who sponsored our horses at the 1995 Cheltenham Festival and also at Liverpool. I was delighted that his enterprise and support was so amply rewarded with our successes and increased orders for him.

Equine flu and the virus are a constant worry for modern

trainers. I suspect it has always been around in a lesser form. The main difference today is the much greater numbers of horses involved. Twenty-five was a big team for my father. When Peter Cazalet was leading trainer he barely had forty horses. Fred Rimell, too, worked with a similar number. Now, with most leading yards having seventy or eighty in training, the virus can spread like wildfire before anyone has a chance to halt it.

When flu vaccinations became compulsory in 1980, I rang one of my owners, Captain Johnny Macdonald-Buchanan, a loyal supporter and a man I sometimes turned to for advice. I explained to the Captain, who was senior steward of the Jockey Club at the time, that it was wrong to force vaccinations on us. For the next twenty minutes I was reduced to holding the phone at arm's length while he gave me a piece of his mind. By the time the conversation ended, I thought it was also the end of a long and happy relationship. Three months later the Captain rang back to apologise. I had, it seemed, caught him at a bad moment.

I was old-fashioned about such training issues, having been brought up to resist change. Father was very set in his ways, and I suppose I was the same. Although I disagreed with compulsory vaccinations at the start, I think the change has proved more or less successful. However, Josh Gifford, for one, begs to differ. My father was so suspicious of vets, quacks, dentists, physios and back specialists that he avoided them as much as possible. Nor did he much approve of injections or anything like that. Today we have someone in almost every day through the winter to check the horses' backs and ensure that everything is in place, while the vets are here most days, too.

I am learning to move with the times and believe that there should be passports with up-to-date vaccinations for every horse and pony in the country. At Jackdaws Castle we keep the horses on paper to reduce dust and associated allergies. Every box has an infra-red light which can be used when the weather turns cold.

Each Tuesday morning we test the blood of every horse that is running in the next week. In addition, our vet looks into the lungs with an endoscope. These tests are analysed that day at their lab and the results are faxed to us. We are looking at two particular readings, blood and muscle enzymes: they are now an important guide to health. We also carry out tracheal washes where necessary. With so many horses stabled together you have to try to eliminate as many problems as possible.

The old days of saying, 'Well, I think he is all right, let's run,' are gone. Now you have to check every detail. If not, you risk the real chance of causing damage by running horses while they are wrong. Then it is too late. Usually, the tests give you a warning in time, although in our second season at Jackdaws Castle we failed to detect a low-grade bacterial infection which affected some of the horses around December.

If you do not take advantage of modern science to safeguard the health of your horses, you risk causing untold damage. The main problem today, I suspect, is that trainers get after their horses too quickly. In the past people like Ivor Anthony would have a horse around for a year or more before thinking of training it properly. They were not under any pressure from owners, so they took their time schooling and handicapping a horse. Horses do not have many easy races now, because owners tend to want their jam yesterday, not tomorrow.

I do not believe in molly-coddling jumpers. That approach is counter-productive. They are tough, outdoor animals, and should be treated accordingly. The only time we shut the top doors at Condicote was in a horizontal blizzard driving straight into the boxes. Even horses turned out in winter are fine provided they have plenty of food, fresh water and some shelter.

Apart from the virus the other constant nightmare for jumping trainers is the never ending problem of leg injuries. If you train jumpers, you have to accept it will happen to a high proportion of your horses at some time; only a handful avoid it. For the vast majority, the enormous strain on tendons and joints leads to injury that invariably requires twelve months' rest if it is to heal satisfactorily. The old-fashioned way of treatment is bar firing, which involves running a red-hot iron across the tendons to encourage healing. Some trainers swear by firing, but it is a practice that I find a bit gruesome and only turn to when all else fails.

Time is the best healer, whatever you decide to do. I have had a certain amount of success with injecting the tendons, which has the advantage of being painless. Other methods of treatment including split tendon operations and carbon fibre implants have not impressed me.

My father fired horses, if necessary, and also believed in

blistering their legs, which encourages the healing process. He handed down his blister recipe of tar and soft soap, which is what I use today on minor injuries. Going round evening stables checking the horses is always fraught with tension. The last thing you want to hear is your head lad ask you to feel a particular horse's leg. Then you know you have a problem.

Prevention, of course, is better than cure and if I have the slightest concern about the going being unsuitable at racecourses I do not run my horses. One moment's impatience can ruin a horse and cost two years of his career. It is never worth the risk. In my book you are never wrong not running; there is always another day. My travelling head lad Jeremy Willis and assistant Alan King know they have my full backing to pull any horse out at any time.

The staff at Jackdaws Castle deserve the best wages and conditions. That is what they get. For a long time all my lads were under twenty-five; a lot of them still are. At first it was a deliberate policy so that I could teach them my way of doing things. I am not saying it is the right way but it suited me. If an older, experienced lad comes along who does not conform to my views, then I would be beating my head against a brick wall. There cannot be any short cuts for stable lads. My father always used to say that if your lads are happy, then the horses will be happy and you will win races. But, if your lads are unhappy, then your horses are likely to be miserable, too, and you will win nothing.

Schooling is a vital part of my training programme and the part I enjoy most. I take a great pride in it. There is nothing to beat the pleasure of educating a horse that has never left the ground. Every one will jump; some will do it better than others, but if they are physically sound and are given confidence to do it properly they will come to enjoy it.

Years ago, while I was riding, I was appalled to hear that the Jockey Club had decided to bring in one plastic fence as an experiment at Stratford. The type they were considering had a steel frame that could have caused untold damage to horses. When I rang General Feilden, the then senior steward, at seven in the morning to express my dismay, I received a major rocket for waking him up. By the time I had finished he promised me that the plastic fence would not be in use at Stratford later that day.

Fences should be made of wood and birch that will give under extreme pressure. I remember Al Hashimi breaking the timber frame of a fence at Ascot a few years ago. Afterwards the horse was fine, but if the base of the fence had been constructed of steel it could have been a different story. Something had to give and it would not have been the fence.

Some of the worst falls come when horses step into an open ditch, chest the fence and turn a somersault. The first thing that hits the ground is their head. However, a lot of ditches have been filled in more recently, making them less hazardous. Water jumps, too, are shallower today. Previously if your horse dropped his hind legs into the water, he often damaged his back, sometimes with fatal consequences. Today there is only a small lip at the rear, with the result that horses are less likely to injure themselves. I do not agree with those who would like to see all water jumps removed. At racecourses like Aintree, Ludlow and Newbury, where they are positioned in front of the stands, they offer a superb spectacle.

At Jackdaws Castle I start the youngsters off by walking and trotting them over lines of telegraph poles on the ground, gradually increasing in size to tree trunks. You can usually tell at once the ones who are going to be the best jumpers. Mysilv was electrifying; Broadsword, in contrast, was totally inept at first. When they are reasonably proficient, they move on to popping over purpose-made flights of baby hurdles placed on one of our all-weather surfaces to save wear on the schooling grounds. This is particularly useful when the going at home dries up, though I also school regularly over hurdles on grass.

Later, when they start over fences, we are very lucky to be able to have four individual schooling areas, one for each year, divided by fast-growing hedges. So the ground we used last season ('94–5) has three years to recover before we need it again. We are able to do this by using portable fences that can be moved with a forklift.

Buying the right type of horse is a crucial part of training. Once, like many trainers, I used to buy the odd horse on spec, without an order, and then try to find an owner for it. The snag to this method is that it requires nerves of steel, convincing powers of persuasion and a particularly friendly bank manager. It is, as I discovered many years ago, a very easy way of losing money and now I prefer to wait until an owner comes along with a firm order. Sometimes I am asked to join the judging panel at sales, held at Doncaster and Goffs, at Kill, where our brief is to choose the horse in the catalogue that we believe will make the best chaser.

Trainers tend to go for their own individual type. Josh Gifford, as I often remind him, likes big plain horses, which, to be fair, have done him very well. I had a few disasters with big backward youngsters in the past who looked as though they would make up into decent racehorses and often did not.

Although good racehorses come in all shapes and sizes I like to try to pick an untried horse that is as nearly correct in conformation as possible. I put this ahead of pedigree and have in mind what I would call a 'Rimell' horse, the sort Fred and Mercy would have bought in the past. Something in the mould of Gay Trip or Very Promising, an athletic mover around 16.1 hands high, standing four square, with quality and a bold outlook.

If I buy a horse I have to like it, because I am probably going to see it almost every day of the year. Breeding comes into it; size and correctness, too. I learned an important lesson from my father when he called at Condicote late in his life to see a youngster I had just bought in Ireland. He took one look and asked if I had bought it in the dark. I had ignored, he pointed out, the fact that it had the most terrible hocks. I had to admit that I had fallen for the Irish vendor insisting that it had typical Menelek hocks.

Colin Smith's readiness to handle all financial affairs at Jackdaws Castle allows me to concentrate on training the horses. He deals with the owners direct over training fees and all other bills, and decides what to pay the lads, though he is always ready to discuss these matters with me. Basically I liaise with him on finances when necessary, but am happy not to be the paymaster. It makes my life much easier. All our lads are salaried; their wages go straight into the bank each month. I warned Colin that the system would not work but, as usual, he has been proved right.

In 1994 the charge for a horse in training at Jackdaws Castle rose by £2 to £37.50 a day plus VAT. Owners enjoy the advantage of a thoroughly modern set-up, with an all-in fee that covers shoeing and all veterinary care. There are positively no hidden extras. Transport to the races is a standard £143 wherever a horse runs. We have two modern horseboxes, one that can carry six, the other four.

We also allow a few friends with eventers or point-to-pointers to use our all-weather gallops provided they appear after eleven, unbox at the top of the farm and do not go on the grass. Mark Phillips trained the Spanish Olympic event team here two or three days a week, the Americans swear by it and Andrew Hoy, an Australian, was a frequent visitor before the Olympic Games. They all know they can bring horses to the peak of fitness here. Only the British have been missing.

You cannot win if your luck is out, which probably explains why I am extremely superstitious. In racing we say if you see a load of straw you are sure to draw, but if it is a load of hay you are sure to pay. It is always a great plus if I manage to drive under a railway bridge just as a train is passing overhead. That is supposed to guarantee a winner. I also spit on my hand for luck every time I see a magpie.

I would not dare to go racing in anything other than red socks, a superstition started on the day I finally broke my duck at the Cheltenham Festival in 1986. On the one day I did forget to wear them, the owner of my fancied runner that afternoon took this omission as a bad omen and, sure enough, his horse was beaten. I wore the NH Jockeys cricket team tie every day until 1993, and also feel lost without my trusty sheepskin coat, which I wear everywhere in winter. My first one was stolen from my car in London in 1963. Eighteen months ago we spotted it on the back of a member of the Jockey Club, no less, at Windsor. Dinah was convinced it was mine from the stitching she had done on it all those years ago, and confirmed her suspicions when we returned home that night and checked with some of our old photographs. I have had two more sheepskin coats since then, one of which is now in the museum at Cheltenham racecourse.

A trainer is only as good as the staff he employs, and I am lucky to have an exceptional team helping me at Jackdaws Castle. Alan King, my assistant, joined me for six weeks eight years ago, on the recommendation of John Wilson. From the start he made up for his lack of experience with tremendous enthusiasm. Now he is my right-hand man, highly efficient and reliable, from A to Z, and the best judge of going on any racecourse.

Both my head lad, Clifford Baker, and travelling head lad,

Jeremy Willis, joined me straight from school at sixteen. Jeremy was too heavy to make a jockey, but I assured him there is always a good job in racing for people who want to progress. He is a thoroughly reliable travelling head lad, a task I consider to be one of the best in racing. After Clifford rode a winner for Jenny Pitman at Towcester, he took the view that race riding was not for him. I promised him the role of head lad some time in the future if he worked hard, and gave him the job in 1988. My previous head lad Lyn Burrows left abruptly after a major disagreement. We had a fairly volatile relationship throughout the ten years he was with me. He would not go back upon what was said after we both lost our cool and neither would I. So he departed.

Though Warren Marston is now first jockey for Jenny Pitman, he still rides out for me and lives near by. He joined me from David Morley after riding in an amateurs' hurdle race at Liverpool. The first time I had him schooling, he jumped about eighteen obstacles in our paddock. At the end he announced, to my astonishment, that he had never schooled over jumps before.

Initially I could not persuade Warren to give me the courtesy of saying good morning when I appeared in the yard. The best that he would offer was a grunt; that really annoyed me. You can call me what you like, but I expect you to say good morning first. Manners are important. Perhaps Warren was just going through a phase, because he has excellent manners now. When he accepted an offer from Jenny Pitman in the summer of 1994, I encouraged him to take it, but also to maintain his links here. He has developed into a decent young jockey and still rides for me frequently if he is available.

Try as I might, I could not train a winner on the all-weather jumps track at Southwell, despite running some half decent horses there. I remember Warren Marston came back one day playing hell about the surface on the course. I suggested that he put down his views in the form of a report. What he said proved to be absolutely right. I refused to run a horse on the all-weather hurdles track at Lingfield because it was not safe. The combination of a quick, firm surface and unforgiving obstacles proved lethal. I could not bear to see horses hitting the ground hard there and was delighted when all-weather National Hunt racing was shelved.

Robert Massey has progressed well since he rode his first winner on the 150–1 outsider Stylus, and I try my best to give chances to anyone else deserving them. Robert Bellamy is a smashing fellow, bright and articulate, and should find a decent job in racing when he retires. He always gives a hundred per cent, but a broken thigh seriously disrupted his career. I also have a very promising young amateur called Richard Johnson, who performed a splendidly acrobatic rodeo act to claw his way back into the saddle on his way to victory on Sandybraes at Market Rasen early in 1995 after he was all but unseated by a blunder at the last fence. There are a dozen more in the wings who will get their chance sooner or later.

28

A Boxing Day Confrontation

If you are in his team, David Nicholson is the most loyal ally imaginable. Two months into the new season in the late autumn of 1994, he marched to the defence of Adrian Maguire with all guns blazing. Maguire had been grounded for the third time by a questionable and undeniably harsh eight-day suspension for a minor offence at Bangor-on-Dee early in October.

His trainer, forced to shuffle his riding arrangements yet again, did not pull his punches. He described the decision as scandalous and suggested Maguire was the subject of victimisation. More practically, he sought an urgent meeting at Portman Square with Anthony Mildmay-White, the chairman of the Jockey Club's Disciplinary Committee, to state his case behind closed doors.

Five months later, Nicholson was the man in the dock at Portman Square as he came face to face with Mildmay-White again at a disciplinary hearing in an acrimonious case that dominated the headlines in the week before the Cheltenham Festival.

I felt the decision by the Bangor stewards to suspend Adrian for eight days was ridiculous and travelled to London, at my own request, to meet Anthony Mildmay-White, Nigel Macfarlane and my old friend Malcolm Wallace, who had begun his new job as the Jockey Club's Director of Regulation. I explained that I was concerned at the effect on Adrian of all these suspensions. I was able to put my point across in a relaxed atmosphere and felt the meeting was helpful at the time.

Adrian was back from his enforced break in time to seek a second successive victory on Barton Bank in the Charlie Hall Chase at Wetherby at the end of the month. This time they were sailing along in the lead with victory apparently assured when Barton Bank dived through the fourth last fence, an open ditch. The horse was all but down, and virtually came to a standstill, but somehow Adrian stayed on his back. This left Young Hustler well clear. Barton Bank set off in pursuit but fell heavily when he blundered again and came down at the second last fence.

By the time I reached the horse, blood was pouring from his face. Given his past record I imagined he had broken a blood vessel badly but it turned out that he had ripped his face with his own front shoe as he struggled to stay upright. Worse, the front of his face had been pushed in, fracturing several small bones around his nose and damaging his sinuses.

The racecourse vets could not have been more helpful. They stitched him up and within days he was being quietly ridden again. At first, I feared that he would be unable to attempt a second success in the King George VI Chase, but the speed of his recovery soon made that a feasible target. We knew he was the best staying chaser in training. Now he proved to be one of the most resilient.

The day after Wetherby I was delighted to attend a memorable party at Ascot to celebrate the Queen Mother's 400 winners as an owner. Many of those who had trained and ridden for her were there. I was one of thirty-two jockeys who had experienced the pride of riding to victory in the royal colours. The Queen and Princess Margaret were both present, and clearly enjoyed the parade of some of the Queen Mother's favourites including Nearco Bay, her 400th winner, Special Cargo and Sun Rising.

A fortnight later on November 16 it was my turn to celebrate when Sevso, owned by Lord Northampton, became my 1,000th jumps winner in this country as a trainer. Although it was a notable landmark, it seemed an age since Arctic Coral had set me on the road with victory at Warwick over a quarter of a century earlier in January, 1969.

The horses were in superb form in the weeks leading up to Christmas. Several promising new recruits had done well for us, including Silver Wedge, winner of the Queen's Vase at Royal Ascot, owned by Shirley Robins, Martin's Lamp, previously trained by Josh Gifford, and the high-class mare Dubacilla, who was sent to us by Henry and Veronica Cole and kicked off by beating Docklands Express at Sandown. Silver Wedge and Anzum, a nice prospect belonging to Colin Smith and a few of his old schoolfriends, each won four on the bounce by early December. Brownhall, belonging to Roger Wade, proved to be an exciting young chaser.

At the start of the season Graham Roach, a good friend and a hard businessman, decided to transfer two of his promising young horses elsewhere to spread his risk, but I was always confident that Viking Flagship would return to Jackdaws Castle. Because the Flagship is such a stuffy horse, I did not think I would ever have him ready to win first time out, but he surprised us all by hacking up in the Tingle Creek Chase at Sandown on December 3.

On the same day Relkeel completed a rapid hat-trick in the William Hill Handicap Hurdle. It was the easiest success you will ever see in a competitive handicap hurdle. Adrian Maguire spent so much time looking round for non-existent dangers that the horse's owner Roscoe Harvey suggested afterwards that he would be suffering from a stiff neck. At the start of the season the Brig had been keen for Relkeel to go straight over fences, but his sparkling form over hurdles delayed that option for at least twelve months. His rate of progress already suggested that he was a serious contender for the Champion Hurdle.

I was delighted to have such a good horse for the Brig, even more so because I had trained both Relkeel's dam and grand dam for him, neither with much success. By the time Relkeel came into training the Brig, who was already well into his nineties, had given his dam Secret Keel to a farmer in the West Country on the understandable grounds that he could not see much point in continuing to breed for the future.

'David, you want to get on and run my horses. Time is not on my side,' he will tell me on his frequent visits to Jackdaws Castle. He is a remarkable man.

We enjoyed such a purple patch in the run-up to Christmas that a treble on December 17 took me to the fastest half-century of my career. December is the month when all sorts of awards are announced in racing. I was delighted to be voted National Hunt Trainer of the Year by the Horserace Writers' Association at their annual lunch in London and equally pleased that Adrian took the jockeys' award.

As ever there were some inevitable reverses along the way. King of the Lot, such a professional, hurt himself irreparably in the Mackeson Gold Cup and had to be put down. It was a devastating blow, in particular for my assistant Alan King, who had ridden the old horse at home for four years. Carobee, Silver Wisp and Winter Squall all picked up injuries which ruled them out for the rest of the season.

In addition, Moorcroft Boy fractured his neck when he fell heavily at Aintree in November. At first his life was in danger because he seemed to be suffering from partial paralysis, but excellent veterinary care at the racecourse, and later at the Liverpool University Hospital for Large Animals, helped him turn the corner. He made a remarkable recovery and by the spring was fit enough to turn out to grass. Only time will tell if he will race again.

Barton Bank, however, made the speediest possible return from his mishap at Wetherby. The scars on his nose hardly improved his looks, but two schooling sessions confirmed that the injury had not affected his confidence or, crucially, his breathing. There was still the nagging doubt about his jumping, because he is always capable of taking on a fence.

Events at Kempton on Boxing Day stretched us all to breaking point. Adrian had already won a valuable novice chase on Brownhall when he walked out to ride Barton Bank in the King George VI Chase. Until the last fence the race unfolded according to the script. Jumping fast and accurately, Barton Bank led as early as the third fence, and was fully in command as he set sail in the final straight. Another electrifying leap at the third last gave him a priceless advantage, so that heading for the last fence he was fully ten lengths clear.

Adrian had been asking him to stand off at his fences throughout the race and now, seeing a long stride, he did so again. He was in no doubt, so he kicked. Instead the horse put down, crashed through the fence, pitched on to his head and ejected Adrian. He held on to the reins and briefly tried to jump back into the saddle before trudging back disconsolately, a picture of misery.

By the time I reached horse and rider, Barton Bank's owners Jenny and Raymond Mould were already there, as well as Dinah and his lad Gordon Clarkson. It was obvious that Adrian was in a very distressed state. He was so upset he could not speak as the tears ran down his face. My immediate reaction was to put my arm around his shoulders and tell him not to worry, but he was inconsolable.

David Minton had asked a group of photographers to move back to give Adrian a bit of privacy. They did as he requested with the notable exception of Edward Whitaker, who continued to take photographs a few paces away. I should make it clear at this stage that Whitaker, as a *Racing Post* employee, is supposed to be an ally, since I write a column for his paper each Saturday during the winter. What's more, he has been given a free hand to take photos on several visits to Jackdaws Castle. Like most guests, he also joined us in our house for breakfast.

Yet he paid no attention to David Minton's request. Frankly, I took exception to his refusal to move, and when I told him in no uncertain terms to retreat, he still took no notice. He resolutely refused to go away. I appreciate that people have a job to do, but all his colleagues had played ball. Whitaker's was an unwarranted intrusion at a very difficult time for Adrian Maguire.

As a result I lost my cool and swore at him. I used bad language, threatened him and made it crystal clear I would clock him if he did not back off, but contrary to what was suggested in many newspapers the next day, I did not hit him. The worst that happened was that I pushed him away.

I then made my way to the weighing-room where my first job was to lift Adrian's spirits sufficiently in time for him to go out and ride Kadi in the next race. He was so down he did not want to ride again that afternoon, but I pointed out that he had a job to do and told him to pull himself together.

After he finished third on Kadi I was besieged in the unsaddling enclosure by reporters accusing me of hitting Whitaker, which I strongly denied. Some members of the press then abused David Minton with every bit as bad language as I had directed at Whitaker in defence of Adrian. By this stage I was wild. It was just as well Minty dragged me away.

The following morning some newspapers were more interested in our so-called fracas than reporting what happened in the race. The incident was blown up out of all proportion. Even so, when I had calmed down, I rang Edward Whitaker at home and apologised for what happened.

Over the following days I had a tremendous amount of support from people for trying to protect Adrian at Kempton. One message of approval came from an unlikely quarter. Edward Whitaker's uncle rang to express his backing for my actions.

He told my secretary Debbie Hancock that he sympathised with me over his nephew's behaviour, and also offered to speak up for me if the matter was taken further.

Eventually the stewards at Kempton sent on a report to the Jockey Club. As a result of this I was interviewed by one of their investigators. I freely admitted to them that I had used abusive language and expressed my regret at doing so. I heard later that I would face two separate charges at a disciplinary hearing at Portman Square chaired by Anthony Mildmay-White.

That was all in the future. The day after Kempton, Adrian, Dinah and I made a frantic dash by helicopter and taxi to Wetherby for Viking Flagship's assault on the Castleford Chase. We left Jackdaws Castle with plenty of time to spare but ten minutes from the course the pilot was forced to turn back to East Midlands airport, because there was a danger of the rotary blades icing up.

Once we landed, we jumped into a waiting taxi. At this stage, I was still confident that we would reach Wetherby in time for Adrian to ride Seaward and Arthur's Minstrel for me in the opening two races, but when we turned on to the M1 we found ourselves caught up in a massive traffic jam. Urgent measures were required. I did my best to encourage the driver but we were at a standstill. Luckily he had a mobile phone, so we were able to listen to Peter Niven win the second race for me on Arthur's Minstrel. Adrian did not say a word throughout the journey. He was still feeling low after the events of the previous day and had also hurt his knee when he was catapulted from Barton Bank.

I rang Wetherby and made sure that Peter was ready to take over on Viking Flagship if we did not arrive in time. I also requested that the gates were left open so that we would not lose valuable seconds at the entrance. By this point I was all but driving the taxi myself. Horn blaring and hazard lights flashing, we came through the back way into the racecourse and sped right up to the winner's enclosure to discover Peter Niven already wearing Graham Roach's red and white colours.

He would have ridden the horse, too, if officials had stuck rigidly to the rule that you must weigh out not later than fifteen minutes before a race. Instead they showed a welcome display of leniency as Adrian grabbed the colours from Peter, pulled them over his shirt and jumped straight on to the scales in his trousers and shoes. I saddled the horse so quickly that he was not even the last one into the parade ring.

The race was relaxing in comparison. Viking Flagship led three fences out and won with impressive ease by twenty-five lengths. I then felt an icy shiver at the prospect of Adrian failing to weigh in at the correct weight. In addition, he was in so much pain from his knee that he could barely dismount when he returned.

There is no doubt that, if he had ridden earlier in the afternoon at Wetherby, he would not have been able to partner Viking Flagship. After he hobbled to the scales I was relieved to see that he weighed in without any further dramas. If anything he was a little heavier than his official mark of 11st. 10 lbs.

Adrian was trailing Richard Dunwoody in their continuing duel for the jockeys' championship until, in January, his great rival was suspended for thirty days for causing intentional interference at Uttoxeter. I am sorry to say the punishment was fully deserved because it was Richard's third similar offence inside a year. A week after that race, riding Luv-U-Frank, he was also in the wrong in pushing up the inner of Adrian Maguire's mount King Lucifer at Ascot. His antics caused my horse to strike into the back of a runner in front of him. Luckily no serious harm was done and King Lucifer still won.

Afterwards I asked Adrian why he had not prevented it happening by shutting the door on Richard as he tried to force his way through. He replied that he had to think of protecting his licence since every incident and manoeuvre now appears on camera. In my day Richard would have been well and truly done if he had tried to come up someone's inner like that, but there were not many cameras in use then.

Richard Dunwoody's long, enforced break from racing in midwinter gave him ample time to reflect on the furious schedule he had been maintaining over the past few years. He returned a changed man, with a different set of priorities. It soon emerged that he was not prepared to charge around the country in his usual relentless pursuit of winners.

While Richard was away in February, Adrian reached a famous landmark with his 500th winner, less than four years since he won on Omerta at the Cheltenham Festival as an unknown young amateur. No one else in the history of the sport has made such a rapid start. It is an unbelievable achievement set against the strike-rate of jockeys in earlier days.

29

The Flagship and a Festival treble

David Nicholson suffered three serious reverses in rapid succession in the final tense days before the 1995 Cheltenham Festival. It was a difficult period which tested his resolve to the limit. When he travelled to London a week before the Gold Cup to face the stewards of the Jockey Club on two charges relating to events at Kempton on Boxing Day, you could almost sense the first flutter of vulture wings among the gathered newsmen in the corridors of Portman Square. At the end of a hearing that lasted more than four hours, the trainer was fined £1,500 for violent and improper conduct, and for bringing racing into disrepute.

When it was over, Nicholson had the option of slipping away through a rear exit to avoid the massed ranks of waiting pressmen. Instead, typically, he chose to meet them face to face to give his version of events.

Three days later came the shocking news that Adrian Maguire's mother Phyllis had died suddenly at her home in County Meath, in Ireland. Before flying home to be with his family, the distraught young jockey advised David Nicholson that he could miss all or part of the forthcoming Festival.

On Monday morning, the eve of the biggest jumps meeting of the year, slight heat was discovered in the tendon of Relkeel's off fore leg. All season the preparation of this outstanding young prospect had passed without so much as a hiccup. Now he would have to miss the Champion Hurdle, for which he was widely quoted as favourite or second favourite on the opening day of the Festival.

The media played up my appearance before the stewards at a

time when I would have preferred to concentrate my thoughts on my horses. Some newspapers, assuming my guilt before the trial, speculated on the extent of the punishment they felt I was likely to face. Others, disgracefully in my view, suggested that my behaviour at Kempton matched that of the French soccer star Eric Cantona when he attacked an irate fan with a flying kick to the chest after being sent off at Crystal Palace.

During the long hearing I said only three words: no, no and no. This was in response to questions about whether I had hit Edward Whitaker. No less than five witnesses including Ed Gillespie, Managing Director of United Racecourses, Cornelius Lysaght, from the BBC, and Dr Michael Allen told the stewards that they had not seen any blows struck. I was particularly grateful that two members of the public, Anne Vale and Elaine Wellsford, took the time and trouble to confirm to the stewards that I had not hit Edward Whitaker.

I thought it was significant that only one witness, another photographer, came forward to support Whitaker's story. I was delighted to be cleared on that charge. All the way through I categorically denied striking him, but I was surprised and disappointed at the severity of the fine for threatening Whitaker and using obscene language. It was certainly a bit harsh when you consider that Jenny Pitman was let off with a fine of only £200 after thumping Jamie Osborne outside the weighing-room at Ayr in 1990.

One wag, who is not an admirer of Whitaker, suggested I should have been fined £3,000 for not hitting him! Others argued that, given his behaviour, I was fully entitled to have a go at him. Immediately after the inquiry I felt that I was owed an apology by people who had publicly accused me of striking Whitaker, but now, as far as I am concerned, the matter is closed. Life has to go on.

Adrian Maguire, as the youngest of ten children, was espe-cially close to his mother, and was badly shaken by her death on Saturday night. When he rang me before leaving for Ireland on Sunday, I tried to give him my full support, and said I would not expect him to return until he felt he was ready to ride again. I was happy to leave the decision to him.

Grief affects people differently. Most of all I was anxious to avoid putting him under any undue pressure at such a tragic time. At first I was hoping that after his mother's funeral on the Tuesday he might consider returning for the third day of the Festival on Thursday, but as the days passed he knew that his mind and his heart were not in tune with the business of race riding. I began to make emergency plans to find cover for him, and fortunately came up with some pretty good substitutes.

The first priority seemed to be to book a top-class jockey for Relkeel in the Champion Hurdle on Tuesday, but that was no longer necessary after we found a bit of heat in his off fore leg on Monday morning as he was being tacked up. You cannot take chances with a sore spot like that, so there was no question of his running the following day. It was a bad moment for everyone at Jackdaws Castle. Hopefully we will have a few more chances in the Champion Hurdle, but time is not on the side of his owner Brigadier Roscoe Harvey.

I drove straight round to see him at his home near Stow. He was brilliant about the whole business when I told him the bad news and, typically, was more worried about the effect on everyone else. Inevitably, the horse's late withdrawal hit him hard in the following days, but within weeks he responded by asking me to find him a three-year-old to run over hurdles in the autumn. As the race turned out, I have to doubt if Relkeel would have beaten Alderbrook, who was undeniably impressive, but I like to think that Relkeel would have been second. Initially I hoped that the horse would recover in time for Liverpool, but I later decided to put him away for the summer.

Relkeel's unfortunate absence left me unusually quiet on Champion Hurdle day. After seeing my only runner Strong Beau finish unplaced, I volunteered to drive our party home in the new Range Rover I had just been given for a year for helping the company with some promotional work on the latest model. As we tried to leave the racecourse we became tangled up in some traffic cones. The next thing I knew a policeman was crawling under the vehicle trying to free a marauding cone. This is where a Range Rover comes into its own. I simply touched a button and it rose up as if on stilts until it was clear of the obstruction. The police involved were not particularly impressed, but luckily they did not breathalyse me.

I set off for Cheltenham on Wednesday believing I had sound chances with all three of my runners. I had booked the Irish champion Charlie Swan for Viking Flagship in the Queen Mother Champion Chase, and also hoped he would be able to ride my exciting new recruit Putty Road in the opening Sun Alliance Novices' Hurdle. Charlie had won on the horse in Ireland, and was keen to renew the partnership, but was unable to break a previous pledge to partner another runner in the same race. So Norman Williamson stepped in for the ride on Putty Road.

In January Sir Philip Harris had rung me out of the blue to ask me to find a Cheltenham horse for his wife. I had met him years earlier through his long association with David Broome, and he had also tried to purchase Mysilv privately before her sale in May, 1994. I flew to France with Dinah to look at a suitable horse for Lady Harris. A deal was struck, too, but the horse subsequently failed to pass the vet. We then turned our attentions to the attractive grey Morceli, an exciting recruit to fencing, but he was not for sale at any price.

Putty Road, a tough, genuine character, who clearly stayed well, was our third choice. This time I travelled to Ireland with David Minton to meet the horse's owner Jim Ryan, and concluded the purchase over lunch at the Mount Juliet Golf Club, where David and I had once played cricket when it was the McCalmont family home.

Putty Road then won decisively at Warwick on his debut for Lady Harris. Cheltenham was a much stiffer test but he proved more than equal to the task. He was challenging when he made a slight mistake at the last hurdle, but showed great resolution on the hill to catch Berude Not To just before the winning post. This was one mission accomplished to the entire satisfaction of the owner, yet as I stood in the winner's enclosure I must admit my thoughts were for Adrian Maguire.

Just over half an hour later Viking Flagship walked out to defend his crown as the champion two-mile chaser. Though he had not won since Wetherby at Christmas, he had been unlucky to fall at Newbury, where he was apparently in command, and had needed the run at Kempton when he was narrowly beaten by Thumbs Up. We had endured a few little problems with the Flagship but he is a real toughie and I had never lost faith in him. On the day I was extremely bullish about his chance. He arrived at the Festival with all guns blazing, led approaching the second fence and readily drew clear of Deep Sensation on the run-in.

I was absolutely thrilled at the jaunty manner in which the

Flagship proved his critics wrong, and deeply upset that poor Adrian had not been in the saddle to enjoy the fruits of all his hard work through the winter. He has made the horse what he is over fences and has always looked after him in two seasons' racing. Charlie Swan came back saying he had never jumped the last fence at Cheltenham so fast. After making sure that Charlie weighed in, I felt so shaky that I sat down to drink a glass of iced water on my own. Contrary to public impression, I am a pretty emotional person.

The next two hours passed like a blur before it was time for me to saddle Kadi for the Mildmay of Flete Chase. He, like Viking Flagship, had been beaten at Kempton on his previous run, but earlier in the afternoon Brief Gale advertised the value of that form with a fine victory in the Sun Alliance Chase. I felt my horse was well handicapped in a race that is sometimes won by novices.

Norman Williamson rode Kadi with tremendous patience before producing him with a well-timed challenge running down the hill for the final time. Dublin Flyer, the long-time leader, was still in front at the last but Kadi landed running and was always going to win on the flat.

It was a stunning climax to an unforgettable day. I had enjoyed a double on the Thursday of the 1986 Festival, when I finally broke my duck at the meeting, but three was beyond my wildest dreams. At the start of the week I would happily have settled for one winner.

No one on the course seemed to know if a trainer had ever achieved a treble at the Cheltenham Festival on the same afternoon. Eventually it was discovered that Reg Hobbs, the father of Bruce, had produced three winners on Gold Cup day in 1942. What's more, two of them, Medoc II and Jack Pugh, were ridden by my father on a day when eight races were held. Leafing through an ancient form book much later, I discovered that Reg's three horses earned a total of £1,028. In contrast my trio picked up £145,599.50p. It is an interesting lesson in the advance of inflation.

Wednesday evening of Festival week is traditionally the night that Dinah and I entertain the gang 'in house'. This time we had all the ingredients for an even wilder party. Amazingly I was still upright at midnight having watched the Cheltenham highlights again on television. Whatever the celebrations there is always work to be done the following morning. The first lot of horses pulled out on the dot at seven as usual. It is the only way to run a racing stable. A set routine is vital for horses and lads.

Thursday offered the prospect of further success at Cheltenham. I was two handed in both the Daily Express Triumph Hurdle and the Gold Cup. In addition I was optimistic that Hebridean would run a big race in the Stayers' Hurdle.

With Adrian still at home in Ireland, I booked Norman Williamson, the man of the moment, for Silver Wedge, and Warren Marston for Anzum. They finished third and fourth behind Kissair but were subsequently promoted to second and third when the runner-up Dr Leunt was disqualified after a mêlée at the top of the hill.

Silver Wedge ran his heart out on going he hates but I felt Anzum would have gone close but for missing the break; he certainly made up a tremendous amount of ground in the second half of the race. It is just reward for Colin Smith to have a decent young horse. Hebridean was then just pipped for third place in the Stayers' Hurdle.

David Bridgwater was my first choice to replace Adrian on Barton Bank. You have to be brave on this horse and David was the ideal candidate. As a precaution, he came over to Jackdaws Castle on Tuesday morning to jump three fences on Barton Bank. Horse and rider were enjoying a fine race and were travelling very well just behind the winner Master Oats, until coming down at the last ditch, less than a mile from home. It was a typical Cheltenham ditch fall and so disappointing.

We all know Barton Bank is a top-class horse, but there is a serious flaw in his jumping, which may stem from the time he smashed his withers when he fell over backwards as a four-year-old. Some trainers at Lambourn call on jumping gurus like Yogi Breisner to school their horses, but though I have turned to Lars Sederholm for advice in the past, I am not a great believer in this trend. I am, however, always open to practical suggestions.

With one of my contenders out of the Gold Cup, it was exciting to see Dean Gallagher making stealthy progress on my other runner Dubacilla. She tended to drop herself out in the early stages, and had done so again now, but in the final three quarters of a mile she was the only one to offer any sort of threat to Master Oats. For one heady moment at the second last fence, I thought that she was going to come through to win, but she had worked so hard to keep up in the race that she had nothing left to offer at the end.

Even so I was thrilled with Dubacilla's gutsy performance in taking second place. It was a run that meant so much to Henry and Veronica Cole, who were still on cloud nine days later. I cannot possibly claim that Barton Bank would have won if he had not fallen, but I fancy he would have finished in front of Dubacilla.

On the Sunday after Cheltenham Adrian Maguire rang to say he would be back in action the following day. He popped in on Monday morning to school some horses before travelling on to Uttoxeter, where he immediately resumed the winning habit with a typically forceful ride on Greville Again, a nice young prospect belonging to Stan and Hilda Clarke. At first I was not sure if he had prevailed, but one thing is beyond dispute: Adrian's strength in the saddle ensured that the nose of Greville Again was in front in the tightest possible photo-finish.

I found it very moving to be there at Uttoxeter and witness my jockey come back in such resolute fashion after his bereavement. His victory on Greville Again gave me nearly as much pleasure as my treble at Cheltenham the previous week.

Viking Flagship sealed another superb season with as brave a victory as you will ever see in the Mumm Melling Chase, over two and a half miles at Liverpool. The horse is invariably better two days after a race than before, and he was jumping out of his skin after Cheltenham. Really, there was nowhere else to go with him except Liverpool, and I hoped he would stay the extra half mile, though I could not be certain about it.

The drying ground, officially described as good to firm, was a worry, too, since Viking Flagship had suffered from leg trouble in the past. Alan King walked the course, and felt it was good fast going, without any jar, so I was happy enough to let the horse run.

As I watched the race unfold with David Minton from a position on the steps of the Queen Elizabeth Stand, the thing that stood out in my mind was the positive attitude of Adrian Maguire on the Flagship. Yet I heard later that he did not want the horse to run, because he thought the ground was a bit too firm, and was uncertain if he would stay the distance.

You would not have known that he had any doubts from the dashing way he rode Viking Flagship.

The manner in which horse and rider attacked the fences was quite breathtaking. They were so long at the first ditch in the back straight it was heartstopping. The Flagship is an extremely clean, accurate and fast jumper. That is him. All the photographs of him show the same athletic ability to cross a fence at speed. Yet as he was swamped by Deep Sensation and the favourite, Martha's Son, immediately after the last fence, I did not think he could get up to win. Even on the line I did not know if he had forced his head in front of Deep Sensation.

It was a desperately close finish, but Alan King was confident and so were one or two others who assured me he had won. I wanted to hear the result of the photo and see his number in the frame before I was sure. Josh Gifford, the trainer of Deep Sensation, was convinced his horse was beaten, even though he had battled all the way up the run-in.

The horses were back in the winner's enclosure before the judge's decision was announced. I don't mind admitting that when the Flagship's number was called out first I leaped into the air with delight. I love to see a champion and he is an outstanding one, so you can imagine my pleasure at learning that he had been voted the Cartier Champion Chaser for 1994–5. When he was also named Murphy's Chaser of the Year, I put back my holiday by a week so that I could attend the Whitbread National Hunt awards dinner, where Silver Wedge was chosen as the Castle Eden Juvenile Hurdler of the Year.

Yet I returned from holiday to find a letter from Bill Robins announcing that none of his horses, including Silver Wedge, would be returning to me in the autumn. In anybody's language it was disappointing news because I could hardly have been more successful for the Robins. Several people have asked me if I will run the Flagship over longer distances in the future. It is possible that he could stay three miles, but why up him in distance when he is the best at two miles? I do not believe I will ever see a better horse race than his thrilling victory at Aintree. It was unbelievable. Adrian was really pumped up afterwards, too. In a subsequent interview he observed that if he came back in another life he would like it to be as Viking Flagship.

I hoped that the Flagship's victory at Liverpool had sealed a second trainer's championship for me, since I ended the three-day meeting with a lead of £174,740 over Martin Pipe. I do not take these things for granted but Michael Stoute, for one, did not have any doubts. I was touched when he rang on Sunday morning to congratulate me on retaining my title. It was something, he added, that he has not yet achieved.

On Saturday Dubacilla ran out of her skin to finish fourth in the Grand National on her last appearance for me. Once again she finished with a flourish, and just for a moment, as I saw her staying on strongly after the last fence, I thought she might do it. I had hoped she would have been able to lie a bit handier through the race, and Dean Gallagher did save precious ground by keeping to the inside. Twelve months earlier her half-brother Just So had finished a close second to Miinnehoma in the National. Now she had added to the family's reputation by taking fourth prize.

Within days she was on the way back to Henry Cole's farm in Somerset, before heading for Ireland where she was covered by Jurado, a son of Alleged, at the end of June, and is in foal. Dubacilla was a delight to train. When Henry rang me the previous autumn to enquire about our training fees at Jackdaws Castle, I thought he might be put off by the cost, yet he called back within the hour to say he was bringing her straight up. Dubacilla won handsomely on her debut for me at Sandown, ran in all the big races except the King George VI Chase, was placed in the National and the Gold Cup, and earned over £70,000 in prize money. It would be nice to think I might train some of her offspring one day.

The weather changed so completely in late March and early April that the ground on almost all racecourses was transformed from one extreme to another. As a result I found myself rapidly running out of ammunition. Some of my horses were tired after a long season. They needed a holiday and so did I.

Adrian Maguire, however, was all set to push Richard Dunwoody to the limit in their continuing duel for the jockeys' championship, until his season ended prematurely on Easter Monday as he stood two winners ahead of Richard. Adrian broke his right arm when Desert Fighter crashed through the wing of a hurdle at Hereford. It was cruel luck. He deserves to be champion and will be one day. He has played an enormous part in our success over the past two years.

The idea when we came to Jackdaws Castle was to train better class horses with improved facilities, and we have achieved that. I like to think that Colin Smith is satisfied with what we have achieved in less than three years since the move. In that time we have trained 277 winners over jumps in this country from our new quarters. The horses have earned the mighty total of almost £2.3 million in win and place money.

What of the future? All I have ever wanted to do in life is ride and then train. I expect I would be unemployable at anything else. So I hope to continue at Jackdaws Castle for a few more years at least.

As you may have noticed by now, I like things done properly. If I think something is wrong, even if it is nothing to do with me, I have a habit of pointing it out. Winning is not everything to me, but trying to win is. That is the way I have always been, though sometimes in the evenings, over a glass of brandy, I do laugh at how seriously I take it all.

David Nicholson's Career Statistics

Riding Record – Flat

Season	Wins
1955	1

Riding Record – National Hunt

Season	Wins	Rides
1954–55	1	2
1955–56	5	31
1956–57	6	81
1957–58	7	110
1958–59	25	157
1959–60	36	284
1960–61	57	397
1961–62	35	381
1962–63	37	355
1963–64	34	444
1964–65	58	402
1965–66	53	393
1966–67	63	421
1967–68	36	352
1968–69	33	332
1969–70	11	169
1970–71	21	226
1971–72	21	197
1972–73	29	156
1973–74	15	113
	583	

Also:
France 2
Norway 1
Sweden 1

Training Record – National Hunt

Season	Wins	Win Prize Money
1968–69	2	510
1969–70	7	1,734
1970–71	3	817
1971–72	9	3,586
1972–73	24	9,241
1973–74	20	6,342
1974–75	28	15,445
1975–76	29	26,369
1976–77	38	29,880
1977–78	34	30,377
1978–79	19	22,137
1979–80	28	33,459
1980–81	47	84,836
1981–82	67	127,191
1982–83	64	116,807
1983–84	50	107,392
1984–85	17	38,396
1985–86	22	115,241
1986–87	42	126,863
1987–88	50	214,421
1988–89	39	122,979
1989–90	42	147,133
1990–91	55	218,243
1991–92	63	363,233
1992–93	100	492,420
1993–94	81	555,355
1994–95	96	649,257
	1,076	

Also:
Belgium 2
France 1
Ireland 4

Training Record – Flat

Season	Wins	Prize money
1970	10	3,934
1971	2	544
1972	1	436
1973	2	552
1974	1	263
1977	1	3,414
1980	3	6,052
1981	1	2,523
1982	1	918
1983	2	3,422
1985	1	1,125
1986	1	966
1992	1	2,040
1994	1	33,285
	28	

Index